**Publisher and Creative Director:**
B. Martin Pedersen

**Chief Visionary Officer:**
Patti Judd

**Design Director:**
Hee Ra Kim

**Designers:**
B. Martin Pedersen
Hee Ra Kim
Hiewon Sohn

**Associate Editor:**
Colleen Boyd

**Contributing Editor:**
Patti Judd

**Publisher's Assistant /Designer:**
Claire Yuan Zhuang

**Writer:**
Maxim Sorokopud

**Interns:**
Maggie Herrera
Lauren Letarte
Ella York

**Japanese Advisors:**
USA: Toshiaki & Kumiko Ide
Japan: Taku Satoh
Sakura Nomiyama

**Chief Executive Officer:**
B. Martin Pedersen

**Cover Image:**
"Sagmeister SVA, Take it On"
Design: Stefan Sagmeister &
Jessica Walsh
Photography: Henry Leutwyler
Retouching: Erik Johansson

**Published by:**
Graphis Inc.
389 5th Ave., Suite 1105
New York, NY 10016
Phone: 212-532-9387
www.graphis.com
help@graphis.com

**ISBN 13:** 978-1-954632-38-7

Dear Graphis Readers,

Welcome to an issue celebrating the mastery of creative pause and purposeful innovation. From Stefan Sagmeister's transformative sabbaticals to Mark Braught's magical illustrations, these pages showcase visionaries who understand that great creative work demands both boldness and reflection. Join us as we explore how these distinguished creators across Design, Advertising, Photography, and beyond are reshaping the boundaries of their crafts.

**DESIGN:** Graphis Master **Stefan Sagmeister** (US) proves that stepping away can lead to stepping forward, using sabbaticals as catalysts for groundbreaking ideas. Meanwhile, **Paul Garbett** (AU) approaches design as an act of optimism, crafting wayfinding systems and exhibition spaces that point toward a brighter future.

**ADVERTISING:** Early exposure to *Star Wars* and Steven Spielberg's films ignited **Ariel Freaner**'s (US) creative passion, leading him into a creative career where he now develops powerful, imaginative campaigns for clients such as Bill Melendez Productions and the Red Cross.

**PHOTOGRAPHY:** Graphis Master **Stan Musilek** (US) celebrates feminine beauty through his lens, capturing both glamour and artistry in his distinctive portfolio. **Eric Melzer** (US) trains his camera on humanity's spectrum, from neighborhood athletes to environmental champions, always keeping the human element in sharp focus.

**ART/ILLUSTRATION: Mark Braught** (US) brings magic to the page, most notably in his enchanting work for the *Harry Potter* series. His collaboration with Roger Sawhill at UP-Ideas demonstrates how creative partnerships can elevate storytelling through illustration and design.

**EDUCATION:** At the **Academy of Art University**, **Thomas McNulty** (US) challenges students to dive deep into design methodology, combining research, strategy, and execution to develop tomorrow's creative leaders.

**PRODUCTS:** The skies are evolving with the **HX50** (UK) helicopter's luxurious reimagining of personal flight and the **VoloCity Air Taxi**'s (DE) promise of revolutionary urban transport. On the ground, the **Daytona SP3** (IT) pays homage to racing heritage, while the innovative **Halfbike** (BG) invites us to rethink personal mobility.

**ARCHITECTURE:** The **House on Lake Como** (DE/IT) demonstrates how thoughtful renovation can honor history while embracing modernity, while the **Majamaja Off Grid Village** (FR/FI) shows us how sustainable living can be both beautiful and self-sufficient.

Within these pages, you'll discover how creative minds across disciplines are reshaping our world, one bold idea at a time.

Warm regards,

B. Martin Pedersen
*Publisher & Creative Director*

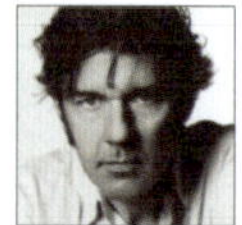



Stefan Sagmeister has designed for clients as diverse as the Rolling Stones, HBO, and the Guggenheim Museum. He's a two-time Grammy winner and has also earned practically every important international design award. Stefan talks about the large subjects of our lives, like happiness or beauty, how they connect to design, and what that means to our everyday lives. He spoke five times at the official TED, making him among the three most frequently invited TED speakers. His books sell in the hundreds of thousands, and his exhibitions have been mounted in museums worldwide. His exhibit, "The Happy Show," attracted over half a million visitors worldwide and became the most visited graphic design show in history. A native of Austria, he received his MFA from the University of Applied Arts Vienna and, as a Fulbright scholar, a master's degree from Pratt Institute in New York.

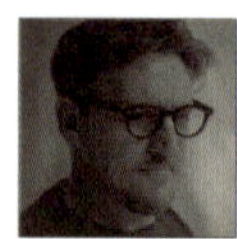

**Introduction by Jessica Walsh**

Jessica Walsh is a creative director and founder of &Walsh. She has received distinctions such as *Forbes'* "30 Under 30" and *Ad Week's* "Top 10 Visual Creatives." She lectures at creative conferences and universities internationally. Her work has been featured in numerous galleries, books, and magazines. She has led branding and campaign work for Netflix, Google, Snapchat, TED, Apple, Beats, Bombas, the Aldrich Museum, and the Jewish Museum, among many others. She founded Ladies, Wine & Design, a global initiative with chapters in over 280 cities aimed at championing and mentoring creative women and fostering women's growth into leadership roles. Jessica also started Let's Talk About Mental Health, a website and Instagram account to start dialogues around mental health, creating a safe space for others to share their stories. Her project, "40 Days of Dating," received over 30 million readers and international recognition. The film rights to "40 Days of Dating" were originally bought by Warner Brothers. Her book, *40 Days of Dating: An Experiment*, was released by Abrams and is available online and in bookstores worldwide.

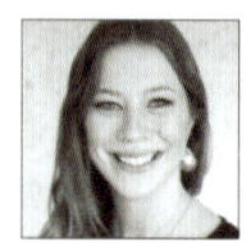



Paul Garbett is a graphic designer, illustrator, and image-maker. He co-founded Studio Garbett, a multidisciplinary design practice in Sydney. They work primarily with clients in the arts, culture, and built environment arenas, believing that curiosity and empathy are key to more effective and engaging design outcomes. Paul was born in South Africa and moved to Australia in 1998, where he is an active member of the design community involved in lecturing, exhibitions, and teaching. His work has been widely published and exhibited and has won awards from prestigious acronyms like AGDA, D&AD, DINZ, and TDC. He has been a member of AGI since 2015.

**Introduction by Yvette Dal Pozzo**

Yvette Dal Pozzo is passionate about working closely with artists, writers, and curators to bring ambitious projects to fruition. As director of the Goulburn Regional Art Gallery since 2021, Yvette has commissioned major artworks and exhibitions, created partnerships with leading art institutions, and secured funding to undertake major capital work projects to expand the Gallery's exhibition footprint. Yvette runs a diverse artistic program, including exhibitions, programs, education, collection management, and commissioning public art. Yvette formerly worked at the National Gallery of Australia, where she worked on major exhibitions and publications. She has also held appointments across the commercial and public art sectors.

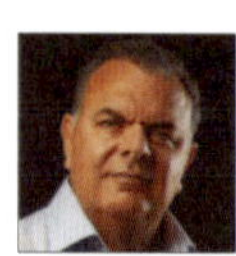



Ariel Freaner has over 35 years of experience in creative development, illustration, and design. He is the principal and founder of Freaner Creative & Design, an award-winning, San Diego-based full-service firm offering creative, digital, and graphic design services, including web and app design, editorial and print design, branding, and 3D development, among many other services. Freaner Creative & Design's multilingual, cross-border commercial campaigns in English and Spanish have distinguished it from many Southern California firms. It works with a diverse spectrum of clients in North America, Latin America, and abroad, earning multiple awards and numerous international and industry awards from various prestigious organizations, including the Davey Awards, Graphis, the International Design Awards (IDA), the American Institute of Graphic Arts (AIGA), the Society of News Design (SND), and *Print* magazine. In 2023, Freaner Creative & Design received five Emmy Awards for art direction, visual effects, and sound design. In 2024, they received two Emmy Awards for audio and sound design and eight nominations for art direction, visual effects, and long-form commercial production. Freaner Creative & Design's US clients include the County of San Diego, the City of San Diego, Motorola, the US Navy, Fujitsu, Eclipse Mobile Entertainment, Clarion Mobile Entertainment, Laura Scudder, *The San Diego Union-Tribune*, and Todd Gloria's successful San Diego mayoral campaign. Freaner Creative & Design's international clients span a wide range of industries and sectors, from the Mexican Red Cross, Fujitsu Latin America, Clarion Latin America, Uniradio, Calimax, the XXI Ayuntamiento de Tijuana, LINTEL, Las Colinas Industrial Park, *ZETA Weekly*, and TBWA Mexico, among many others. This diverse client portfolio is a testament to their versatility and ability to adapt to different client needs and industries. Ariel Freaner's dedication to the design industry extends beyond his professional achievements. He has served as a mentor to design students for more than 35 years, offering invaluable career advice to numerous educational organizations, including the Art Institute of San Diego, Cuyamaca College, San Diego City College, the San Diego City School District, and ITESO in Guadalajara, Mexico. His participation in multiple congresses and design expositions throughout the United States, Paris, China, and Mexico, both for students and commercial clients, is a testament to his commitment to fostering the next generation of design talent.

*(Opposite page) Bike Path Bentonville by Stefan Sagmeister*

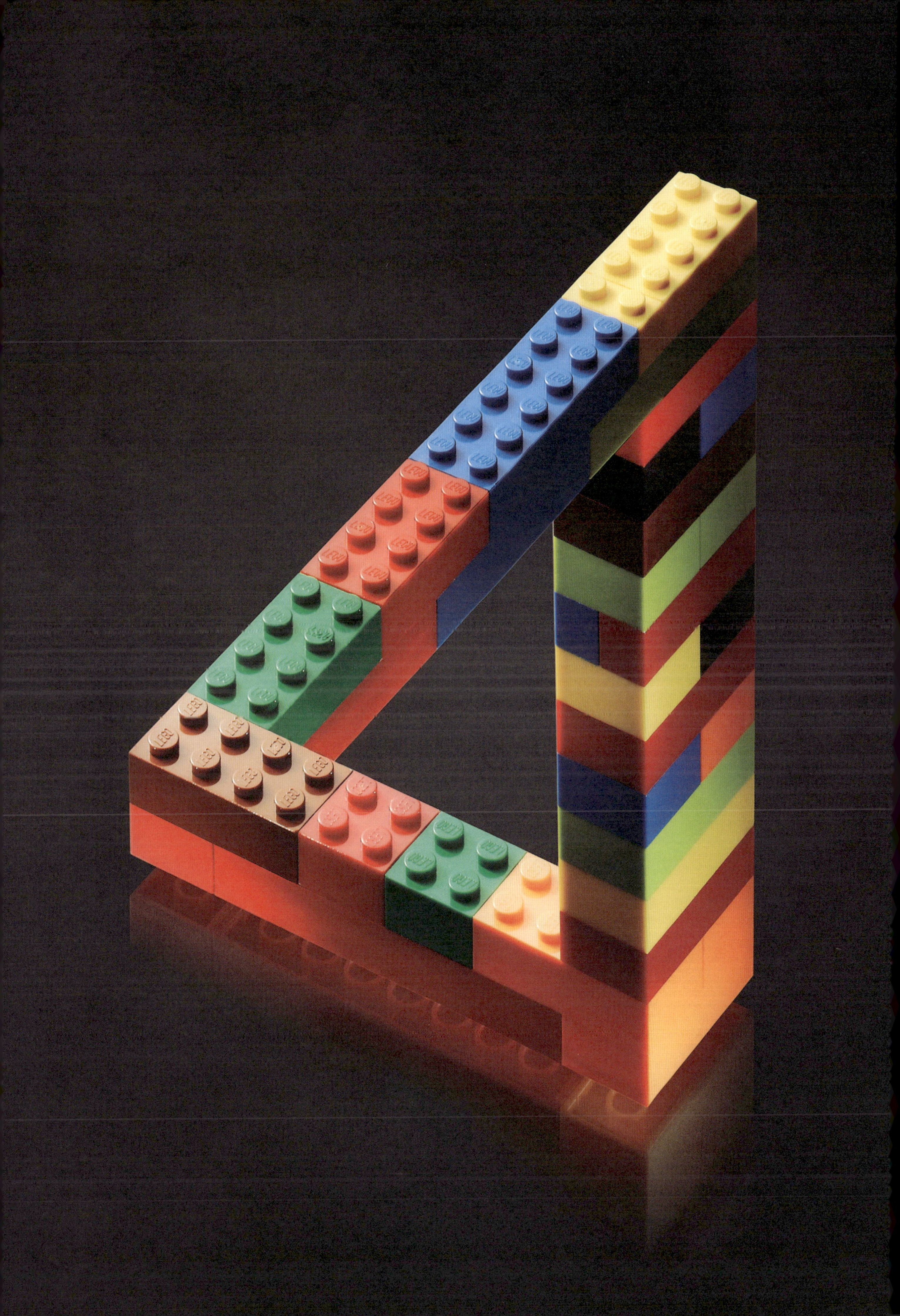

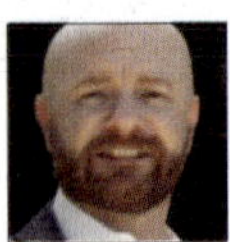
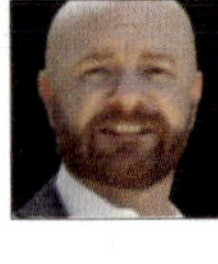

### Introduction by Adrian Kwiatkowski

Adrian is the vice president and partner at Bartell & Kwiatkowski (formerly Bartell & Associates). Before joining Bartell & Associates in 2011, he was the vice president of government and public affairs at The Monger Company for over ten years. During his career, he has been the project manager for numerous high-profile, controversial public policy campaigns, including the San Diego Needle Exchange Program, the San Diego Strong Mayor Campaign, and the Seal Protections in La Jolla. He has provided pro-bono political and strategic consulting to the San Diego chapter of the American Lung Association in successfully advocating for the Smoke-Free Beaches and Parks Ordinance. Adrian has extensive experience representing high-profile clients such as General Dynamics NASSCO, Carnival Corporation & Plc, the Corky McMillin Companies, and the Seal Conservancy and manages numerous non-profits. He grew up in San Diego and lives in the neighborhood of Mission Hills with his husband, Ray Thomas, and their two dogs, Archer and Liberty.



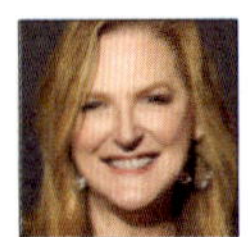

### 62  Stan Musilek (Graphis Master) / USA

Stan Musilek was born in Prague before Prague was cool. As a child, he turned his mother's pantry into a dark room and relentlessly photographed the neighbors. Eventually, his family fled Czechoslovakia for Germany, where he studied mathematics at Heidelberg University. He then moved to the United States, earning an MFA in photography from the Academy of Art University in San Francisco and playing as a midfielder for the University of San Francisco's men's soccer team, winning the Division I NCAA championship. Stan soon opened his own studio in San Francisco. A second studio eventually followed this in Paris. He has won numerous awards throughout his career and loves making his clients laugh.

### Introduction by Patti Judd

An award-winning creative director, accomplished marketing and film executive, and co-founder of the San Diego International Film Festival, Patti Judd joined Graphis as chief visionary officer. A key initiative was forming the Graphis Industry Advisory Board to promote greater industry insights and connections globally. Patti blends business savvy gained from 20+ years at her agency with the entertainment biz acumen garnered from working in music and film. Her studio, Judd Brand Media, champions her passion for creating innovative work, receiving over 100 awards in design, advertising, and marketing. Her work includes notable global brands such as WME, Disney, Mattel, the Montreux Jazz Festival, Century 21, Aramark, Service America, and Hilton, alongside numerous emerging brands, recording artists, and filmmakers. Her influence goes from helping launch a major live music venue, where she was a key player in its growth, to one of the top live jazz venues in the world to co-founding the San Diego International Film Festival. She holds two executive producer credits for a children's TV series on Nickelodeon and a feature film in association with the BBC, which premiered at Sundance (acquired by Universal Pictures). Currently, she is in development as executive producer on an exciting new animated children's series. Patti's nonprofit work includes being a foster youth board member and a past president of an arts and culture board benefiting Balboa Park, the largest urban cultural park in the US. Recently, she was awarded as an Altruist Honoree by *Modern Luxury* magazine.

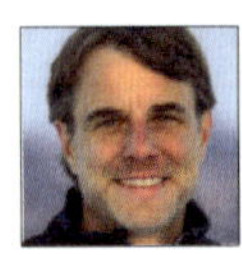

### 78  Eric Melzer / USA

Eric Melzer's curiosity and adventurous spirit have taken him from local basketball courts to the Amazonian rainforest in search of personal, authentic images. His publication credits and clients include *The New York Times*, *The Guardian*, The IHT, NRG, Cummins, Flex, Jera Americas, 3M, APM, UHG, CWT, the Glacier Conservancy, the Montana Department of Tourism, and more. His commercial photography focuses on climate change mitigation. His personal work celebrates local communities and good health through images of neighborhood play. His work has earned multiple awards from CA, IPA, AI/AP, the Color Awards, ASMP, and Graphis. He's lived in many places domestically and abroad and currently makes his home in Minneapolis, Minnesota.

### Introduction by Michael Cina

Michael Cina is a multidisciplinary artist and creative director. He leads Cina Associates, creating distinctive visual identities, typeface design, and art for international clients. His work, which has earned a Grammy nomination and an Emmy, extends into painting and is exhibited worldwide, reflecting his passion for visual expression and thoughtful artistic direction.



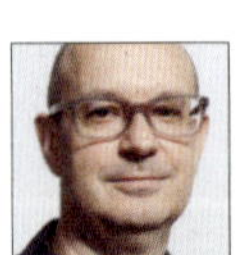
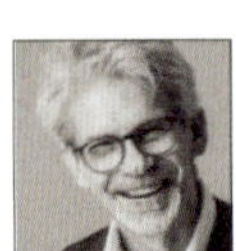

### 94  Mark Braught / USA *Portrait by Georgia Zumwalt*

Mark Braught studied graphic design at the Minneapolis College of Art & Design and graduated with a BFA from Indiana State University in 1979. He has lived and worked in Georgia since 1991. He joined Roger Sawhill to create what is now UP-Ideas in 2007. Mark's wide-ranging experience encompasses the design of books, identities, packages, collateral, exhibitions, and illustrations. His clients have included IBM, General Housewares, Churchill Downs, Warner Bros., the State of Indiana, the Cincinnati Zoo, the Women's League of Indiana, Citibank, ProServe, and AT&T. Mark's work has been recognized and received numerous awards from the NY Art Directors Club, *Communication Arts* magazine, *Print* magazine, the Society of Illustrators (NY and LA), Graphis, and other regional and local organizations. He has served as the president of the Indiana Art Directors Club, a board member of the Graphic Artist Guild (Indiana), and is a member of the Society of Illustrators, the Society of Typographic Arts, the Society of Children's Book Writers & Illustrators, and the Illustrators Partnership of America. Mark has lectured at institutions and organizations nationwide and has taught at the University of Georgia, the Portfolio Center, Ivy Tech Community College, Hollins University, and the Creative Circus.

*(Opposite page) Global Warning Poster by Paul Garbett*

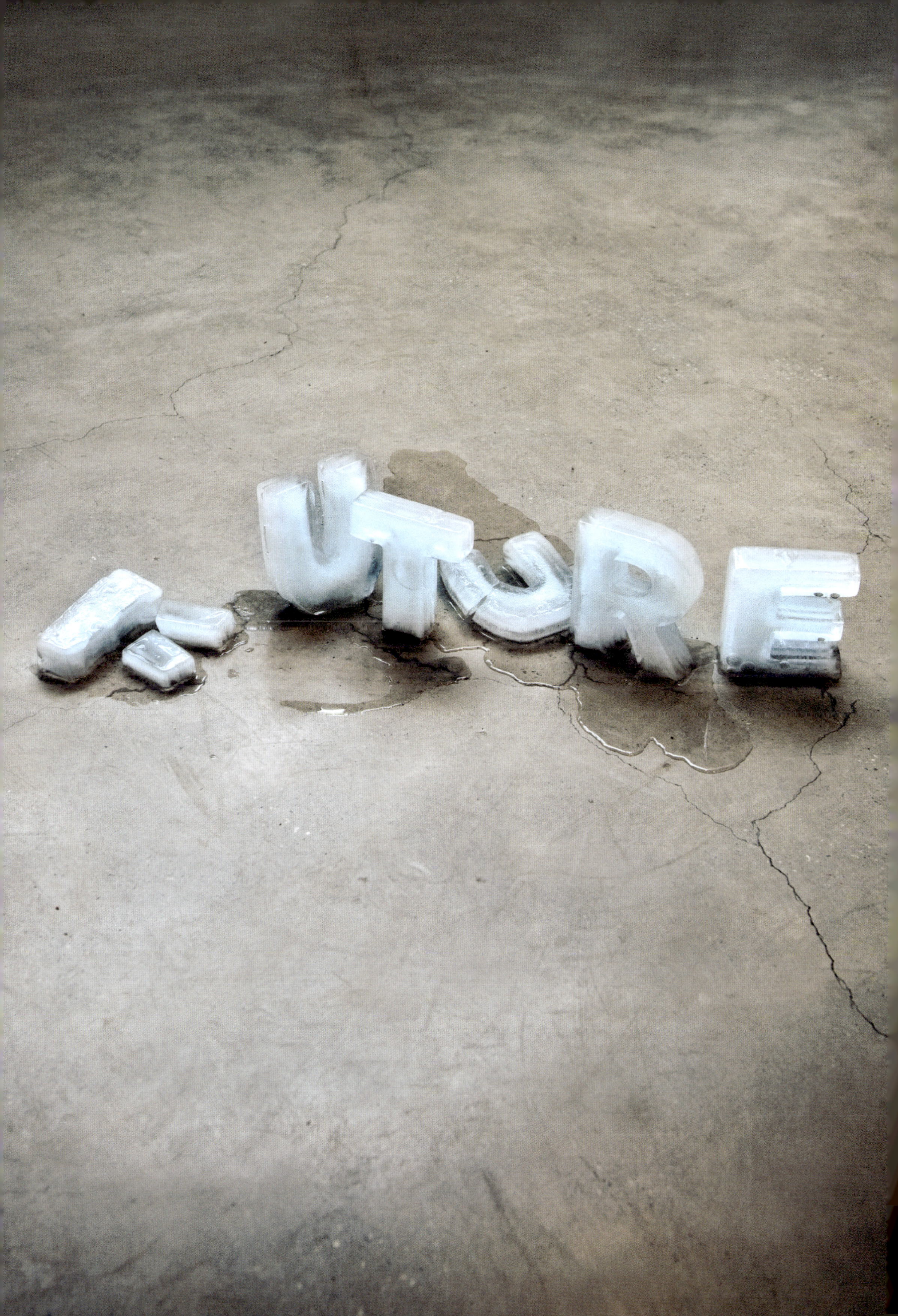

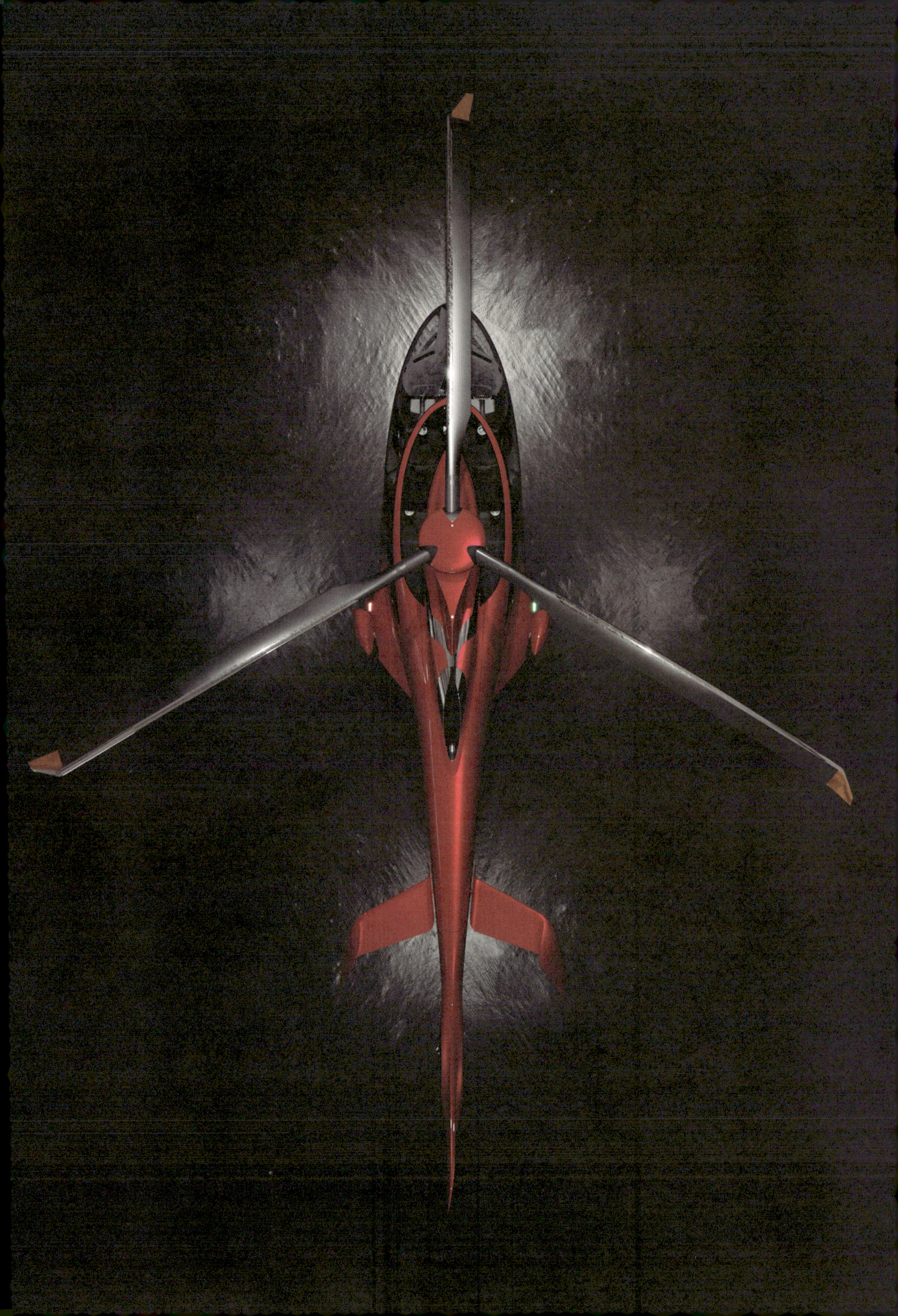

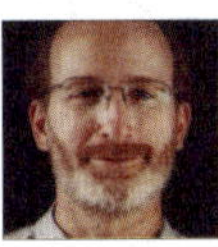

**Introduction by Roger Sawhil**
Roger Sawhill is a graphic designer with 40+ years of experience under his belt. At age 12, he knew he wanted to design logos. He progressed from paste-up and artboards to mouse and keyboard. This led to teaching computer and logo design classes at corporate training centers, the Portfolio Center, and the Creative Circus. His teaching career spanned 32 years, and he has taught well over 5,000 students. Since 2007, he has partnered with Mark Braught in their small design firm, UP-Ideas. Roger also has a strange pumpkin-carving obsession.

**PRODUCT:**

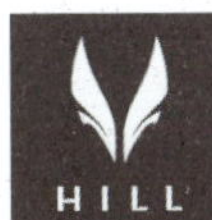


All Hill Helicopter vehicles and engines are designed and built in the company's UK factory, ensuring that the HX50 is as British as can be. The result is that the HX50 is the world's fastest-selling helicopter.

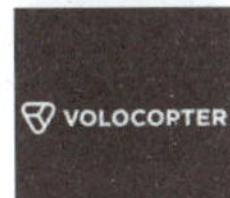


Since 2011, Volocopter has continually improved its initial VoloCity air taxi prototype, conducting thousands of test flights in the process. It envisions the vehicle being used in cities across the world. It is building a technological ecosystem to ensure that it performs safely and to a high standard across a range of environments.

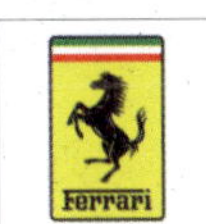


Ferrari is synonymous with luxury sports cars and the very best in motoring excellence. To date, it is responsible for by far the most Formula 1 wins of any automobile company. The Daytona SP3 is a prime example of Ferrari creating an exciting vehicle.

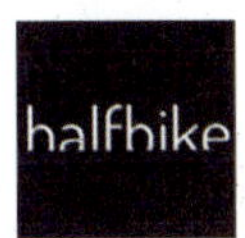


Halfbike describes creator and founder Martin Angelov as a pure minimalist. After a successful architectural career, he reestablished himself as an inventor focused on products that facilitate urban utopias. After years of prototypes and enhancements, he teamed up with a friend from architecture school, Mihail Klenov, to finesse the design and raise over $1 million in funding to bring Halfbike to the world.

**ARCHITECTURE:**

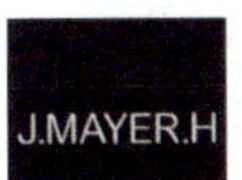


J. Mayer H. und Partner Architekten mbB considers the relationship between the human body, technology, and nature to be a key consideration in its design work. The detailed preservation of the House on Lake Como showcases how to do this in a way where technology is muted in favor of highlighting heritage.

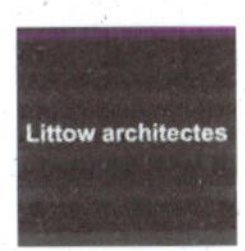


Littow Architectes founder Pekka Littow envisioned the Majamaja Off Grid Village as a "concrete response to the global trend towards sustainable construction and living." The finished village would go on to win a Dezeen Award in 2024 in the Small Project category.

**EDUCATION:**

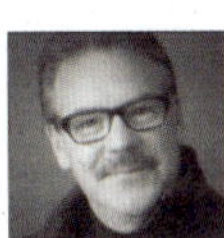


Thomas McNulty has been a brand and package design consultant for over 30 years in the United States and Europe. He served as the associate director and design educator of the School of Graphic Design at the Academy of Art University in San Francisco and received his degree from the ArtCenter College of Design. Thomas has successfully managed and directed many multinational brand and packaging programs, including Anheuser-Busch, Apple, Raychem, Oracle, Charles Krug Winery, Trinchero Family Estates, Anomaly Vineyards, Lynch Vineyards, Coca-Cola (Ireland), Kraft Foods, Mrs. Fields, Otis Spunkmeyer, and Safeway, winning numerous awards and recognition for design excellence from the likes of American Corporate Identity, Communication Arts, Graphis, Graphic Design USA, International Packaging, *Print* magazine, CMYK, and the Design Business Association. His company, Profile Design, was featured numerous times as a leading graphic design agency in the San Francisco Graphic Design Showcase publication.

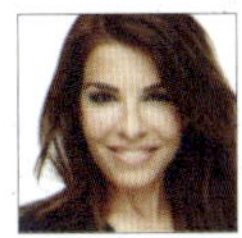

**Introduction by Anna Villano**
Anna Villano is the executive director of the School of Brand Communications and the School of Graphic Design at the Academy of Art University in San Francisco, where she teaches graphic design and advertising courses. Anna has led numerous collaborative student projects with renowned brands such as Adobe, Apple, NBCUniversal, VinFast, and Athletic Brewing Company. A leading expert in branding and advertising, she has worked at top agencies like Deutsch, FCB, and VaynerMedia, developing successful campaigns for brands like Taco Bell, Sonic, and Procter & Gamble. She is also a partner at INTENT, a branding and strategy agency.



*(Opposite page) HX50 by Hill Helicopters*

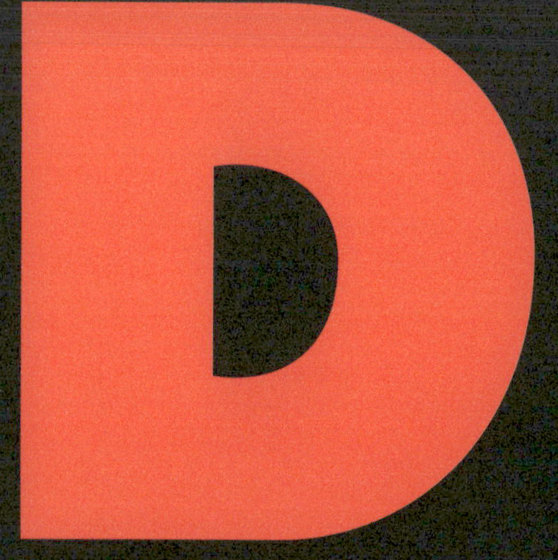

**DESIGN**

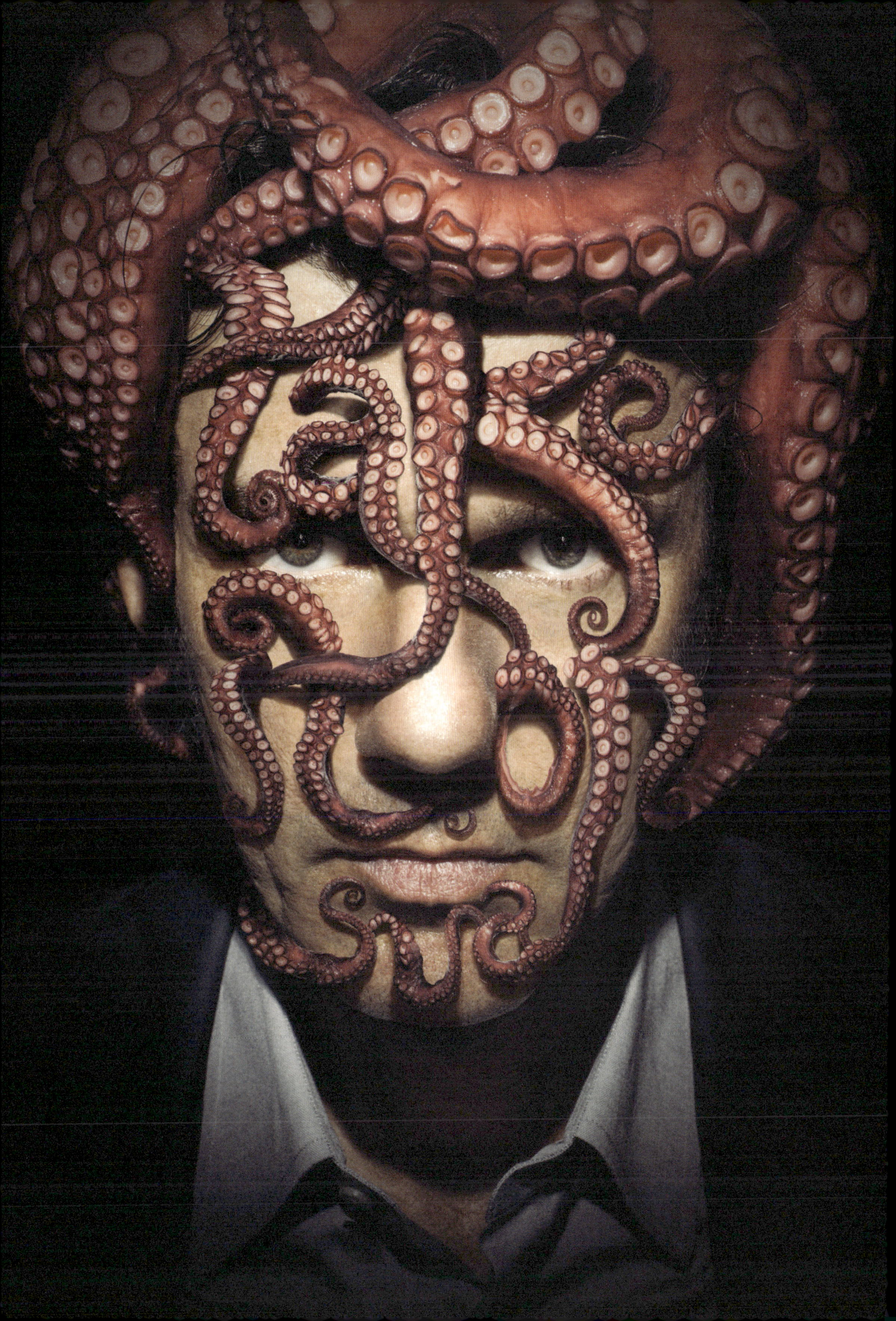

# Stefan Sagmeister: The Importance of Sabbaticals

I LOVED WORKING WITH STEFAN. IT WAS GREAT TO SEE FIRSTHAND HIS CONCEPTS AND SKETCHES AND HOW HE APPROACHES EACH PROJECT. THERE IS FREEDOM AND EXCITEMENT IN CREATING ART FOR STEFAN.

**Raxenne Maniquiz,** *Freelance Graphic Designer & Illustrator*

ALWAYS CURIOUS AND WITH A SINCERE AGENDA TO IMPROVE OUR EXPERIENCE, STEFAN ENCOURAGES DIALOGUE, THOUGHT, AND EXPLORATION.

**Bela Borsodi,** *Artist & Photographer*

STEFAN IS MUCH LIKE HIS WORK: INSPIRING, CREATIVE, INTELLIGENT, HUMOROUS, WISE, AND CURIOUS. ON TOP OF THAT, HE IS ONE OF THE KINDEST SOULS I HAVE EVER MET.

**Linus Lohoff,** *Freelance Art Director & Graphic Designer, Linus Lohoff Art Direction*

THIS ARTISTIC ICON IS SOMETHING OF A GRAPHIC DESIGN DAREDEVIL. THROUGH HIS WILDLY INVENTIVE WORKS, HE CHALLENGES CONVENTIONS AND COMMUNICATES IDEAS THAT CAN ALTER THE WAY WE PERCEIVE SOCIETY.

**Dan Rubinstein,** *Journalist & Podcaster, The Grand Tourist*

HIS ARTISTIC VISION THREADED HIS EMPATHY FOR THE HUMAN CONDITION THROUGH HIS LOVE FOR BEAUTY AND CREATED UNEXPECTED AND WELCOMED MOMENTS OF REFLECTION FOR PATIENTS AND CAREGIVERS USING TORONTO'S HOSPITAL TUNNELS.

**Garfield Mitchell,** *Chair, Weston Family Foundation*

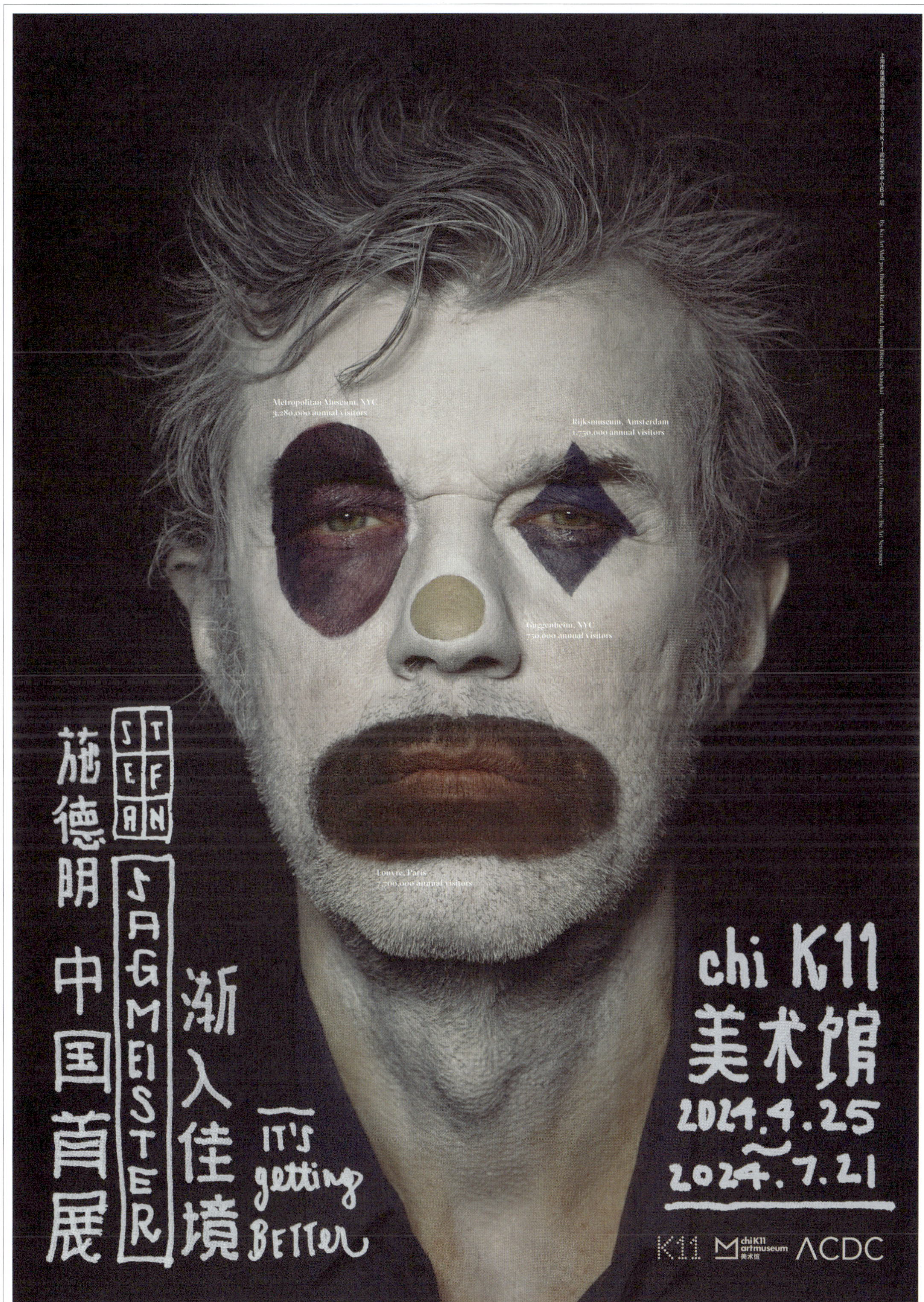


*(Page 9) Sagmeister SVA, Take It On. Design: Stefan Sagmeister, Jessica Walsh. Photography: Henry Leutwyler. Retouching: Erik Johansson.*
*(Above) It's Getting Better, Exhibition Poster in Shanghai. Design: Stefan Sagmeister. Photography: Henry Leutwyler. Make-up: Anastasia Durasova. Date: 2024.*

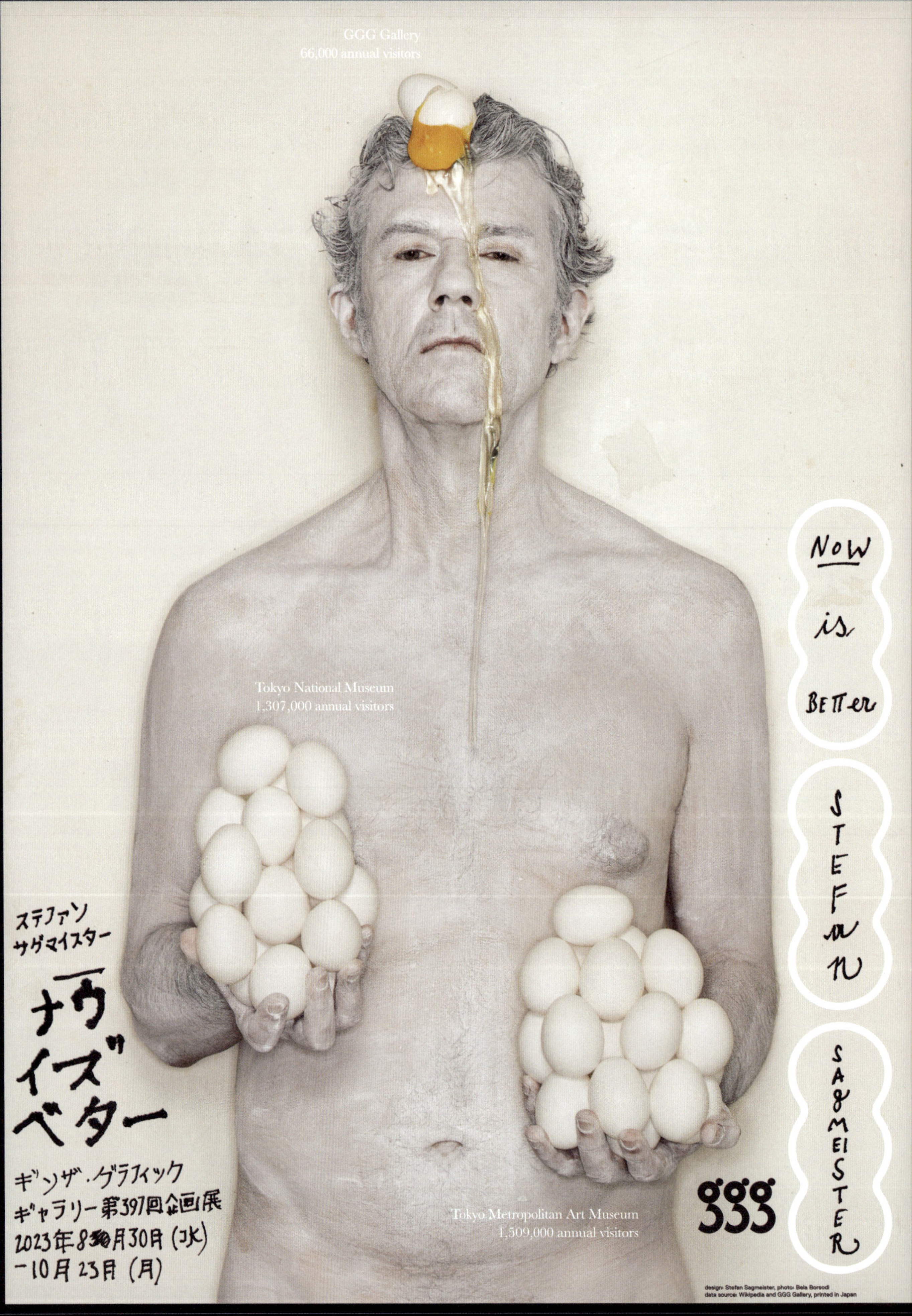

*Tokyo, Now is Better, Exhibition Poster in Tokyo. Photography: Henry Leutwyler. Make-up: Anastasia Durasova.*

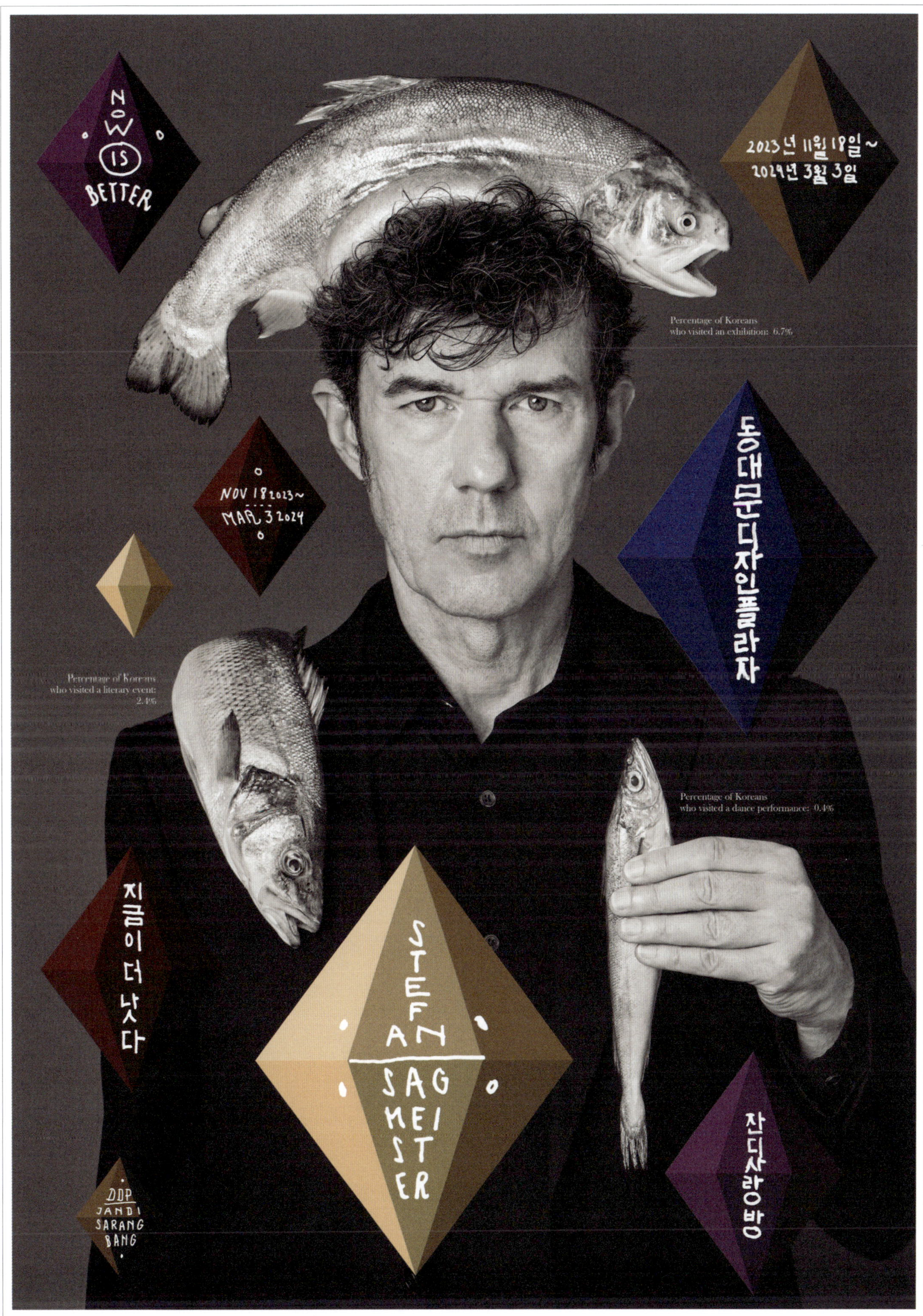


*Seoul, Now is Better. Design: Stefan Sagmeister. Photography: Bela Borsodi.*

Stefan Sagmeister blurs the boundaries between art, design, and philosophy. Known for his provocative and thought-provoking approach, Stefan has redefined what it means to be a graphic designer and is an icon in the industry. His projects, ranging from album covers and immersive exhibitions to art projects, challenge conventions while exploring deeply human themes like happiness and self-reflection. He transforms design into an emotional experience. He has a fearless approach to merging personal and professional creativity. Simply put, there's no one quite like him, and it was an honor to collaborate with him for so many years!

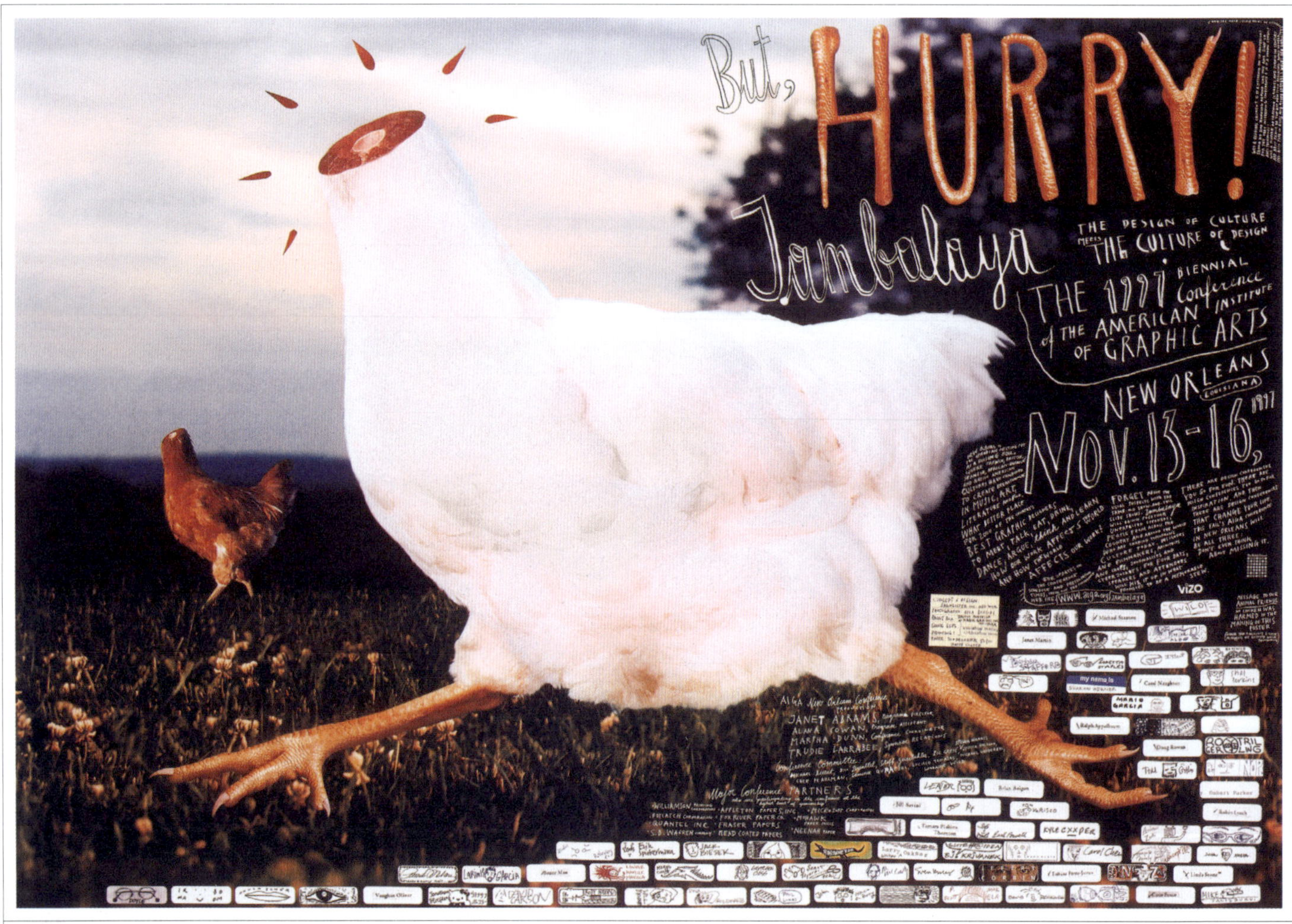


*Jambalaya. Photography: Bela Borsodi. Paint Box: Dalton Portella. Date: 1997.*

## Q&A: Stefan Sagmeister

*Your work is renowned for its ability to transform complex ideas into compelling visual narratives. What drives your creative process when tackling such profound themes?*

It occurred to me during my first sabbatical that I should try to use the language of communication design in areas that are not promotional. The first large project that came out of that thought was the "Things I've Learned in My Life So Far" series. As there was a lot of positive feedback, I continued looking for other areas to explore.

*If you were to summarize your design philosophy in one sentence, what would it be?*

I'm trying to create work that helps and delights people.

*You've built a career on challenging conventions and provoking thought—what's the most significant risk you've taken in your work, and how did it shape your perspective as a designer?*

My first sabbatical. Actually, doing it after building a studio for the previous seven years was very scary; I truly needed to overcome that fear. Sabbaticals ensured that I could continue to see my work as somewhat of a calling instead of a career or a nine-to-five job.

*What question do you feel most encapsulates the essence of your work?*

Is it possible to touch the heart of the viewer with design?

*How has your understanding of design evolved throughout your career?*

Form and beauty took on a completely new importance. When I started out, the only things important to me were the idea and the concept. Over time, I understood that everything works

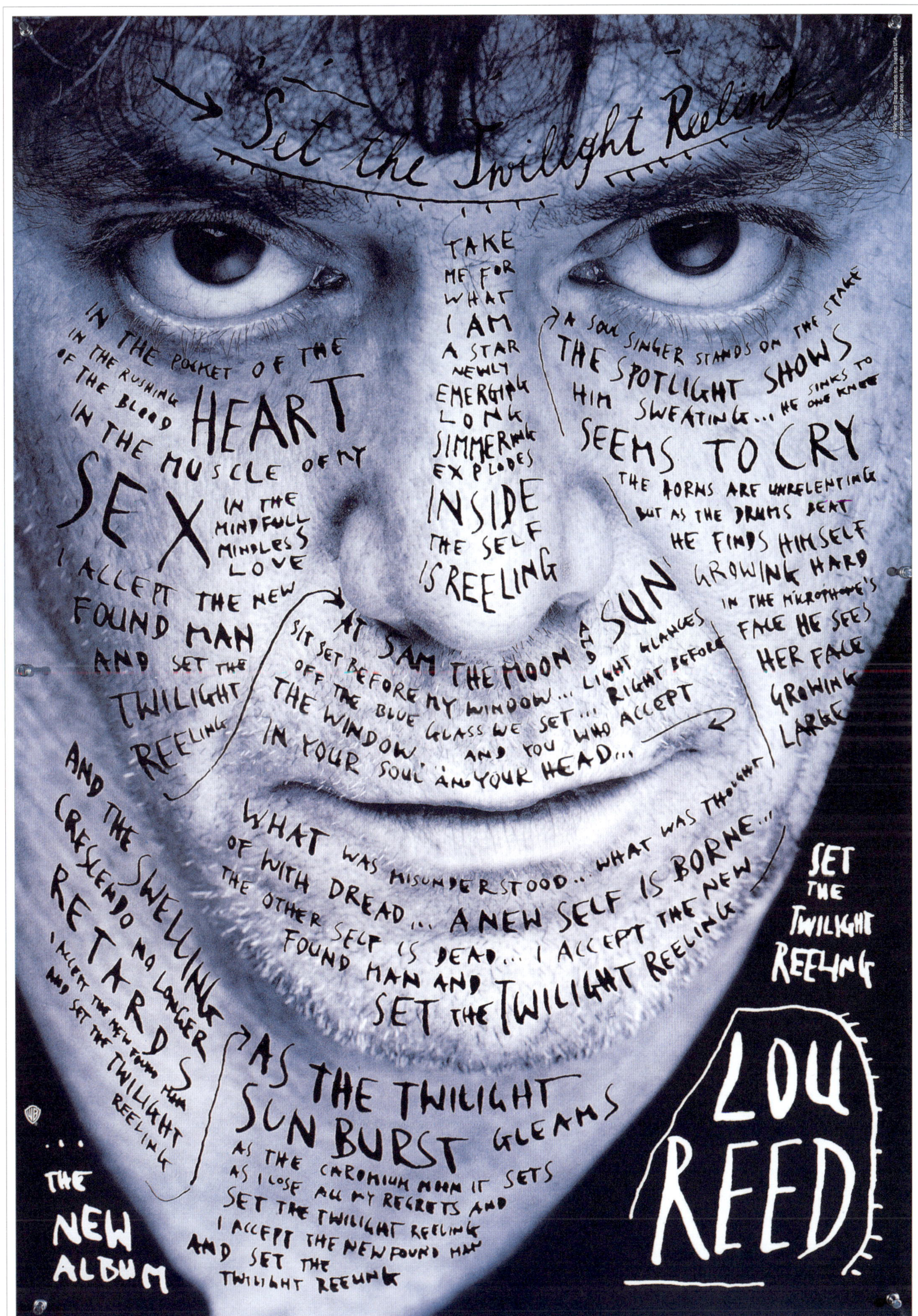


Lou Reed Poster. Art Direction & Design: Stefan Sagmeister. Photography: Timothy Greenfield-Sanders. Client: Warner Bros. Music Inc. Date: 1996.

much better when I take the form (and the color, the composition, the shape, and the materiality) seriously.

*Is there a single moment or project in your career that you see as a turning point?*
For someone on the outside, maybe the series "Things I've Learned in My Life So Far" because it is firmly rooted in graphic design and, at the same time, deeply personal. For myself, defining moments are always the things I'm working on right now, like "The Beautiful Numbers" series that deals with long-term thinking.

If I look at developments concerning the world from a long-term perspective—the only sense-making way—almost any aspect concerning humanity seems to get better. Fewer people go hungry, fewer people die in wars and natural disasters, and more people live in democracies—and live much longer lives—than ever before. 200 years ago, nine out of ten people could neither read nor write; now, it is just one out of ten. The goal behind these visualizations is that viewers might want to place them in their living rooms as reminders that the latest tweets are just tiny blips in an overall relatively healthy environment.

*When you're beginning a new project, where do you find your first spark of inspiration?*
All over the place: it could be a conversation, it could be the limitations, or it could be a term that has absolutely nothing to do with the project at hand.

*What's the biggest misconception people have about your work?*
When we still did commercial work—until five years ago—many students thought we should do whatever we wanted or thought was cool. This could not have been further from the truth; we tried to create work that worked very well for our clients (and very often it did). Now that we don't do commercial work anymore, we still don't do whatever we want but work within a very tight set of limitations.

*You've worked with iconic clients such as the Rolling Stones, HBO, the Guggenheim Museum, Lou Reed, and David Byrne. How do you approach designing for such culturally significant figures and institutions, and what have these collaborations taught you about balancing personal creativity with their unique visions?*
Of course, all these people and institutions come with lots of values and histories that informed a significant part of the content we designed for them. By the time we designed a cover for the Rolling Stones, they had already published two dozen albums and given thousands of concerts.

Right now, the overall process of working on a series such as "Now is Better" is similar to how a song is written. When I visited the bands, we worked within their rehearsal spaces, and it became clear that their songs began with a combination of tiny sparks from many directions: a segment of a lyric, a guitar riff, a bass line, or a particular beat.

Similarly, the pieces in the "Now is Better" series could begin with the discovery of an intriguing data set or a pleasing shape or color scheme before combining all of these factors atop a historical painting.

*Who has been a particularly memorable collaborator or client, and what made that partnership stand out?*
Here is a very long account from my diary about my first meeting with Mr. Mick Jagger:

On Wednesday, a brand new and extra clean stretch limo picks me up at the studio; we are going to Newark Airport. The driver hands over business class tickets for LA, and I have a stupid grin on my face all the way to the airport. Looking out over the New Jersey industrial landscape with the Statue of Liberty at my back, I contemplate if this is one of those "happy" moments I have about once a year. The next morning, Mick's assistant, Lucy, meets me in the bar, gives me a quick rundown on Mick, and we go to the suite. In the elevator, I'm nervous. Mick opens the door and turns around immediately without saying hello, and I feel awkward. Lucy introduces us; he's friendly but busy going through a Sotheby's catalog with Charlie Watts.

"At $9 million, that's a real bargain," he says in a heavy British accent, looking at a Monet painting. "Pity I have no walls left to hang it." I help Lucy open the water bottles while Mick grabs my portfolio and says, "So, you're the floaty one."

"The floaty one?"

"Yeah, all your covers seem to float in the plastic box."

He likes the Lou Reed package and the attention to detail in some of the others, and I can stop being nervous. I ask him about his favorite Stones covers, and he says without hesitation: "Exile on Main Street," "Sticky Fingers," and "Some Girls." These are my favorites as well: "We should have an easy time working together since I would have told you exactly the same covers only in a different order: 'Sticky Fingers,' 'Some Girls,' and 'Exile on Main Street.'" Charlie (in a lowered voice) asks Mick, "What's on the 'Sticky Fingers?'" to which Mick replies, "Oh, you know Charlie, the one with the zipper, the one that Andy did." The stupid, happy grin is back on my face.

Mick shows me the presentation for the stage designs, labeled "The Blasphemy Tour," with a huge Baroque cross in the center of the stage: "Just look at it for style; forget about the title and the cross, we got rid of that." I mention that I'm certainly glad they did 'cause after having had the orthodox Hindus on my back for the use of Hindu iconography on the Aerosmith cover, I have little desire to revisit the religious world and have right-wing Christian groups making bomb threats.

Charlie asks me about my accent, and I tell him all about Bregenz, Austria, that I have lived in New York for eight years, and that I'll fly back there tonight. "Oh, you came here specially for this? So this is like a little vacation then." I tell him I feel like I've won first prize in "The Big Rolling Stones Meet the Band All Expenses Paid Radio Show" contest. They crack up, and I am out of there. I take the limo back to Rizzoli's, get some books on Baroque, meet with the stage designers, and fly out at 8:30. I feel good and am asleep before the plane leaves the ground, having learned no big lesson whatsoever.

*Which clients or collaborators do you think understood and championed your vision best, and how did that impact the final result?*
David Byrne is visually literate, which makes it very easy to work with him. We seem to be interested in similar visual directions. We all but stopped designing album covers after the first sabbatical in 2000—there were just too many other interesting things to design, and music stopped playing the same role in my life as I got older.

*Who have been your biggest creative influences throughout your career, and how have they shaped your approach to design and storytelling?*
Tibor Kalman was the single most influential person in my design life and my one and only design hero. 35 years ago, as a student in NYC, I called him every week for half a year and got to know the M&Co. receptionist well. When he finally agreed to see me, it turned out I had a sketch in my portfolio rather similar in concept and execution to an idea M&Co.

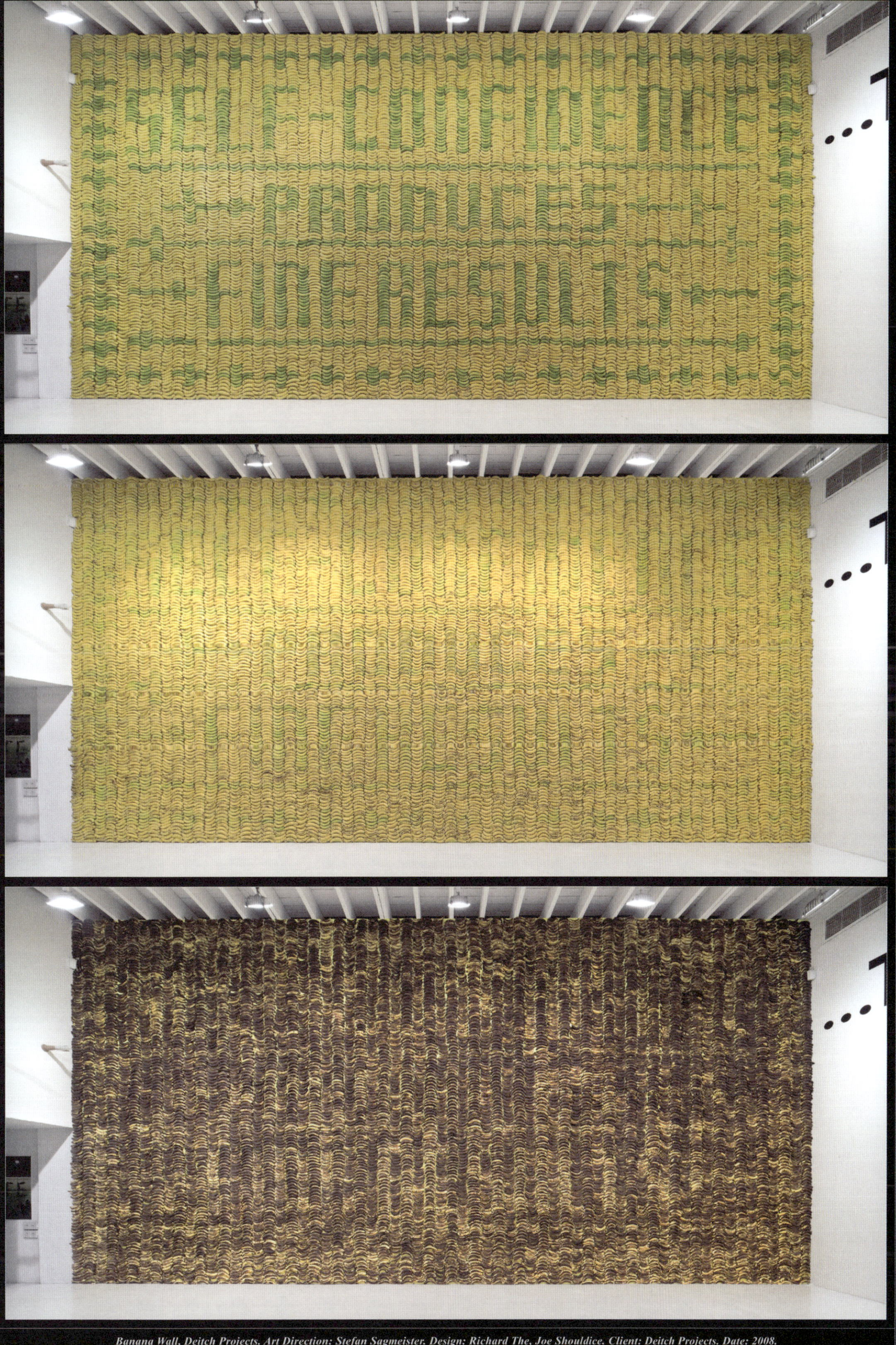



*Banana Wall, Deitch Projects. Art Direction: Stefan Sagmeister. Design: Richard The, Joe Shouldice. Client: Deitch Projects. Date: 2008.*

was just working on: He rushed to show me the prototype out of fear I'd say later he stole it out of my portfolio. I was so flattered. When I finally started working there five years later, I discovered it was, more than anything else, his incredible salesmanship that set his studio apart from all the others. There were probably a number of people around who were as smart as Tibor (and there were certainly a lot who were better at designing), but nobody else could sell these concepts without any changes and get those ideas with almost no alterations out into the hands of the public. Nobody else was as passionate. As a boss, he had no qualms about upsetting his clients or employees (I remember his reaction to a logo I had worked on for weeks and was very proud of: "Stefan, this is TERRIBLE, just terrible. I am so disappointed."). His big heart was shining through, nevertheless. He did good work containing good ideas for good people.

*Are there any artists, designers, or thinkers—past or present—that you constantly return to for inspiration?*
Right now, my influences are likely more coming from the art world: James Turrell, John Baldessari, Ellsworth Kelly, and the Cusco School of Art from the 18th century being classic influences.

*What early life experiences or environments sparked your interest in design?*
I was very lucky as I knew at about 15 that I wanted to become a designer. I had joined a small local youth magazine called *Alphorn* and discovered there that I was much more interested in creating the layouts than writing the articles. Furthermore, I was fascinated by album covers and thought that would be a wonderful thing to do with my life.

*Has there been a particular piece of advice or perspective from a mentor or peer that has stuck with you and influenced your creative journey?*
Tibor had an uncanny knack for giving advice and dispersing morsels of wisdom packaged in rough language later known as Tiborisms: "The most difficult thing when running a design company is not to grow," he told me when I opened my own little studio. "Just don't go and spend the money they pay you, or you are going to be the whore of the ad agencies for the rest of your life," was his parting sentence when I moved to Hong Kong to open up a design studio for Leo Burnett.

*What books, films, or other media have deeply influenced your approach to design?*
Edward de Bono's *De Bono's Thinking Course.* It includes a technique that calls for forming a senseless sentence about a problem in aid of coming up with an idea. For example, if I have to design a lamp, my sentence might be, "My lamp can fly." So I might think wings, a light-up ball that bounces about the room, lights hanging like a mobile... In the end, my lamp will likely not have wings, but I entered the problem from a different angle, avoiding the regular roads my brain normally takes.

*Are there any lesser-known designers, creatives, or colleagues whose work you feel deserves greater recognition?*
Yes, there is a photographer in New York called Bela Borsodi; he has been working for two or three decades and creating fantastic work throughout and, for some reason, has not become as famous as he clearly would deserve.

*Your designs often evoke profound emotional responses—how do you balance aesthetic appeal with emotional depth?*

If I take the "Now is Better" project as an example, data by itself, shown in Excel documents, is cold and communicates with great difficulty. I am trying to make the data dance.

*In an era of AI and automation, how do you see the role of the designer evolving, especially in creating meaningful experiences?*
I do not know. I myself have a rather dull crystal ball. I'm following a number of experts I trust in this regard, and they are split between opinions that this will have more upsides than downsides and people who see a severe danger for humanity.

*You've always embraced vulnerability in your work. What's a moment of personal vulnerability that shaped your creative journey?*
The late Quentin Crisp, British queen extraordinaire and subject of Sting's song "I'm an Englishman in New York," came to visit our students at the graduate department of the School of Visual Arts in New York. Among the very many quotable things he mentioned was that he used to say to journalists, "Everybody is interesting." They came back and said, "Mr. Crisp, this is just simply not true; there are lots of utterly boring people out there." So he had to revise it: "Everybody who is honest is interesting." This has impressed me much and informed many of our projects.

Every designer wants to create interesting work: True honesty is a fantastic strategy.

*Your projects often push societal norms. Do you feel you have a responsibility to use design as a tool for cultural commentary?*
When we created the large exhibit on "Beauty" with the accompanying Phaidon book, we were among the very few in design singing its praises. Since then, more important voices have joined: Jacques Herzog (of Herzog & de Meuron) and Renzo Piano stated the importance of beauty in architecture; in fact, last year, a whole architectural conference and symposium was held under the title of "Beauty." The most famously ugly buildings in New York—Penn Station and LaGuardia Airport—have been revitalized and injected with beauty (not enough, of course). I believe we are on the right track.

*Your use of social media to openly critique design projects is both bold and collaborative. What inspired you to create this platform for public critique, and how do you think it impacts the design community as a whole?*
My Instagram project was largely influenced by the late artist Louise Bourgeois, who was kind enough to have ten people over at her studio every Sunday in order to critique their work. I was one of those critiqued people, and it left a lasting impression on me.

I first copied her idea directly and had ten young designers come into the studio on Mondays. When that became impractical, I switched to Instagram. And, of course, like in every form of teaching, energy flows in both directions.

*What does failure mean to you, and how has it informed your creative process over the years?*
Failure right now seems very much like an overrated strategy. Every second conference speaker talks about the virtue of mistakes and the wonders of failure. I do know a designer who really leans out the window very far; he does take on lots of risks doing large jobs, and when he fails, it is neither pretty nor enjoyable. People lose their jobs, and people get sued. But he does really do good work.

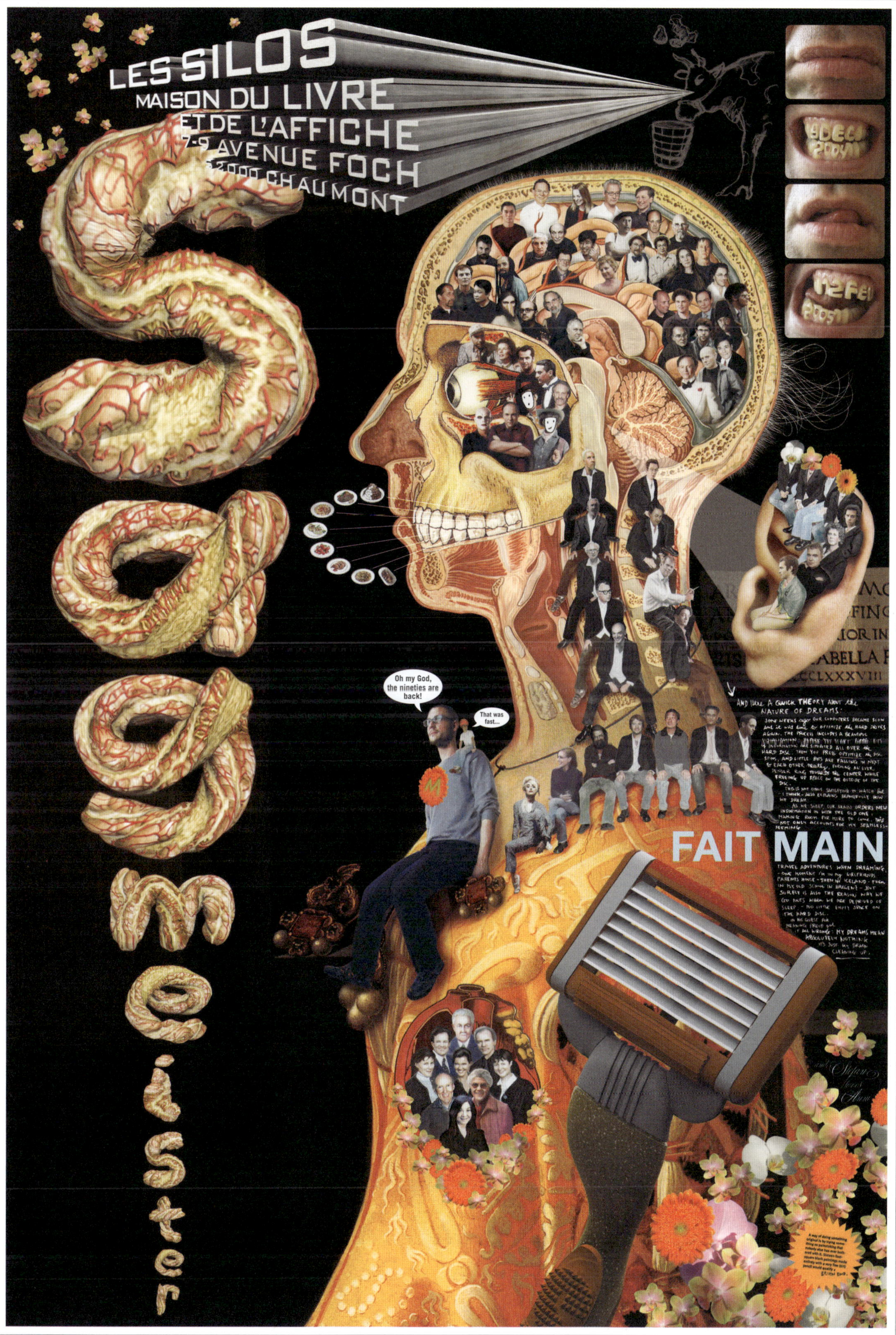


*Chaumont Poster. Art Direction: Stefan Sagmeister. Design: Matthias Ernstberger. 3D Illustration: Aaron Hockett. Illustration: Gao Ming, Mao. Client: Chaumont, France. Year: 2004.*

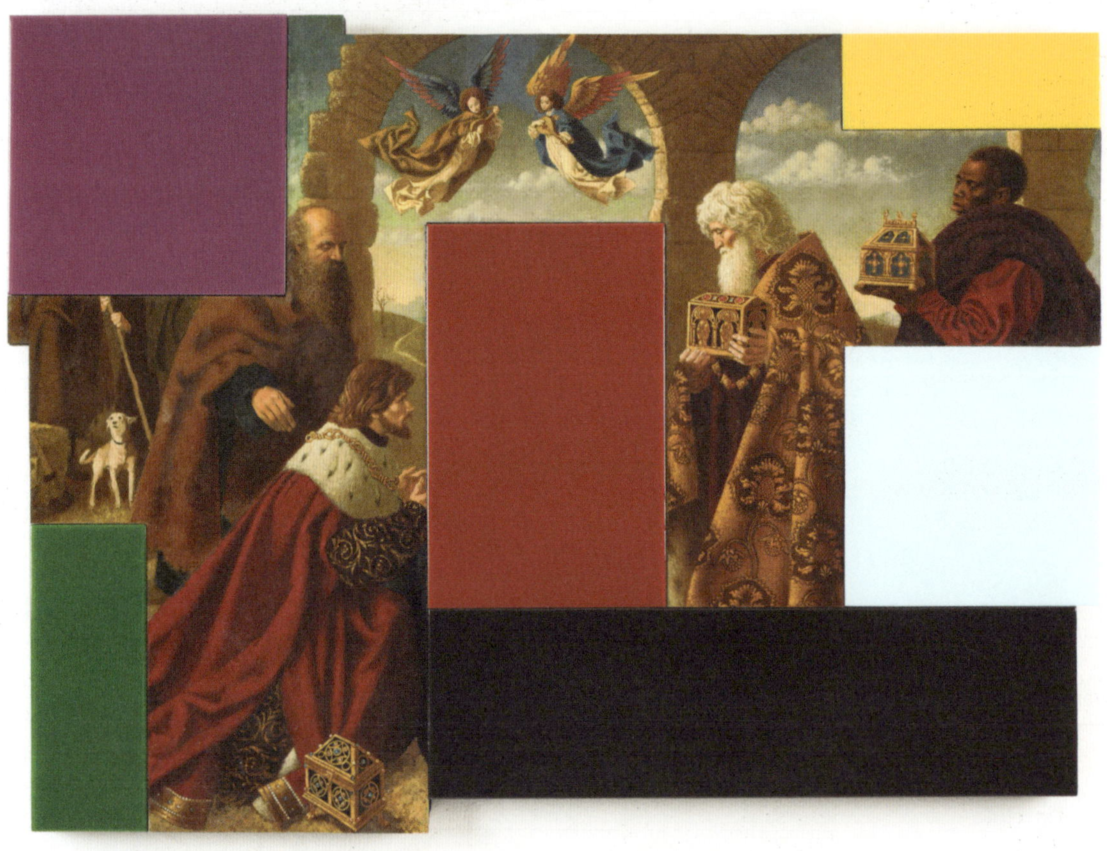

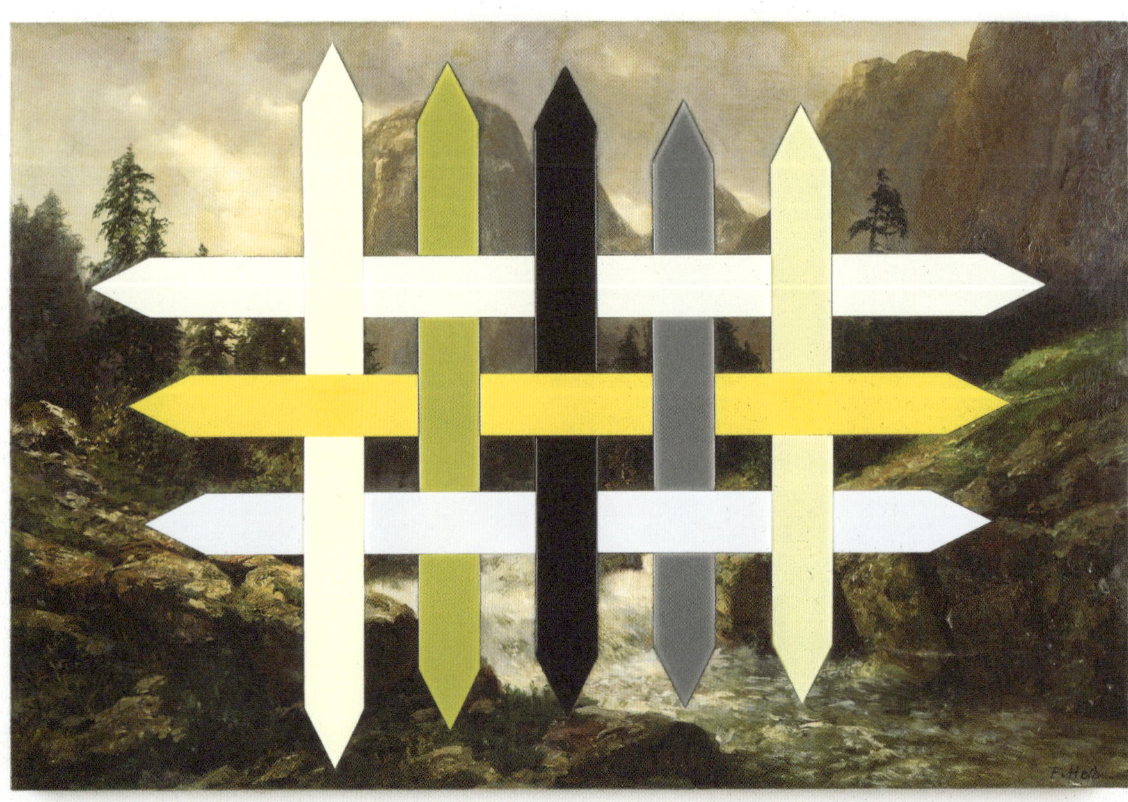

*(Top)* Giving It Away. Social spending as a share of the GDP. France: 32% black shape. Spain: 24% dark red shape. UK: 22% purple shape. US: 19% light blue shape. South Korea: 10% green shape. Mexico: 7% dark yellow shape. Sources: Joseph Moore and Thomas Memecek (2018). OurWorldinData.org.
*(Bottom)* Helping and Healing. Percentage of the population who lives in poverty by country, 2021. Horizontal shapes, from top to bottom: Israel: 17.3%. Japan: 15.7%. US: 15.1%. Vertical shapes, from left to right: New Zealand: 12.4%. UK: 11.2%. Germany: 10.9%. Austria: 10%. Switzerland: 9.9%. Historic painting: F. Held, 19th century, Die Mühlsturzhörner im Berchtesgadener Land.

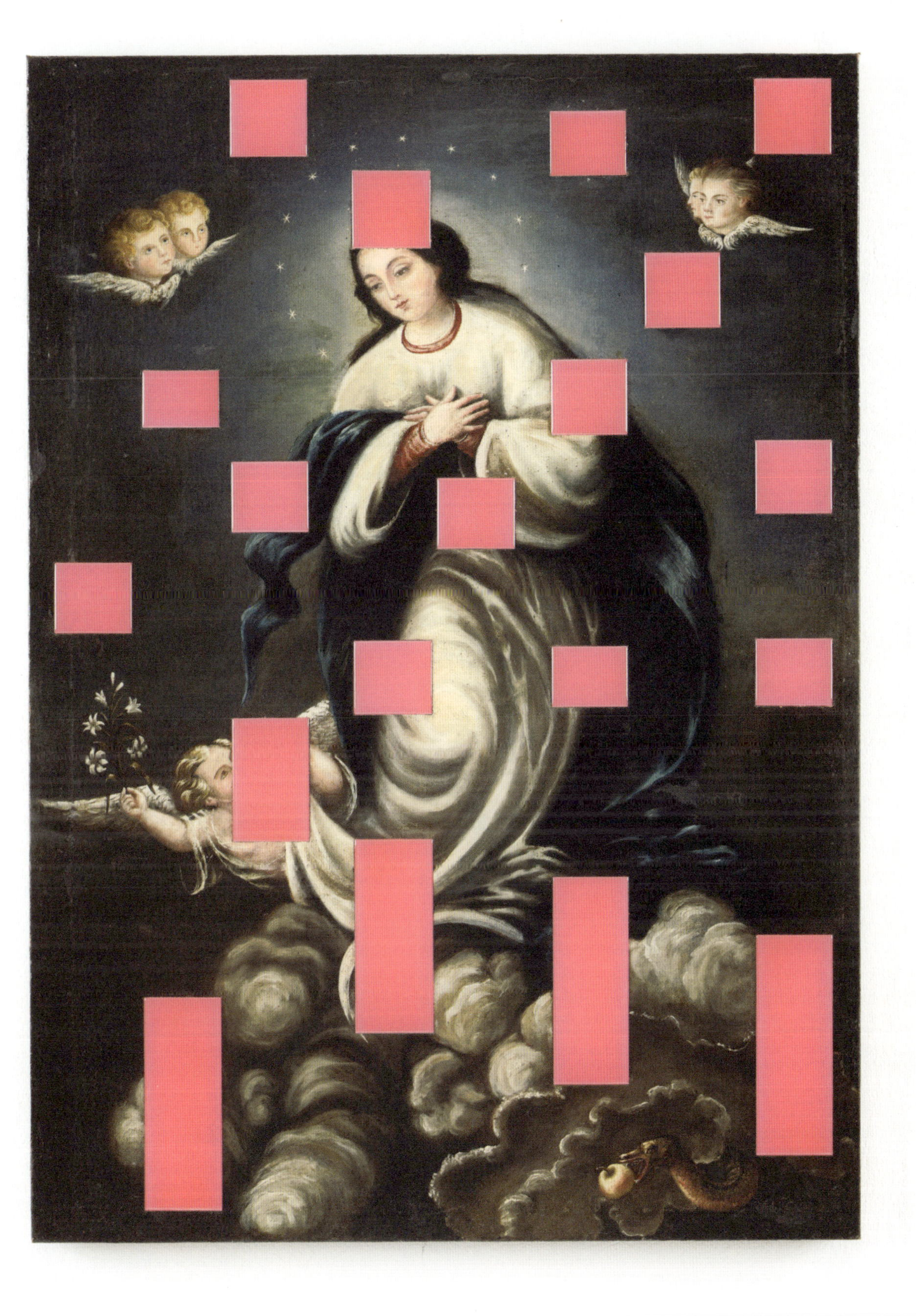

*Burning Brightly. Number of years various artists lived. From left to right and top to bottom: Raphael (1483-1520), 37 years. Vincent van Gogh (1853-1890), 37 years. Georges Seurat (1859-1891), 31 years. Henri de Toulouse-Lautrec (1864-1901), 36 years. Franz Marc (1880-1916), 36 years. Egon Schiele (1890-1918), 28 years. Amedeo Modigliani (1884-1920), 36 years. Yves Klein (1928-1962), 34 years. Eva Hesse (1936-1970), 34 years. Robert Smithson (1938-1973), 35 years. Blinky Palermo (1943-1977), 34 years. Gordon Matta-Clark (1943-1978), 35 years. Jean-Michel Basquiat (1960-1988), 29 years. Keith Haring (1958-1990), 32 years. Andy Warhol (1928-1987), 59 years. Pablo Picasso (1881-1973), 92 years. Louise Bourgeois (1911-2010), 99 years. Bruno Giacometti (1907-2012), 105 years. Françoise Gilot (1921-2023), 102 years. Source: Statista 2023.*

# STEFAN IS A CREATIVE GENIUS WHO SURPRISES WITH UNEXPECTED VISUAL MASTERY, AND HE IS CONTINOUSLY EVOLVING. **B. Martin Pedersen,** *Designer*

*If you could redesign any aspect of the modern world—be it social systems, urban spaces, or technology—what would you tackle first and why?*
The airport security process, because it makes the lives of an unusual number of people a little bit worse.

*How do different cultures influence your work, especially projects that resonate on a global scale?*
I've worked all around the world on different continents and for different cultures. Luckily, significant agreement exists throughout all cultures, for example, about what we find and don't find beautiful. Blue is the favorite color from Iceland to South Africa, from Kyoto to Rio de Janeiro. The circle is the favorite basic shape in every culture in the world.

*With exhibitions like "Now is Better" being overwhelmingly embraced in places like Ukraine, how do you approach creating work for diverse cultural contexts? Do you change your designs to resonate locally, or do you let the audience interpret them on their own terms?*
With the "Now is Better" exhibits, we sometimes include pieces talking about data sets from the local culture, but I have always found that an audience is just as interested in the sets from other cultures.

*Do you see design as a reflection of culture, a tool for shaping and evolving it, or both?*
Design is shaped by culture and is actively shaping it.

*Your work often intersects with art, philosophy, and sociology. How do you see these disciplines contributing to the cultural relevance of design?*
I find the juicy spots are to be found in the cracks between these directions.

*What role does beauty play in culture, and how has this shaped your exhibitions and philosophy?*
We find the things that we know beautiful. From an evolutionary point of view, if we have encountered it before and it has not eaten us yet, we like it. The context in which we see it is important: If we feel safe, we want a larger portion of newness added to what we know. If we are scared, we can only stand a small bit of novelty. I've encountered this phenomenon often with our clients. When business was good, they were ready to take risks. When times were difficult, they would rather do what worked five years before.

*Reflecting on your recent retrospective at SVA, how did revisiting your extensive body of work influence your current creative direction and future projects?*
Hmmm, I am not sure. I have to admit that I am, in general, not such a big fan of retrospective exhibits in design, but it did make sense at SVA with its large student audience. Outside of that, I'd rather create exhibits that make a particular point.

*Your exhibitions, like "The Happy Show" and "Beauty," have been viewed by audiences worldwide. What's your process for turning abstract concepts like happiness or beauty into immersive, physical experiences?*
It's really the core of communication design—looking at a very large subject and trying to communicate in a limited time within a limited space.

*Do you view your exhibitions as extensions of your graphic design practice, or do they represent an entirely different creative outlet for you?*
They are an extension and very much part of my practice. I spent my formative years in Vienna, where art and design got to be very close to each other and where the practitioners insisted there was no difference between the two. Klimt painted and, at the same time, designed posters, and so did Schiele and Kokoschka. In Germany, the faculty of the Bauhaus encouraged their students to be involved in the disciplines of art, architecture, and design simultaneously: Josef Albers designed furniture, tableware, and record covers, even though he was primarily known as a painter. These cultures still influence my ideas today.

*Your book, Things I Have Learned in My Life So Far, is both deeply personal and universally resonant. What inspired you to compile those lessons, and how has their meaning evolved over time?*
About 25 years ago, we started publishing maxims—things I had found in my diary—under the title "Things I've Learned in My Life So Far" in a wide variety of media, like on billboards, magazine spreads, and gallery walls. All these maxims came out of my life and sometimes took on complex typographic forms like letters made out of 6,500 ripe and unripe bananas at Deitch Projects in NYC. These maxims were also published as a book by Phaidon and seem to have had an unintended influence on the flood of typographic wisdom that designers started to flood Instagram with about a decade later.

*In Now is Better, you tackle the topic of optimism. What compelled you to explore this theme, and how did creating the book impact your own outlook on the future?*
I started to think about this subject when I was invited to be a designer in residence at the American Academy in Rome. I worked out of a gorgeous studio and had fantastic lunches and dinners with artists, writers, architects, and archeologists in the courtyard. These were quite salon-like meals with ever-changing pairings of table mates. One evening, I wound up next to a very sharp lawyer who worked at the European court. We got to talk politics, and he told me that what we are now experiencing in Hungary, Poland, and Turkey, as well as in Brazil and the US, is really the end of democracy.

So, after dinner, I looked it up! When did modern democracy start? How did it do over the past two centuries? Where are we now?

Well, in 1823, only one democracy arguably existed: the United States. In 1923, 18 democratic countries had already been established following WWI. In 2024, we now have 96 democratic countries, and, for the first time in human history, more than half the world's population lives in a democracy, so he COULD NOT HAVE BEEN MORE WRONG. Not only are we not seeing the end of democracy, we are living in the absolute golden age of democracy. This was interesting to me: a smart, highly educated person who clearly has no clue about the world he lives in.

*Your exhibitions often engage the audience in unexpected ways, like encouraging them to write on walls or interact with installations. Why is participation so central to your work?*
Well, the more I can make a viewer participate, the higher the chances of communicating something successfully.

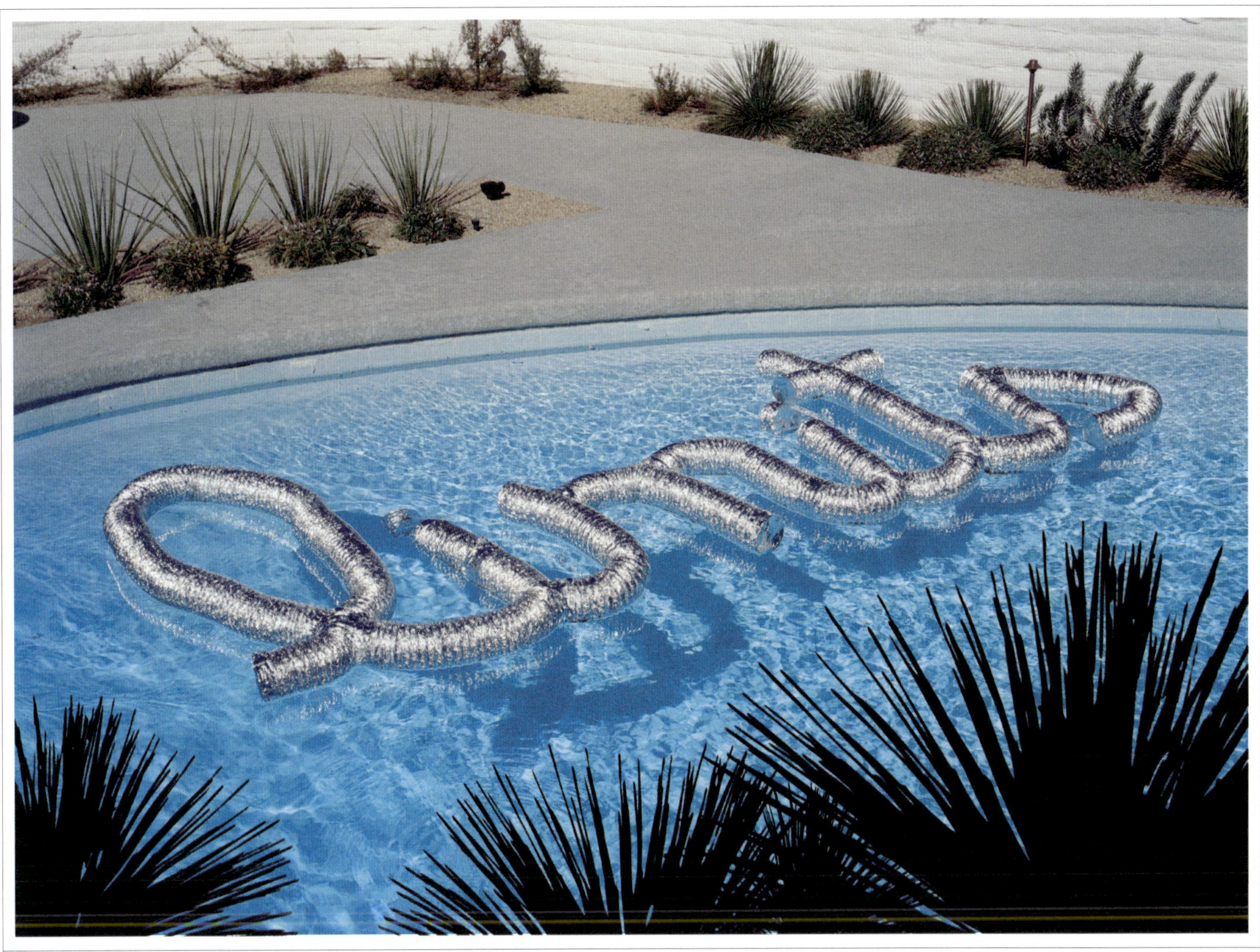



Limits. Art Direction: Stefan Sagmeister. Design: Stefan Sagmeister, Matthias Ernstberger. Photography: Matthias Ernstberger. Client: Art Grandeur Nature. Year: 2004.

**What's the biggest challenge in translating the conceptual depth of your books into exhibitions—or vice versa?**
You can put much more information into a book than an exhibit, so funneling this down to the essentials is essential. And, of course, we can do things in a book that we can't do in an exhibit and vice versa.

**Are there any themes or ideas you've yet to explore in a book or exhibition but feel drawn to in the future?**
I would hope so. I won't be taking on any commercial client projects in the foreseeable future. It is possible that I might feel differently some years from now—I always have incredible difficulties predicting what might get me excited in the future. Still, for now, I will continue to look into myself and see what resonates. As I have been working as a designer for 40 years, I am extremely happy to indulge in this luxury.

**You've discussed the importance of taking sabbaticals throughout your career. How do those breaks reshape your creative process?**
At the beginning of my first sabbatical, I discovered fairly quickly that my initial desire to conduct this year without a plan ("a vacuum of time") was ill-fated, and I came up with a very tight hourly plan. I looked through my diary and wrote down all the instances where I had complained about how busy I was and that I would really like to do "X" if I were not so busy. I added to this list, ordered them by importance into three, two, and one hourly segments, and wound up with a schedule, just like in grade school.

**What advice would you give to others about the value of stepping away from their work?**
I am not in a position to determine what other people should do, but I can say this: I have now talked to dozens and dozens of people who took a sabbatical, rich and poor, singles and families. EVERY single person thought it was among the best things they had ever done in their lives.

**Sagmeister Inc.** www.sagmeister.com
*See his Graphis Master Portfolio at graphis.com.*

# STEFAN IS AN AMAZING PERSON AND A BRILLIANT ARTIST. REALIZING PROJECTS WITH HIM IS GREAT FUN. HE IS EXCELLENT AT CONVEYING PROFOUND MESSAGES IN HIS INIMITABLE WORK.

**Maximilian Hutz,** *Founder & Owner, Galerie Maximilian Hutz*

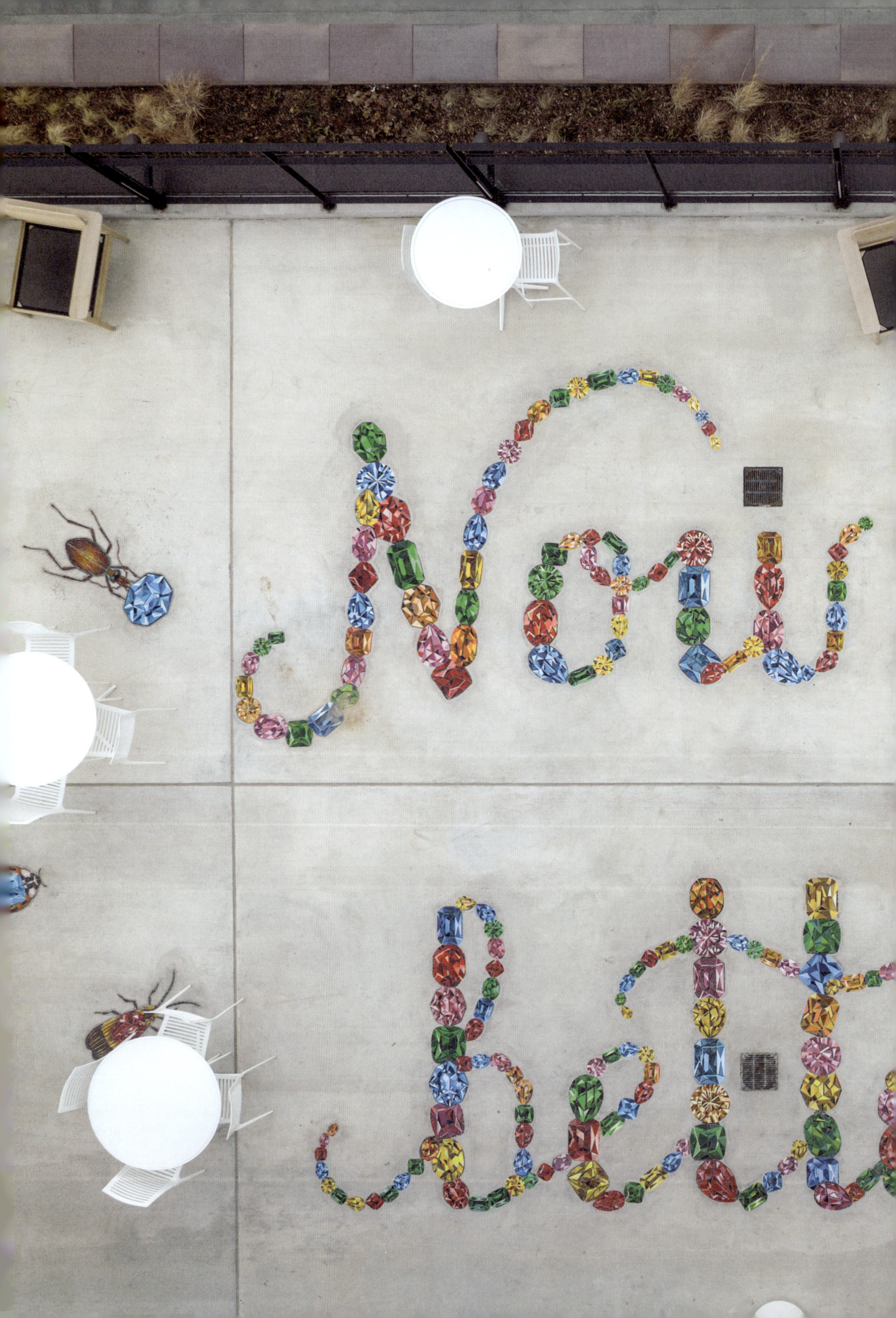

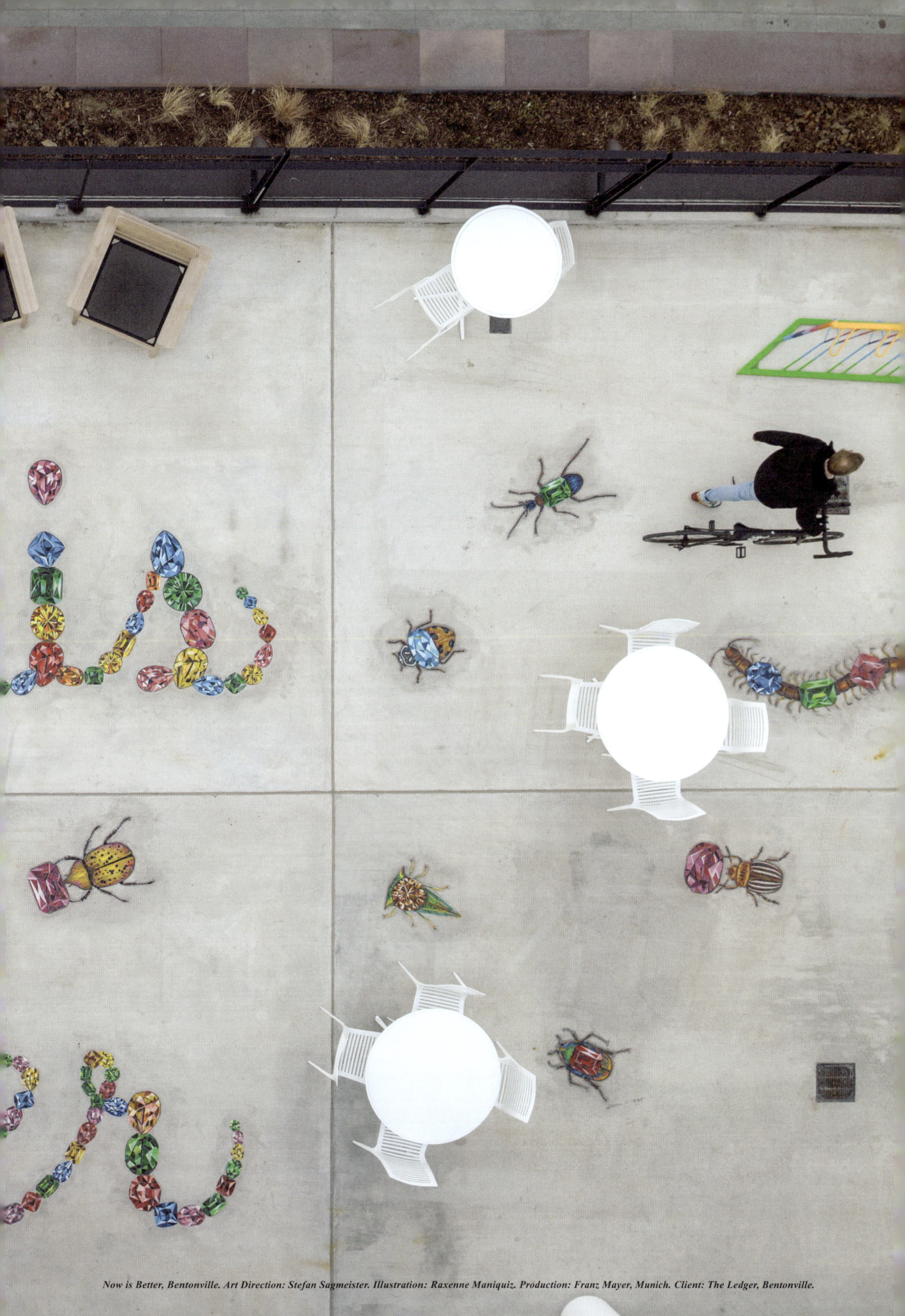

*Now is Better, Bentonville. Art Direction: Stefan Sagmeister. Illustration: Raxenne Maniquiz. Production: Franz Mayer, Munich. Client: The Ledger, Bentonville.*

# **Paul Garbett:** Design is An Act of Optimism

PAUL CREATED A DISTINCTIVE AND BOLD CREATIVE
PALETTE FOR THE WHITE BAY POWER STATION
BRAND. NO ONE ELSE COULD HAVE CREATED
SUCH A FITTING DESIGN—HE IS ONE OF A KIND.

**Annie Tennant,** *Director of Design & Place, Placemaking NSW*

WE HAVE HAD THE GREAT PRIVILEGE AND PLEASURE
OF WORKING WITH PAUL ON A BROAD RANGE OF
INTERIOR PROJECTS OVER THE PAST 15 YEARS
AND ARE ALWAYS EXCITED TO SEE PAUL'S GRAPHIC
DESIGN PRESENTATIONS.

**David Selden,** *Designer & Founder, David Selden Design*

PAUL GARBETT IS ONE OF THOSE PEOPLE
THAT ONE HOPES TO MEET DURING A CAREER.
NO MATTER HOW BIG OR SMALL THE BRIEF,
HIS DESIGN WORK IS CLEVER, INSPIRED,
IMAGINATIVE, AND TRANSFORMATIVE.

**Katrina Cashman,** *Gallery Manager & Senior Curator, National Art School*

HE DESIGNED AN IDENTITY FOR YIRRANMA PLACE
THAT CONNECTED TO ITS HISTORY, ITS HEART
AS A PRECINCT FOR SOCIAL PURPOSE,
AND OUR COMMITMENT TO THE COMMUNITY.

**Suzie Warrick,** *National Communications Manager, Paul Ramsay Foundation*

PAUL POSSESSES THE RARE GIFT OF BLENDING
GENUINE ORIGINALITY WITH BRILLIANT IDEAS,
THEN EXECUTING THEM WITH ABSOLUTE SIMPLICITY
AND FLAWLESS CRAFT IN A WAY THAT LEAVES
YOU THINKING, "I WISH I'D DONE THAT!"

**Lee Selsick,** *Director of Strategy & Design, Next Brand*

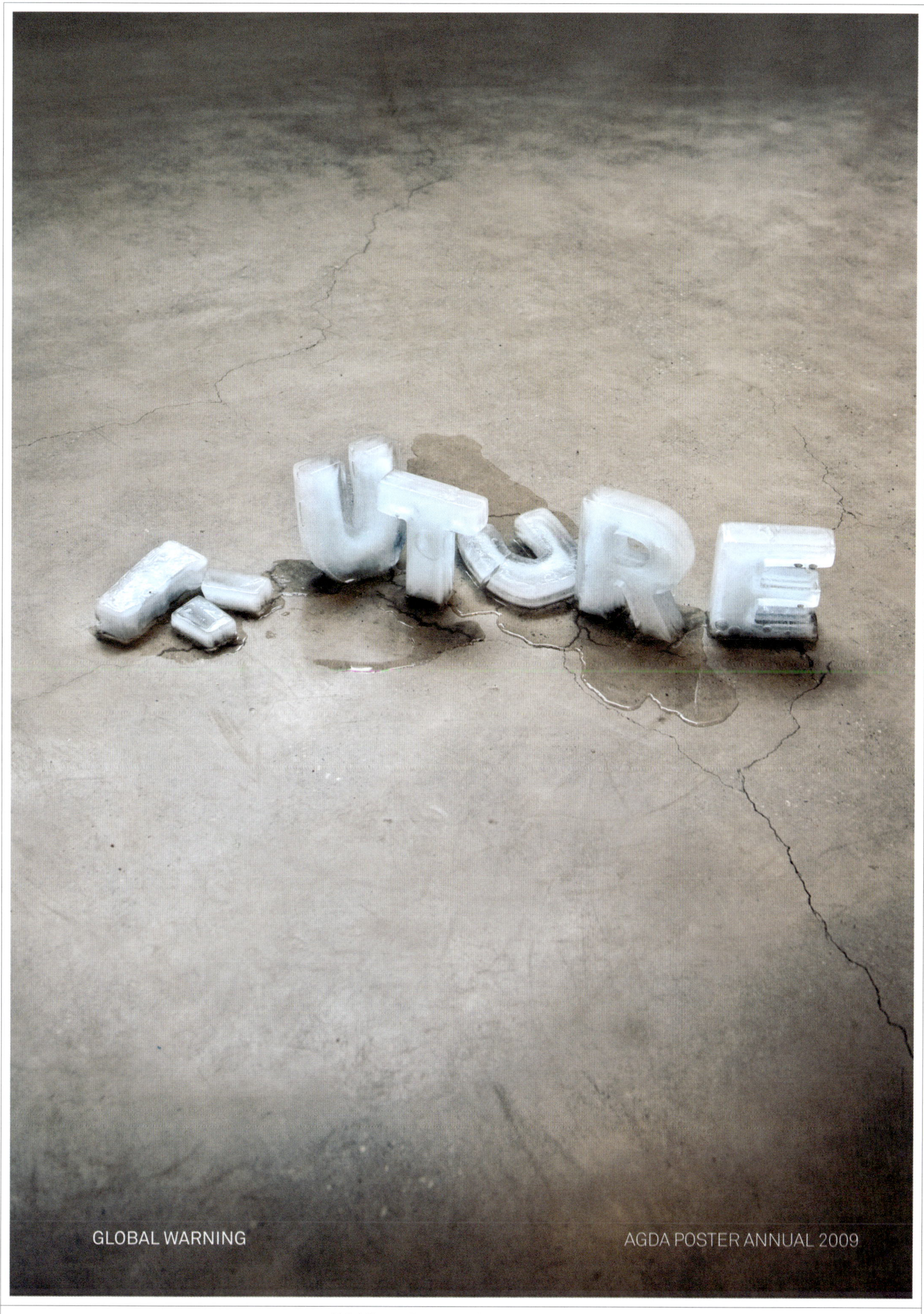


*Global Warning Poster. Australian Poster Annual. 2009.*

# Introduction by **Yvette Dal Pozzo** *Art Gallery Director, Goulburn Regional Art Gallery*

The Goulburn Regional Art Gallery has worked with Paul Garbett of Garbett Design for a number of years on a range of projects from digital to print, publications to signage. Paul is an incredible graphic designer who is sensitive to representing art and artists in the best light possible whilst also meeting the needs of the Gallery by clearly communicating information and intent. He takes creative and fresh approaches to interpreting visual and written information and making the work we do sing through clean and engaging design outcomes. The work he creates is eye-catching and resolved, making the overall look and feel of the Gallery cohesive and engaging.

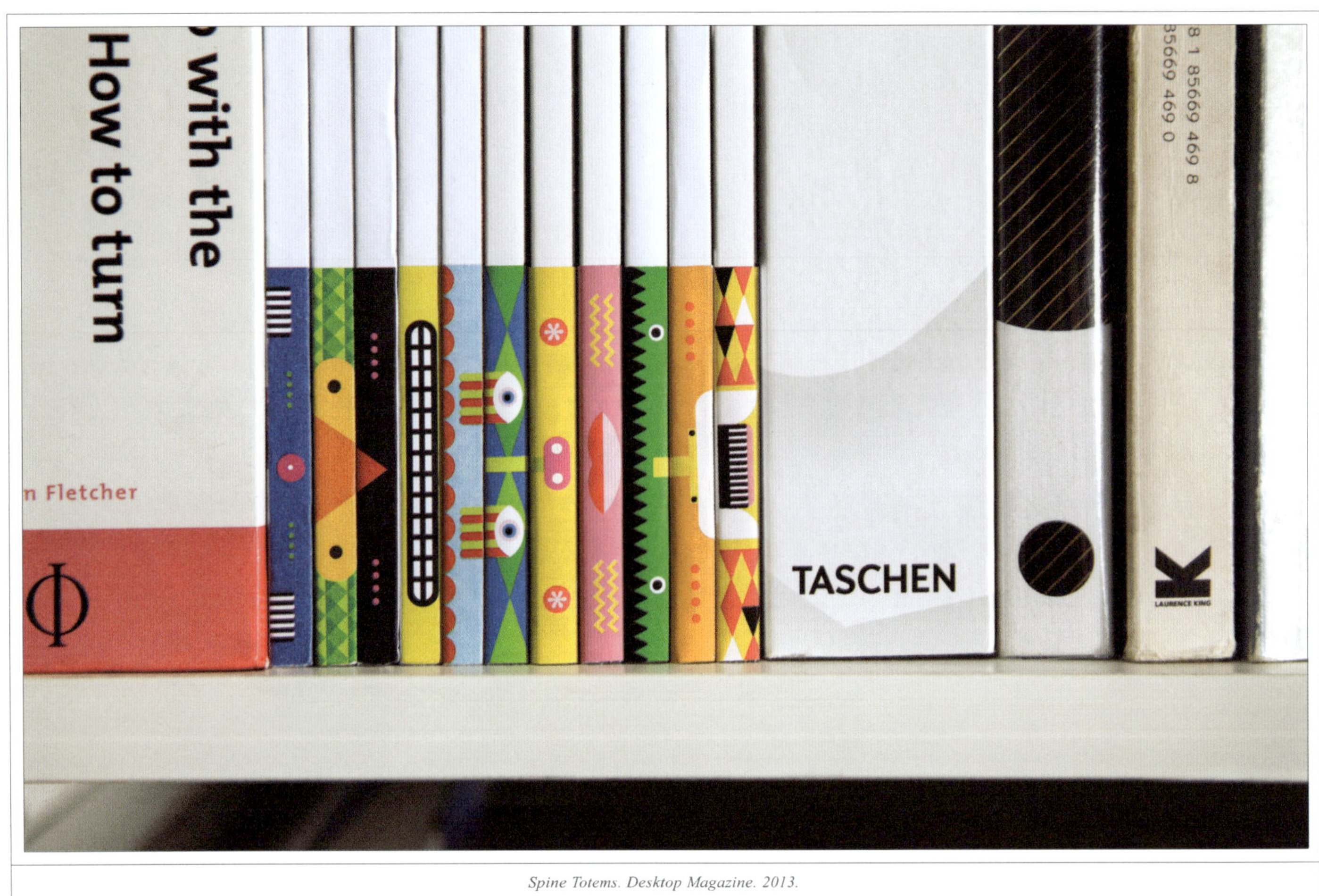


*Spine Totems. Desktop Magazine. 2013.*

# IT'S RARE TO SEE SUCH A VAST BODY OF WORK WITH SUCH AN UNMISTAKABLE STYLE.

**Flavio Carvalho,** *Designer & Art Director, Apple*

## Q&A: Paul Garbett

*What inspired or motivated you to have a career in design?*
As a child, I was always interested in making art and drawing. My earliest design memory is when I discovered an old suitcase in the back of a closet in my house. The suitcase belonged to my deceased grandfather, who had left Germany before WWI. It was filled with old documents, photos, stamps, poetry, defunct currency, and knick-knacks. I was transfixed with this ephemera, and it helped me form a picture of who he was. I later learned that what was in the suitcase were bits of graphic design.

I was fortunate enough to attend an arts high school that offered design as a subject, along with painting, sculpture, photography, printmaking, and drawing. As soon as I heard the term "graphic design," I knew it was what I wanted to do, and that has been my focus ever since.

*What is your work philosophy?*
I've been reflecting on the importance of optimism. Design is an act of optimism because it involves envisioning and, hopefully, realizing a better future. We're always striving to do better and improve upon what's been done before.

Our design approach focuses on creating work that looks beautiful and has a positive impact on people's lives. We take play seriously. Far from being purposeless or unserious, play is creatively productive and foundational to expressing our humanity.

*Who is or was your greatest mentor?*
I've had many mentors along the way, teaching me different things when I was ready to learn them. I am grateful to all of them. Anyone can be a mentor, even people you haven't met in person.

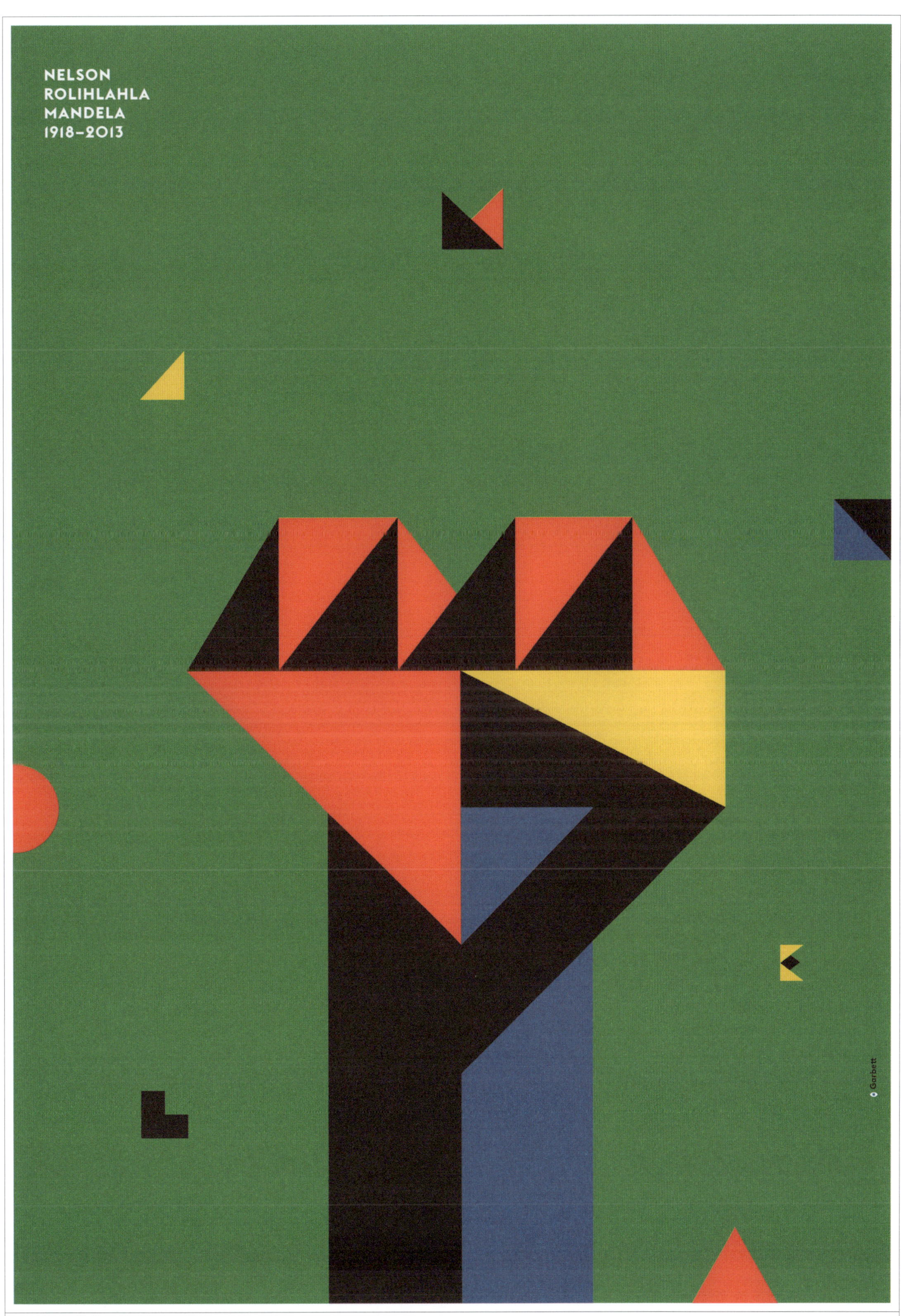


*Nelson Mandela Tribute Poster. Ijusi Magazine. 2014.*

*What is it about design that you are most passionate about?*
It offers possibility and an outlet for useful creativity.

*Garbett Design works on creating digital, print, signage, wayfinding systems, branding, and identity projects. Which is your favorite to work on?*
Lately, we've been focusing more on signage and wayfinding projects, which are an extension of our identity projects. I'm enjoying this work because it allows us to explore 3D spaces, sculpture, and material tactility, which the digital realm doesn't provide. These projects also allow us to collaborate with new kinds of people, such as artists, architects, and engineers, which is very rewarding.

I also enjoy working in the cultural realm, such as art galleries, exhibitions, and placemaking.

*What is the most difficult challenge you've overcome to reach your current position?*
Learning about business processes and that business success is about more than just good design. It is about relationships, building trust and consistency... and luck.

*Who were and are some of your most significant influences?*
Africa, Japan, dogs, my children, Danielle, art, music, books, Graphis annuals, Josef Müller-Brockmann, Isamu Noguchi, Alexander Calder, Henry Moore, Alexander Girard, Tadao Ando, Josef Albers, the Bauhaus, Charles and Ray Eames, Emigre, Alphonse Mucha, Bruno Munari, Kenya Hara, Ikko Tanaka, Tadanori Yokoo, Alan Fletcher, Otl Aicher, Lance Wyman, Stefan Sagmeister, and Marcel Duchamp.

*Who among your contemporaries today do you most admire?*
I love watching people doing what they were meant to do and thriving, anyone who zigs when others zag, idiosyncratic design from Japan and France, the precision of Swiss design, and the clarity of Australian and New Zealand design.

*What would be your dream assignment?*
I've always wanted to create an identity for the Olympics—a good one like Mexico in 1968 or Munich in 1972. However, I'm not sure this kind of singular design vision is possible today as there are so many stakeholders, sponsors, etc.

*Who have been some of your favorite people or clients you have worked with?*
I love working with relaxed but confident people. If you have good chemistry, every part of the process is good, not just the outcome.

*What are the most important ingredients you require from a client to work successfully?*
Friendliness, clarity, ambition, and trust.

*Your work has won multiple awards. Which one means the most to you?*
Awards were a big deal to me when I was younger, but I'm not as concerned with them these days. I always wanted to win the D&AD Yellow Pencil, which was a nice highlight a few years ago.

*What is your most outstanding professional achievement?*
It was a special day when I was accepted into the Alliance Graphique Internationale (AGI); on the same day, I heard that my mother was diagnosed with a terminal illness, so that was an important reminder to have perspective.

*What is the greatest satisfaction you get from your work?*
Knowing that it is doing its job. I also really enjoy the process of being in the flow state, in which time passes and ideas are plentiful.

*What part of your work is most demanding, considering your position?*
Patience.

*What professional goals do you still have for yourself?*
To keep doing interesting things and doing good work. This gets rarer as the years go by because the same things aren't as exciting as they used to be, so you tend to seek out newer, bigger things.

*As someone who has given multiple lectures about design across Australia and New Zealand, what drove you to do this? Is there a specific talk that sticks in your memory?*
I started teaching design part-time because I felt I had a perspective to share and needed financial support in the early years of starting a studio. The first keynote was at AGIdeas in Melbourne in 2009. It sticks in my mind because I was utterly intimidated to speak alongside people like Stefan Sagmeister, Marina Willer, and Harry Pearce. They turned out to be the most lovely and generous people. The big lesson was that they were regular people.

*What advice would you give to students starting out today?*
Travel. Observe, question, be humble, and be open.

*What interests do you have outside of your work?*
My family, travel, art, photography, cinema, music, and books.

*What would you change if you had to do it all over again?*
I would have liked to move to New York or somewhere in Europe for a while to see where that might have led.

*Where do you seek inspiration?*
Everywhere and anywhere.

*How do you define success?*
Success = Do I feel enthusiasm and energy for today?

*Where do you see yourself in the future?*
Traveling and exploring more of the world.

**Garbett Design** www.garbett.com.au

PAUL GARBETT IS A VISIONARY DESIGNER WHO FOLLOWS HIS OWN PATH AND INSPIRES ALL THROUGH HIS CREATIVE JOURNEY.

**Michael Schepis,** *Creative Director, Handle Branding*

AGI Open
Sydney
AGI
2020.agi-open.com
19–
20
September
20
20

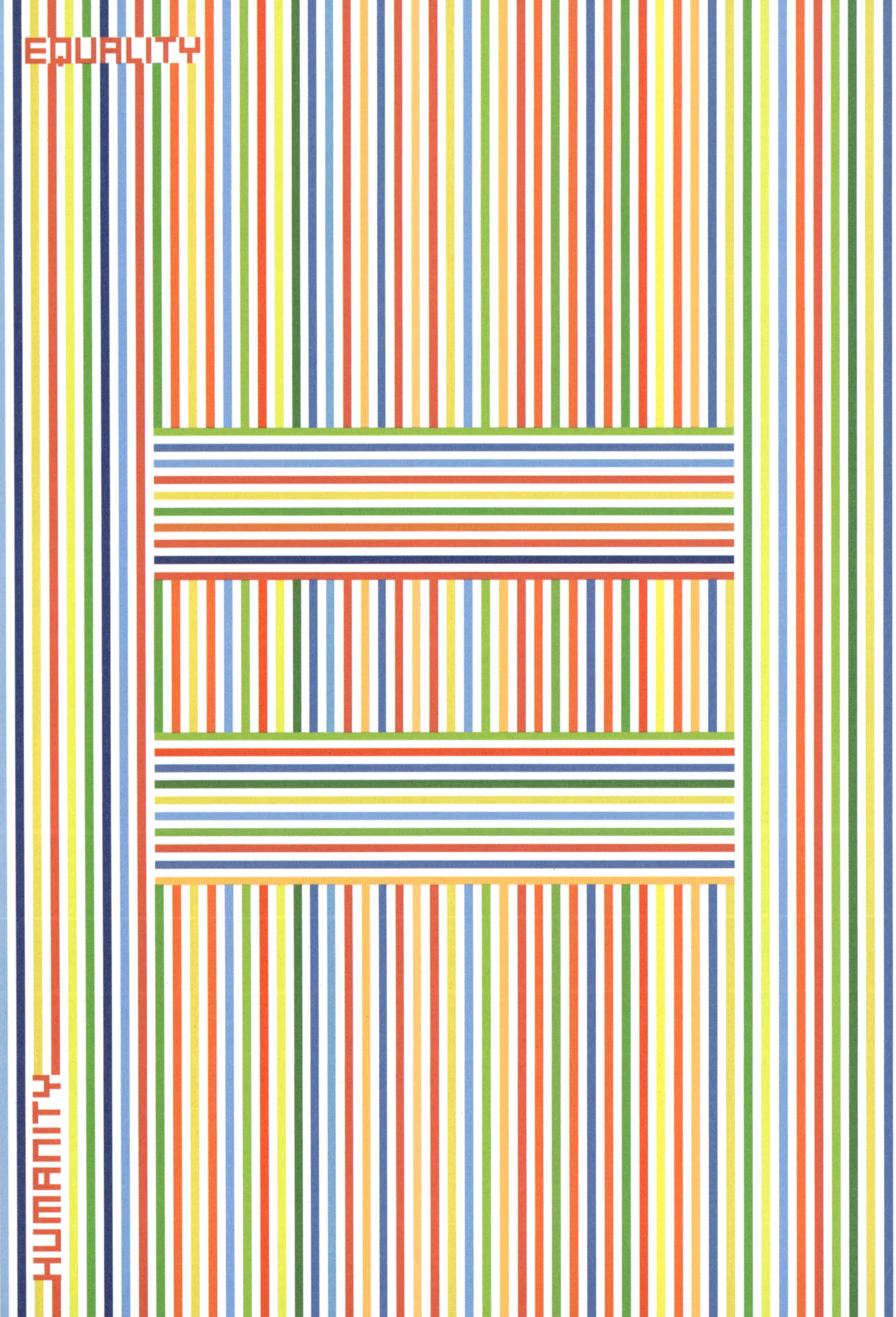


*Humanity/Equality Poster. Eyesaw Exhibition. 2009.*

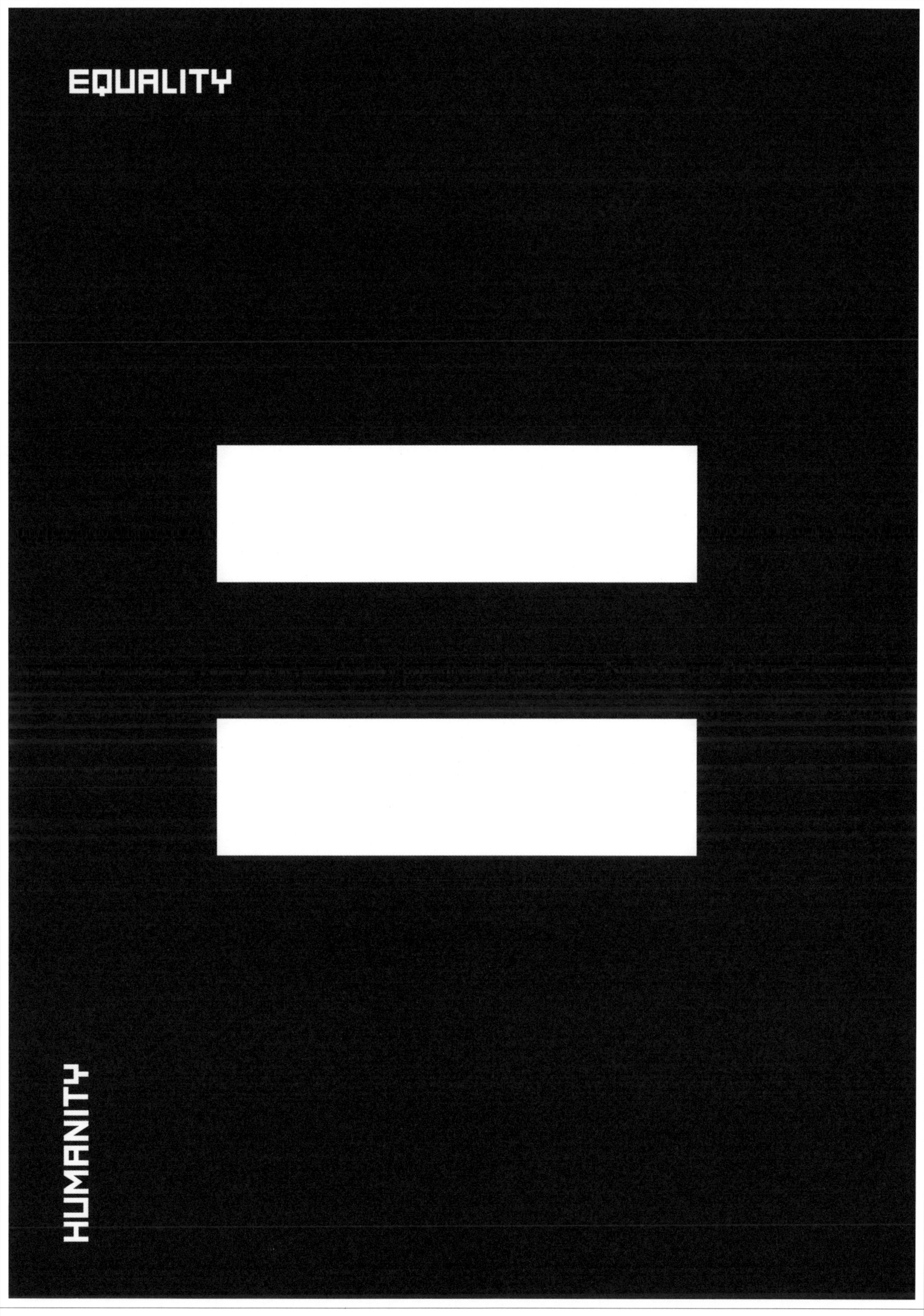


*Humanity/Equality Poster. Eyesaw Exhibition. 2009.*

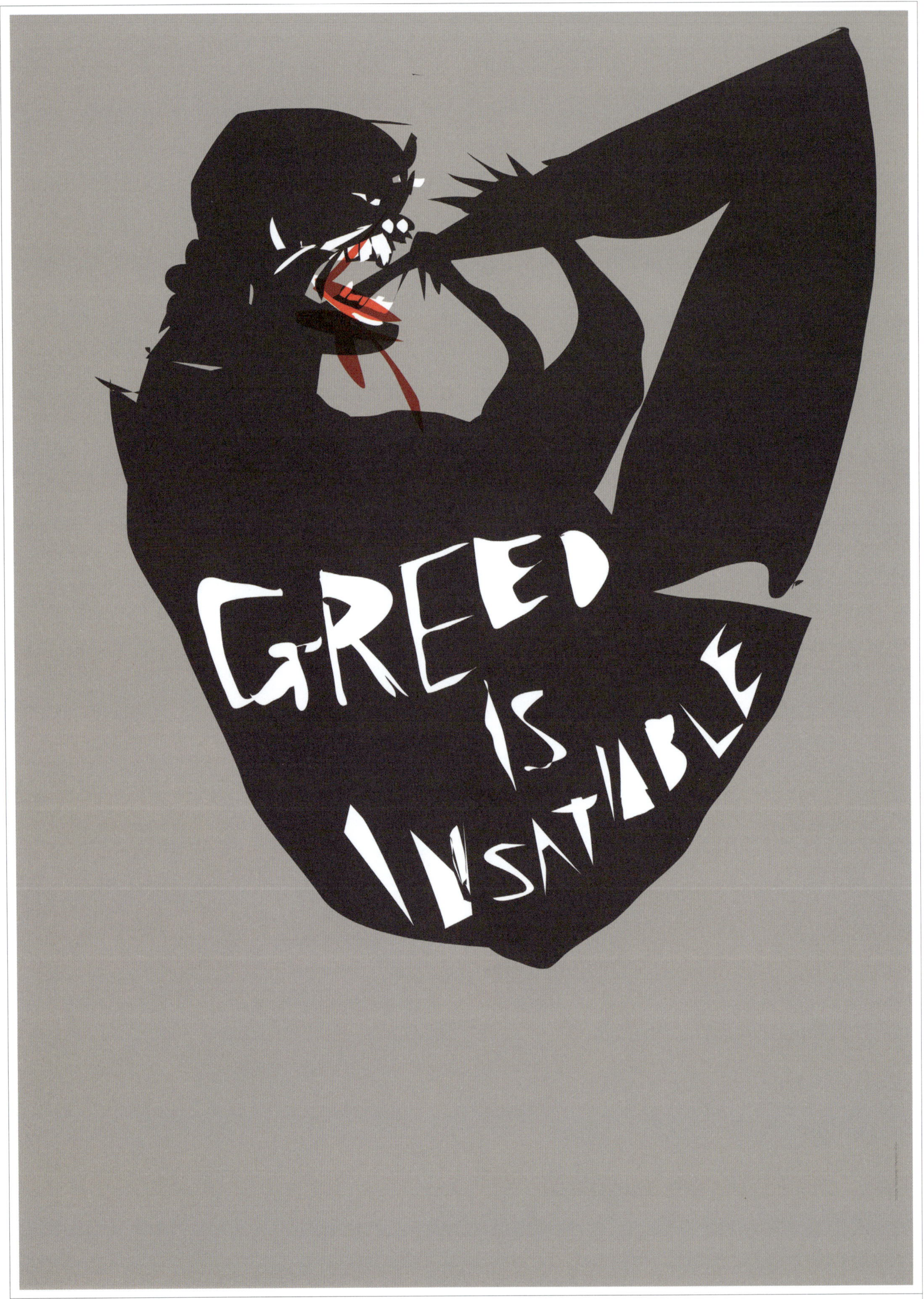


*Greed is Insatiable Poster. 2008.*

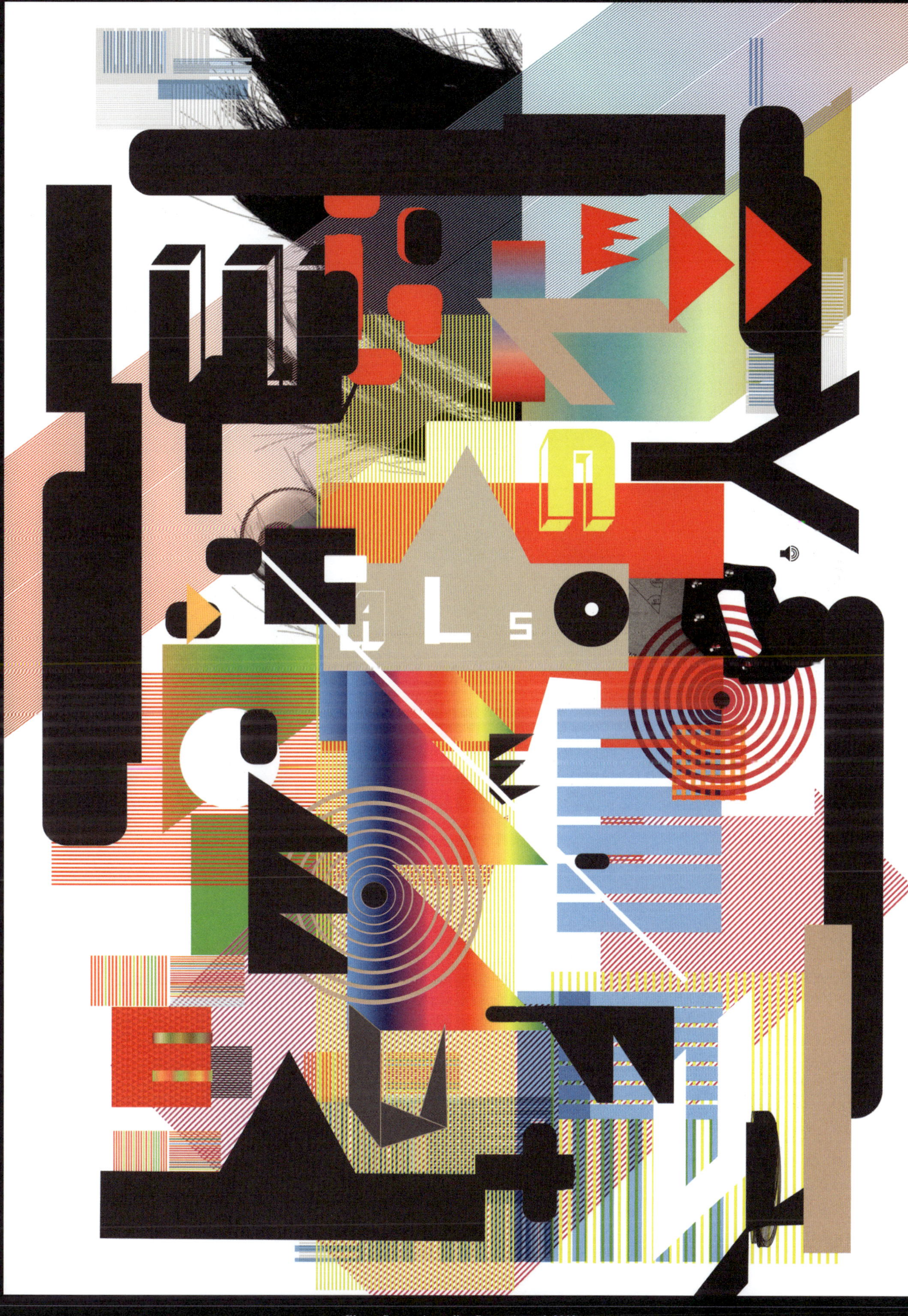



*Eleven Poster, Australian Poster Annual, 2013.*

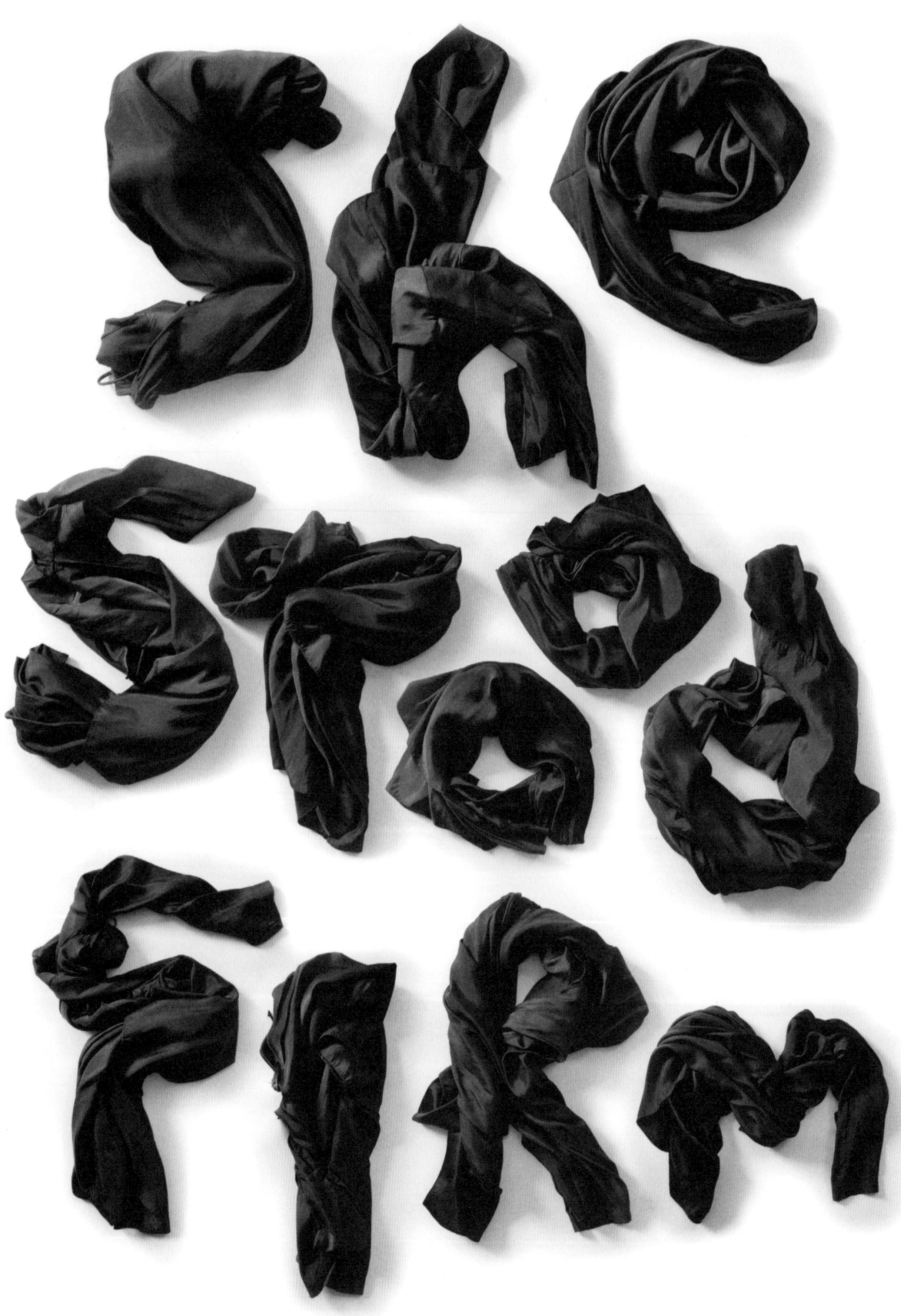




*She Stood Firm. Tribute to Mahsa Amini. Woman Life Freedom Poster. 2022.*

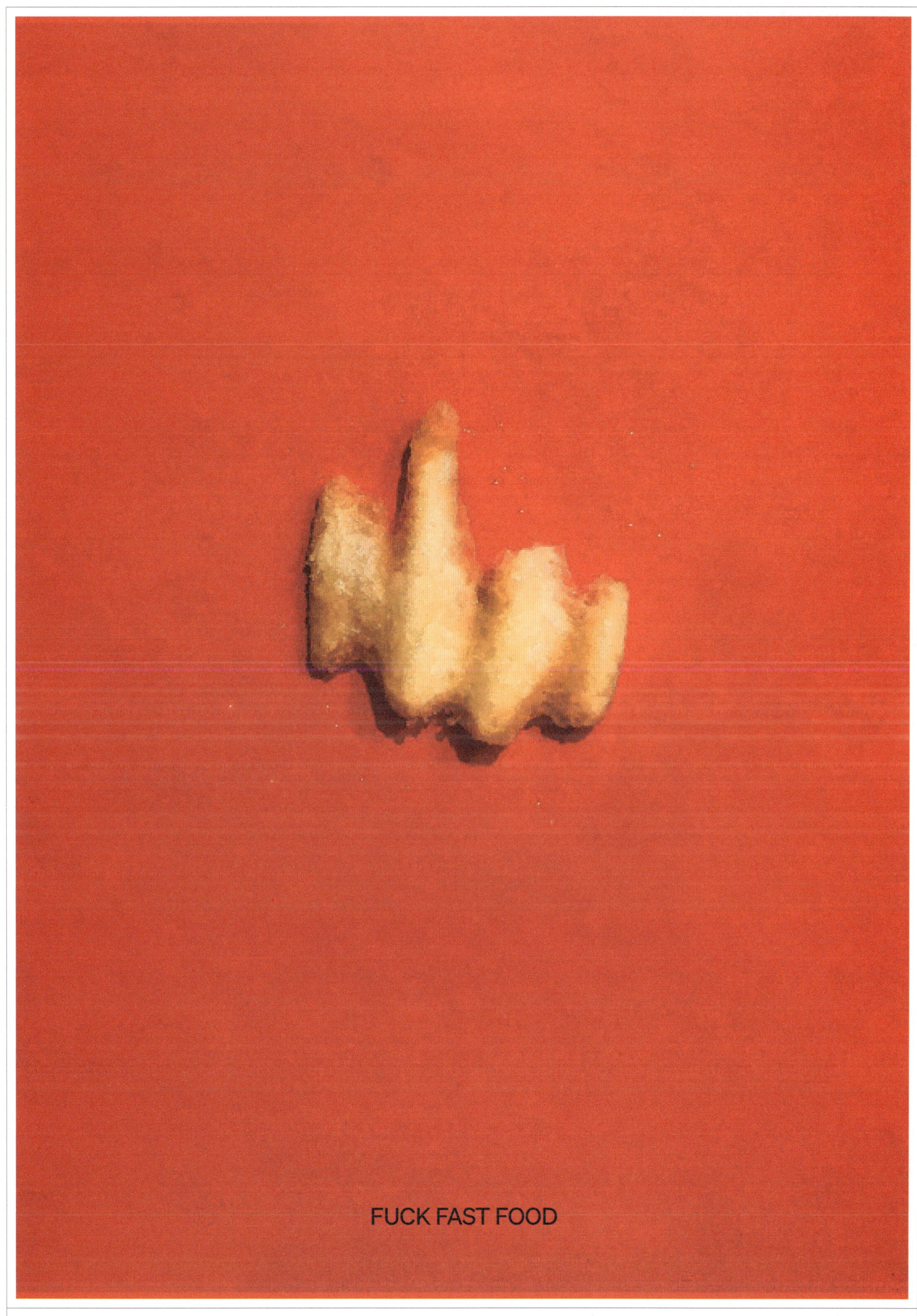


*Fuck Fast Food Poster. 2021.*

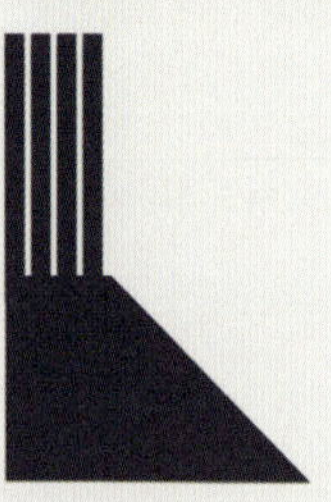
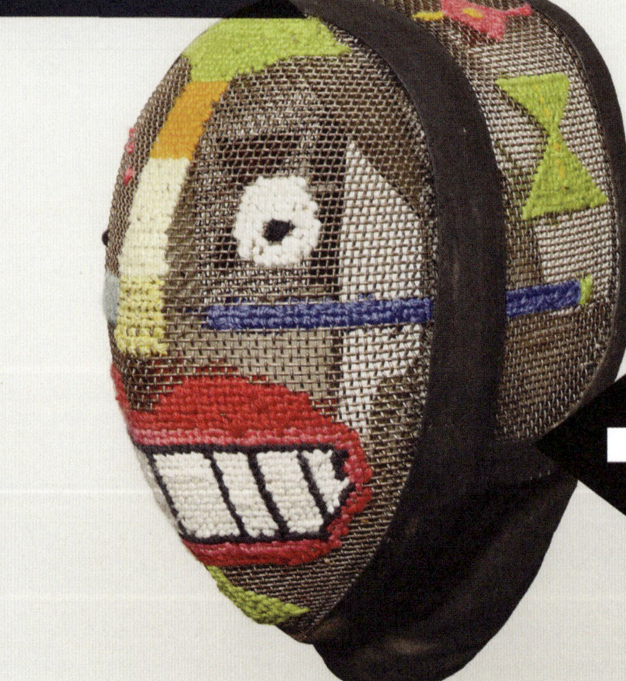


*Masked Intentions Poster. 2013.*

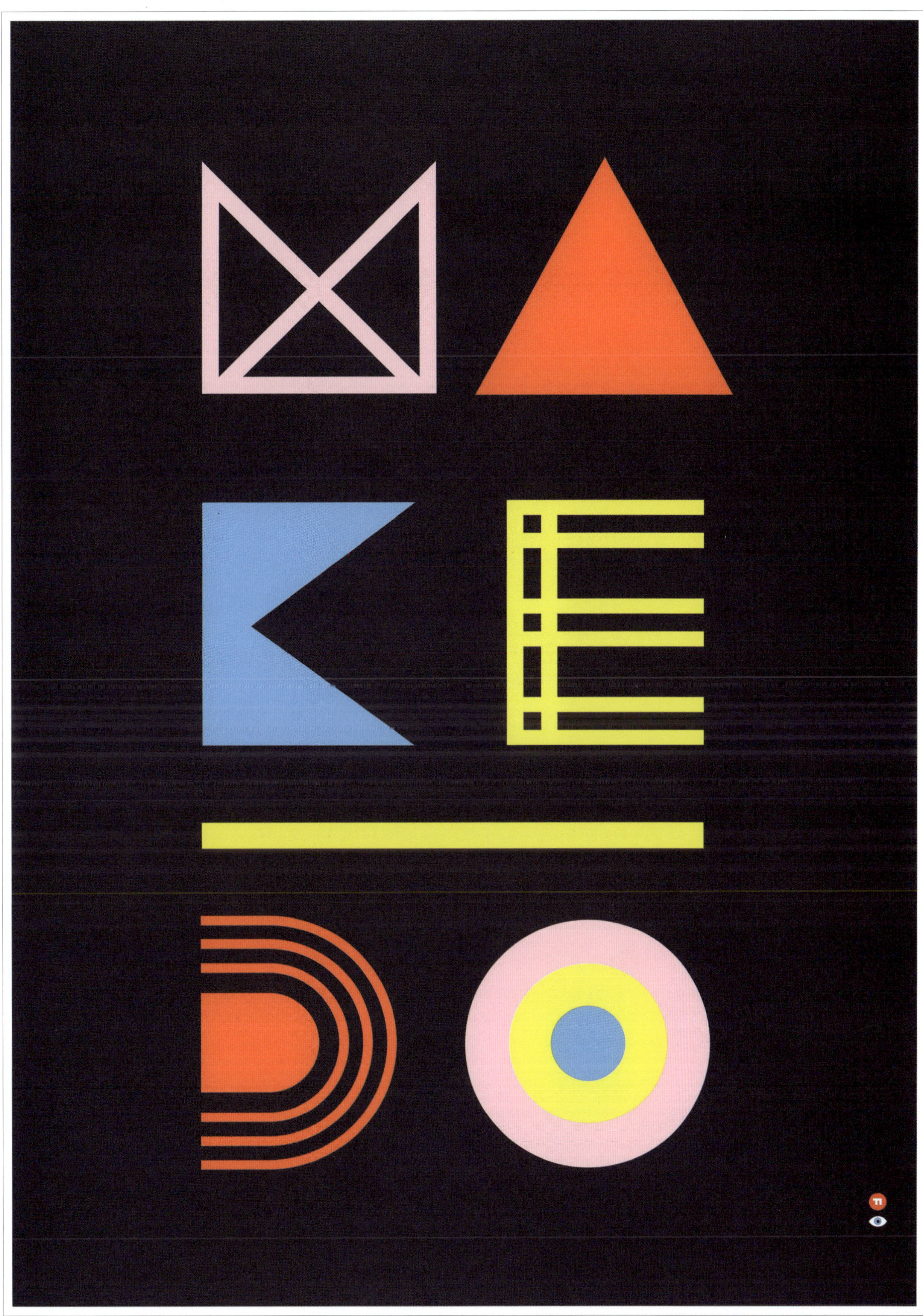



*Make Do Poster. Australian Graphic Design Association. 2011.*

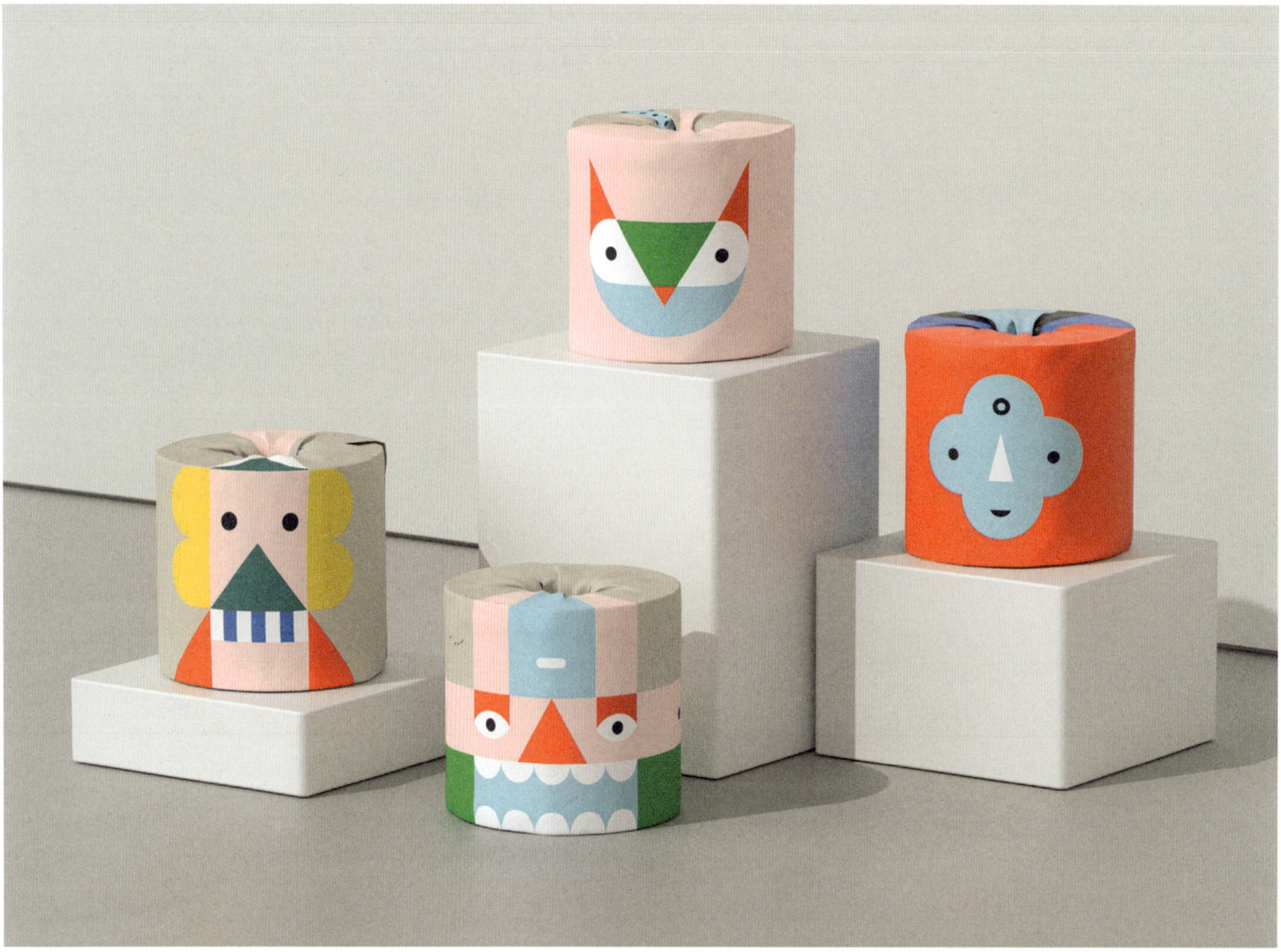

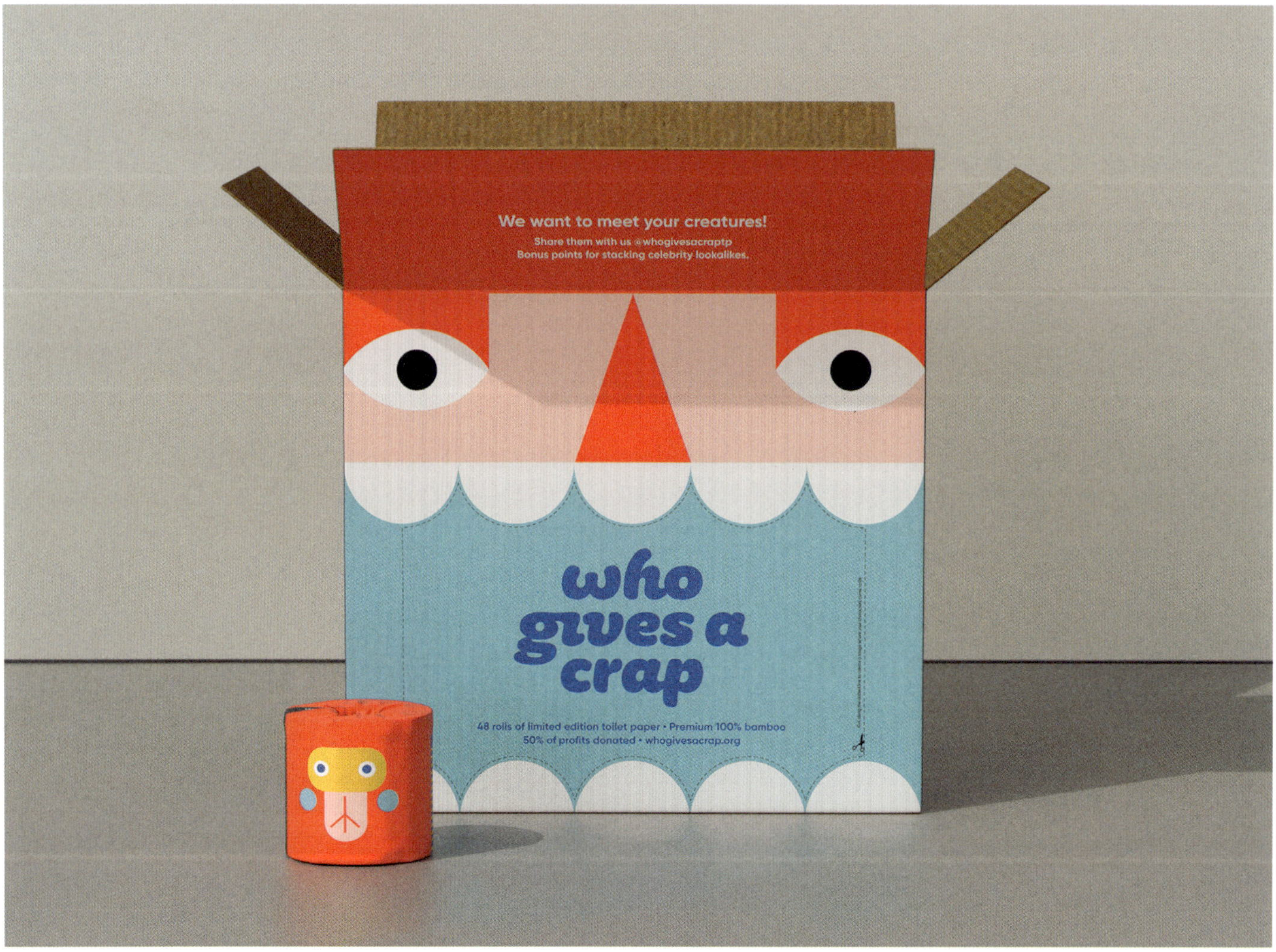

*Play Edition Packaging. Client: Who Gives a Crap. 2019.*

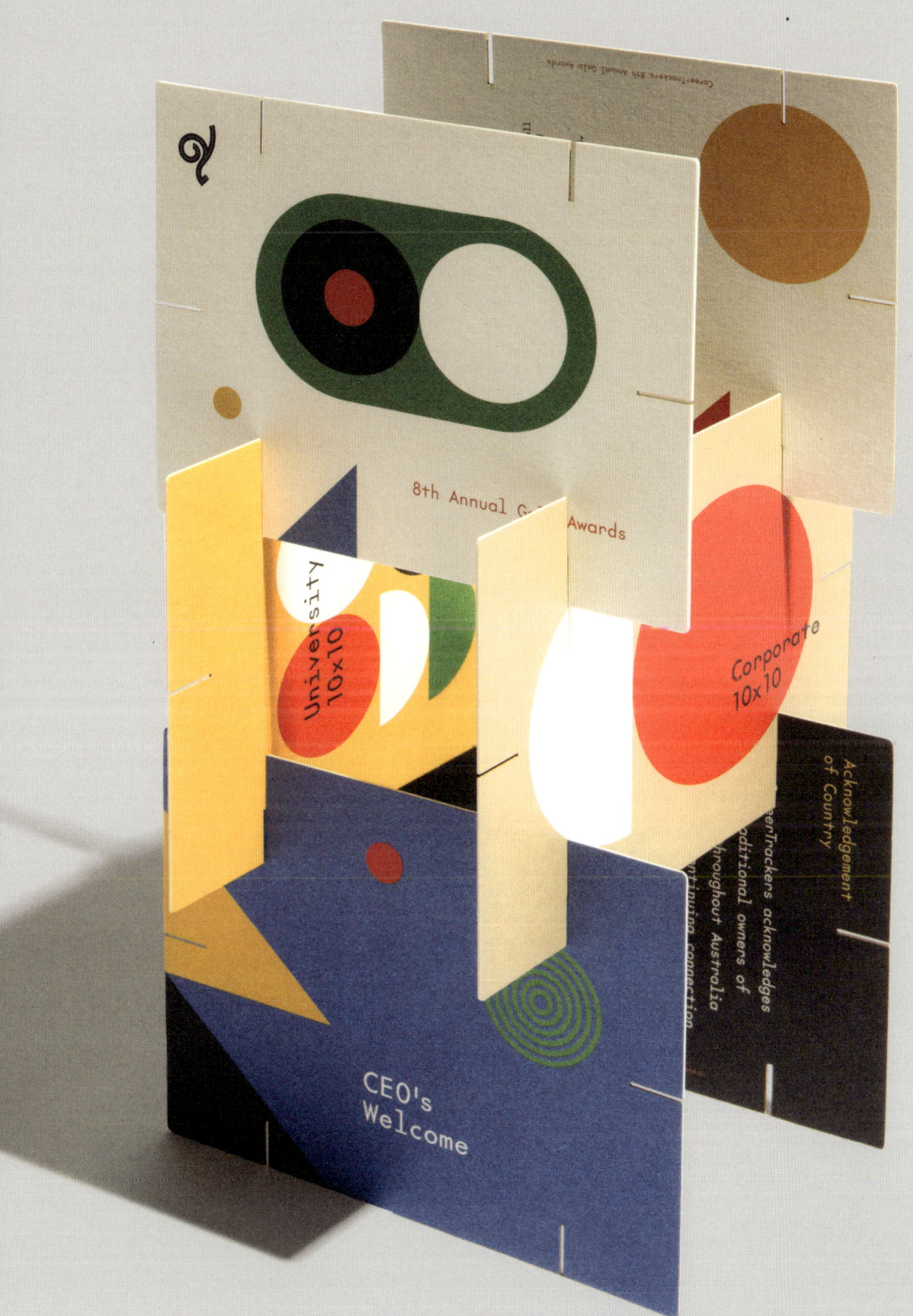



*Awards Evening Identity. Client: Career Trackers. 2019.*

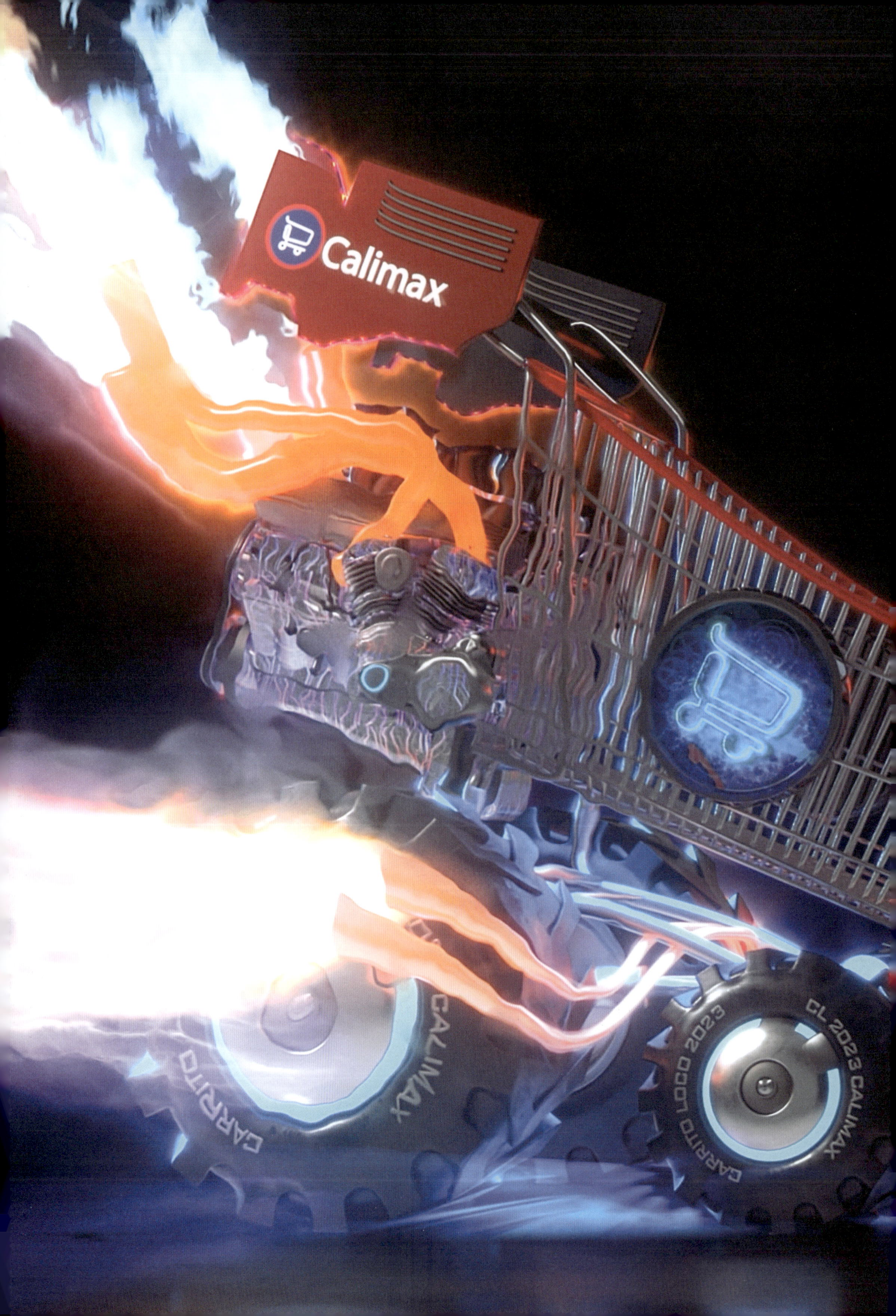

Calimax
CARRITO LOCO 2023
CL 2023 CALIMAX
CARRITO
CALIMAX

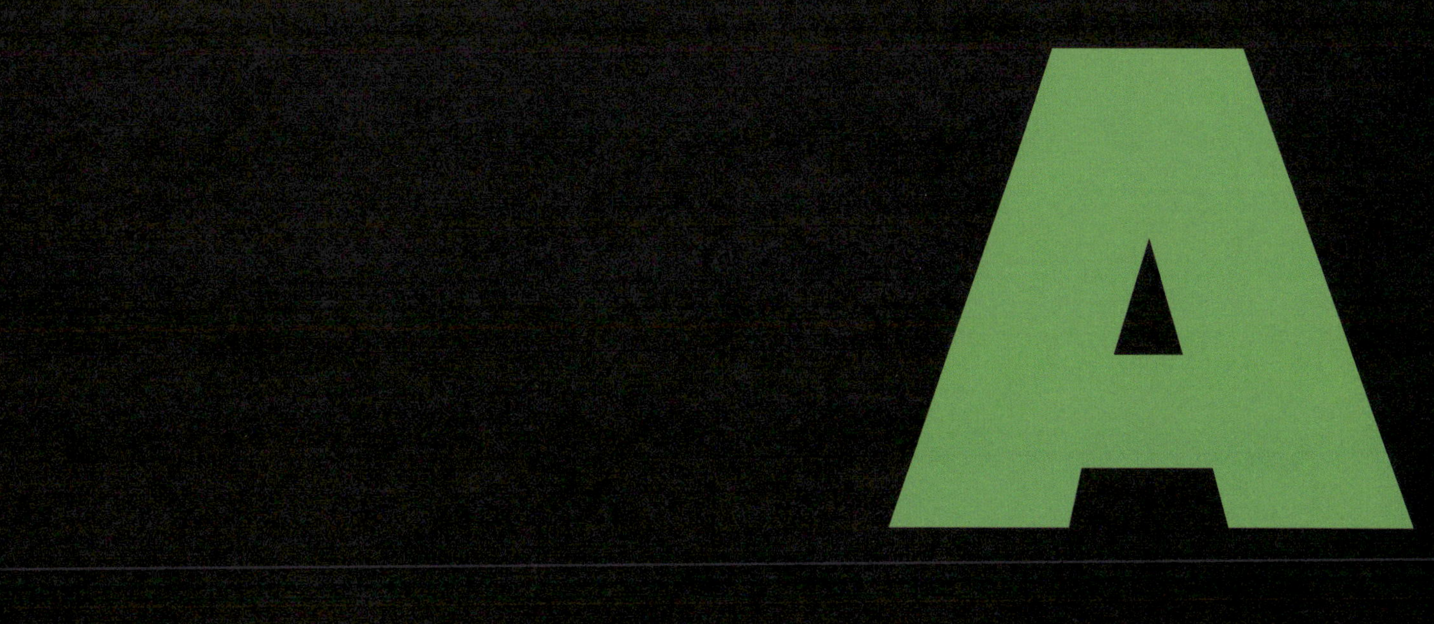

# A

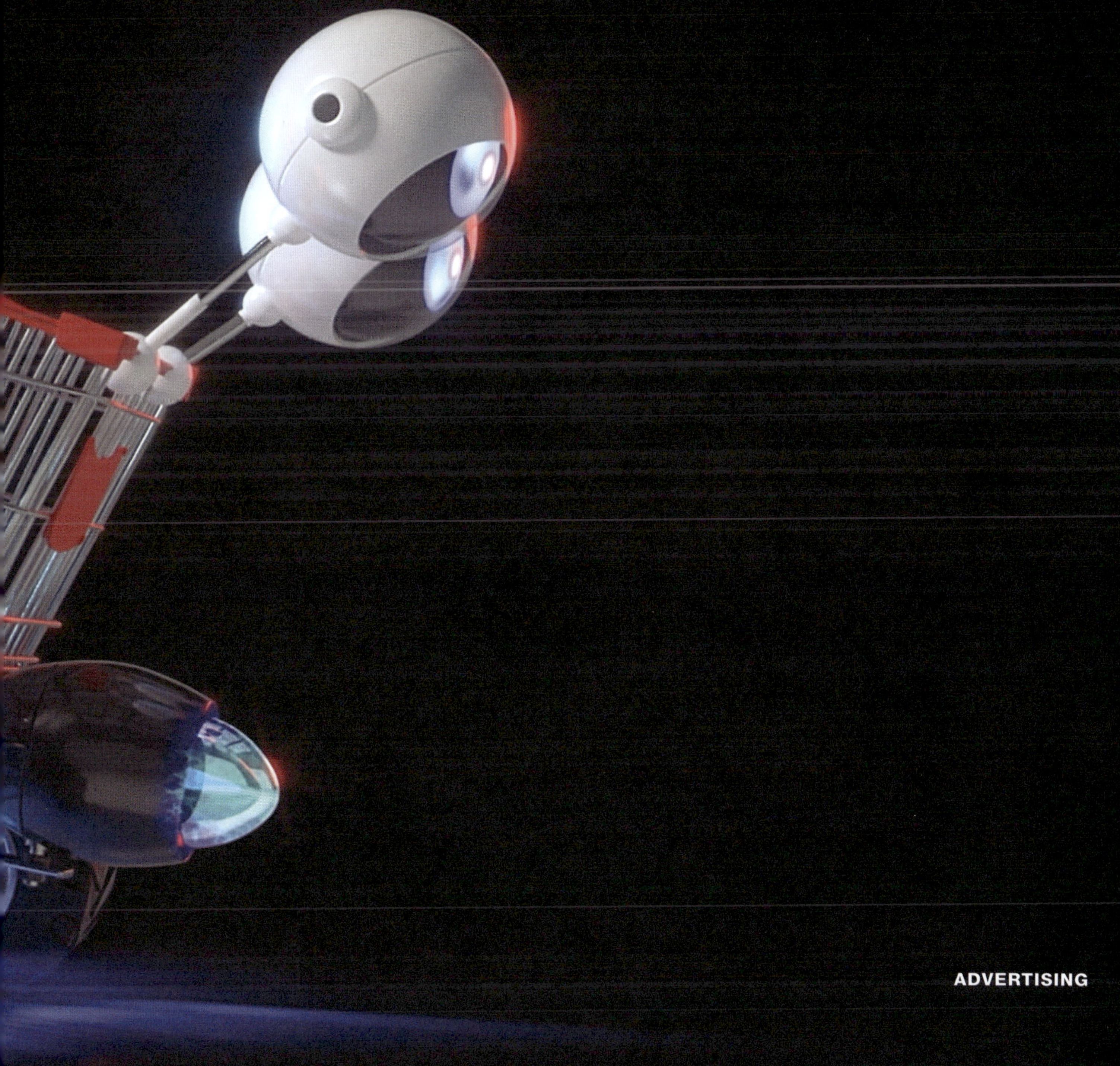

# Ariel Freaner: **Evolving With Advertising**

I FEEL FORTUNATE TO HAVE FREANER CREATIVE & DESIGN AS PART OF MY TEAM. ARIEL'S CREATIVITY KNOWS NO BOUNDS, AND HE IS FUN TO WORK WITH. HE IS A PASSIONATE, KNOWLEDGEABLE DESIGNER WHO IS DESTINED FOR GREAT THINGS.

**Donna Durckel,** *Communications Officer, County of San Diego Land Use & Environment Group*

ARIEL IS THAT RARE DESIGNER WHO TAKES A CONCEPT AND PUSHES IT IN CREATIVE DIRECTIONS THAT ARE SURPRISING, INVENTIVE, AND, ULTIMATELY, MORE EFFECTIVE.

**Steve Walker,** *Communications Director & Special Assistant, County of San Diego District Attorney's Office*

HIS PASSION FOR GRAPHIC DESIGN SHINES BRIGHT — HE CONSISTENTLY GOES THE EXTRA MILE TO DELIVER CREATIVE SOLUTIONS.

**Porfirio Mancillas,** *Program Coordinator of Program Business Intelligence, County of San Diego Department of Agriculture, Weights & Measures*

ARIEL FREANER IS A DEDICATED PROFESSIONAL WHO CONSISTENTLY DELIVERS CREATIVE AND AWARD-WINNING PRODUCTS TO ENSURE HIS CUSTOMERS' SUCCESS AND SATISFACTION.

**Ha Dang,** *Agricultural Commissioner & Sealer, County of San Diego Department of Agriculture, Weights & Measures*

WE'VE CREATED MANY EXCELLENT PROJECTS SINCE I BEGAN COLLABORATING WITH ARIEL IN 2016. HE'S VERY CREATIVE AND KNOWS HOW TO DELIVER WHAT THE CUSTOMER NEEDS.

**Ismael Lopez,** *Human Services Program Manager, County of San Diego Health & Human Services Agency*

ARIEL IS SIMPLY ARIEL — PROFESSIONAL, CREATIVE, KIND, PASSIONATE, WORKAHOLIC, WITTY, BUT, MOST IMPORTANTLY, A GREAT HUMAN BEING. THE WORK HE DESIGNED (PRO BONO) FOR THE MEXICAN RED CROSS TIJUANA CHAPTER PROVES IT.

**Jorge Astiazarán MD,** *President of the Board, Tijuana Red Cross*

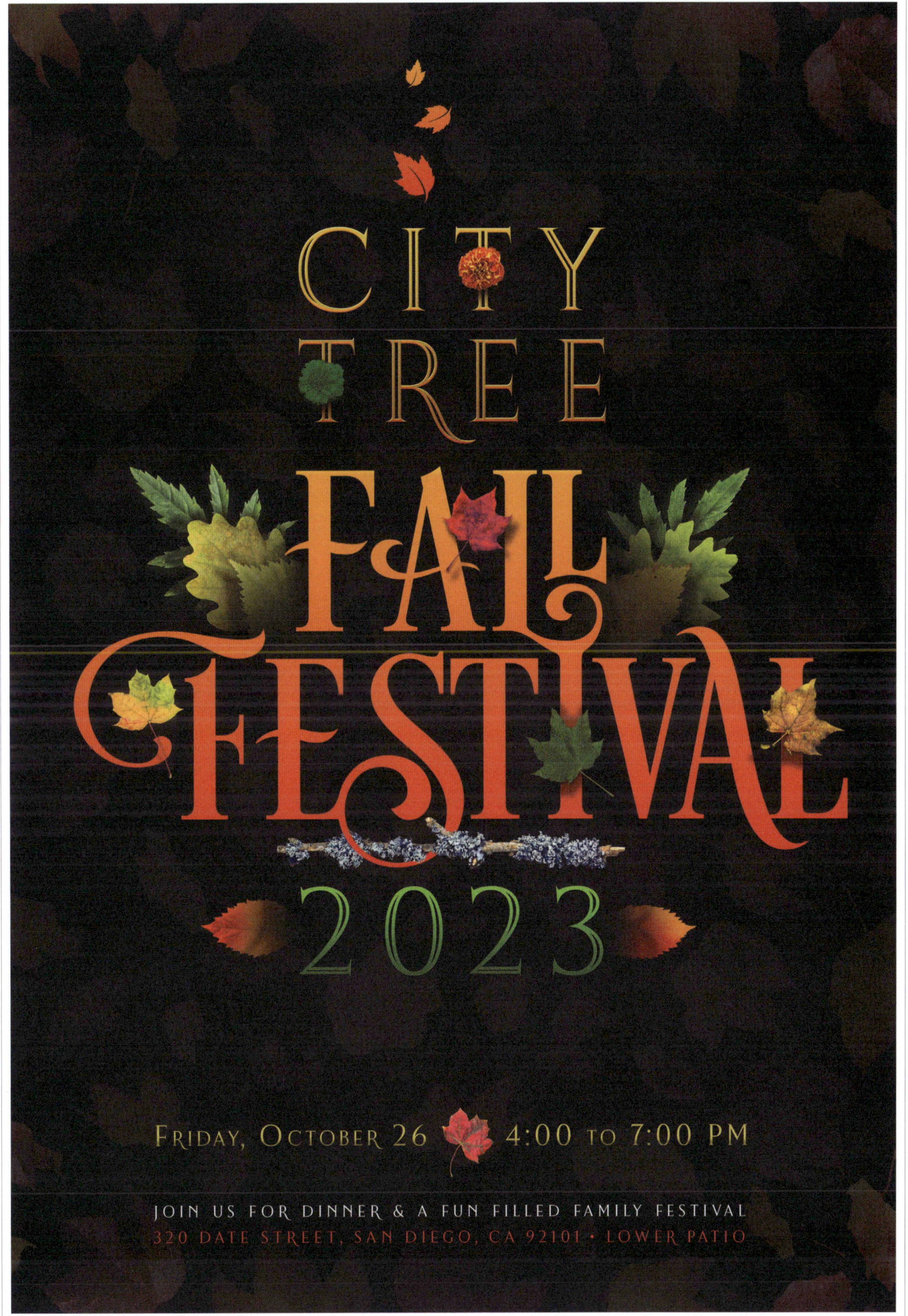


*(Pages 42, 43) Calimax Crazy Cart. Character Design, Illustration, Design: Ariel Freaner. Clients: Jose Fimbres, Ignacio Fimbres, Calimax.*
*(Above) City Tree Fall Festival logo and poster. Illustration and Design: Ariel Freaner. Client: City Tree Christian School.*

# Introduction by **Adrian Kwiatkowski** *Vice President & Partner, Bartell & Kwiatkowski*

Ariel Freaner is an accomplished and well-respected graphic designer. I have known him for over five years, and we have worked together on numerous creative projects of varying complexity. He is knowledgeable and professional and applies his creative abilities to the maximum benefit of his clients and collaborators. Ariel approaches each task with a focus on producing high-quality results filled with elegant designs and organic functions. As a result, he is my go-to graphic designer when I need a job done well, a job done right, and a job done to complete satisfaction.

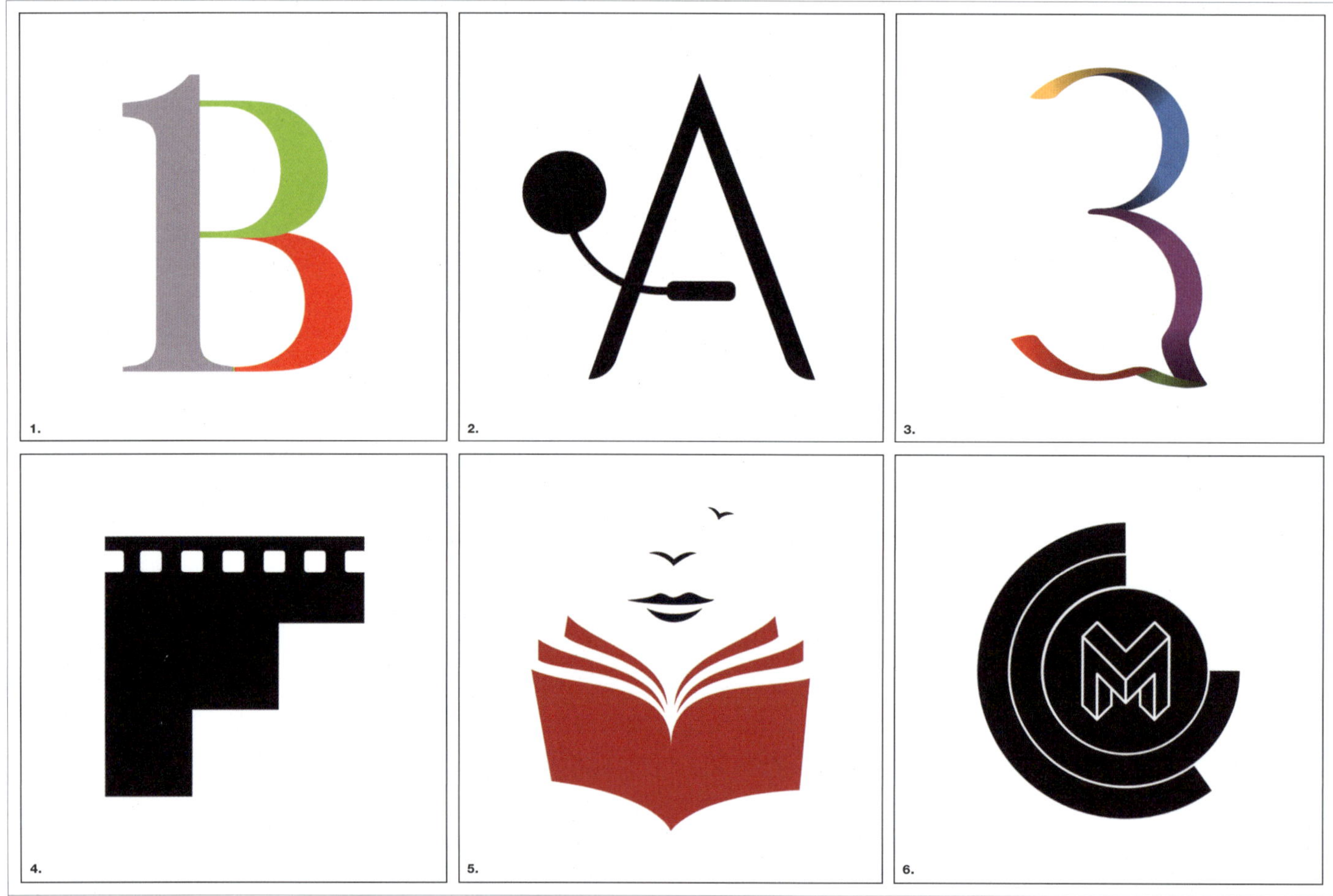

*1. Bernardo Padilla First State of The Congress (Baja California). Design: Ariel Freaner. Client: Congressman Bernardo Padilla. / 2. Access. Design: Ariel Freaner. Clients: County of San Diego Health & Human Services Agency, Terra Berhe. / 3. Tres y Contando poster logo. Design: Ariel Freaner. Clients: Jorge D'Garay, Tres y Contando. 4. Freaner Films. Design: Ariel Freaner. Clients: Freaner Films, a Freaner Creative & Design subdivision. / 5. Tres y Contando logo. Design: Ariel Freaner. Clients: Jorge D'Garay, Tres y Contando logo. / 6. Otay Chamber of Commerce. Design: Ariel Freaner. Clients: Otay Chamber of Commerce, Viviana Ibañez.*

## Q&A: **Ariel Freaner**

***What has inspired or motivated you in your career?***
Since childhood, I have loved to draw and contemplate every visual form, from cartoons, books, and encyclopedias to newspapers, magazines, and advertising. I used to collect packaging just because I was captivated by its appearance. The same thing happened with advertising. When I was a kid, my father and I spent hours reading newspapers and magazines. He was actually reading; I, on the other hand, was looking at the visuals. In his travels to Mexico City, my father always brought me back journals, some *Mafalda* books, and other magazines I loved seeing and reading.

My first, and so far biggest, inspiration (like many other people my age) was seeing *Star Wars* for the first time. That movie changed my life in every direction in the art field. It made me believe I could do so many things without limitations, and somehow, I knew it would involve the arts. Design, illustration, cinema, animation, and special effects became my biggest obsessions. George Lucas became one of my heroes, as did Ridley

Scott after *Blade Runner* and *Alien* premiered. Steven Spielberg soon joined them thanks to similar success with *Jaws, Close Encounters of the Third Kind, E.T., Jurassic Park, Raiders of the Lost Ark, Schindler's List, Saving Private Ryan*, and other films.

Those inspirations and motivations were and continue to be profound, but I also found inspiration closer to home: my own family. When I was 11, I discovered I had an uncle who did animation in Los Angeles. Another uncle who understood my passion for drawing, animation, and everything visual took me to visit him. What a surprise to find out my distant uncle was Bill Melendez, the animator for the *Peanuts* TV shows and movies. I could not believe it; my uncle had done all the Snoopy and Charlie Brown shows! Over the years, I continued visiting him, building a relationship with him, and working with him on several projects. I remember being the first kid (or at least I was told that) to see *What A Nightmare, Charlie Brown!* Once I met my uncle, I knew I could follow my dreams of building a career in illustration and design.

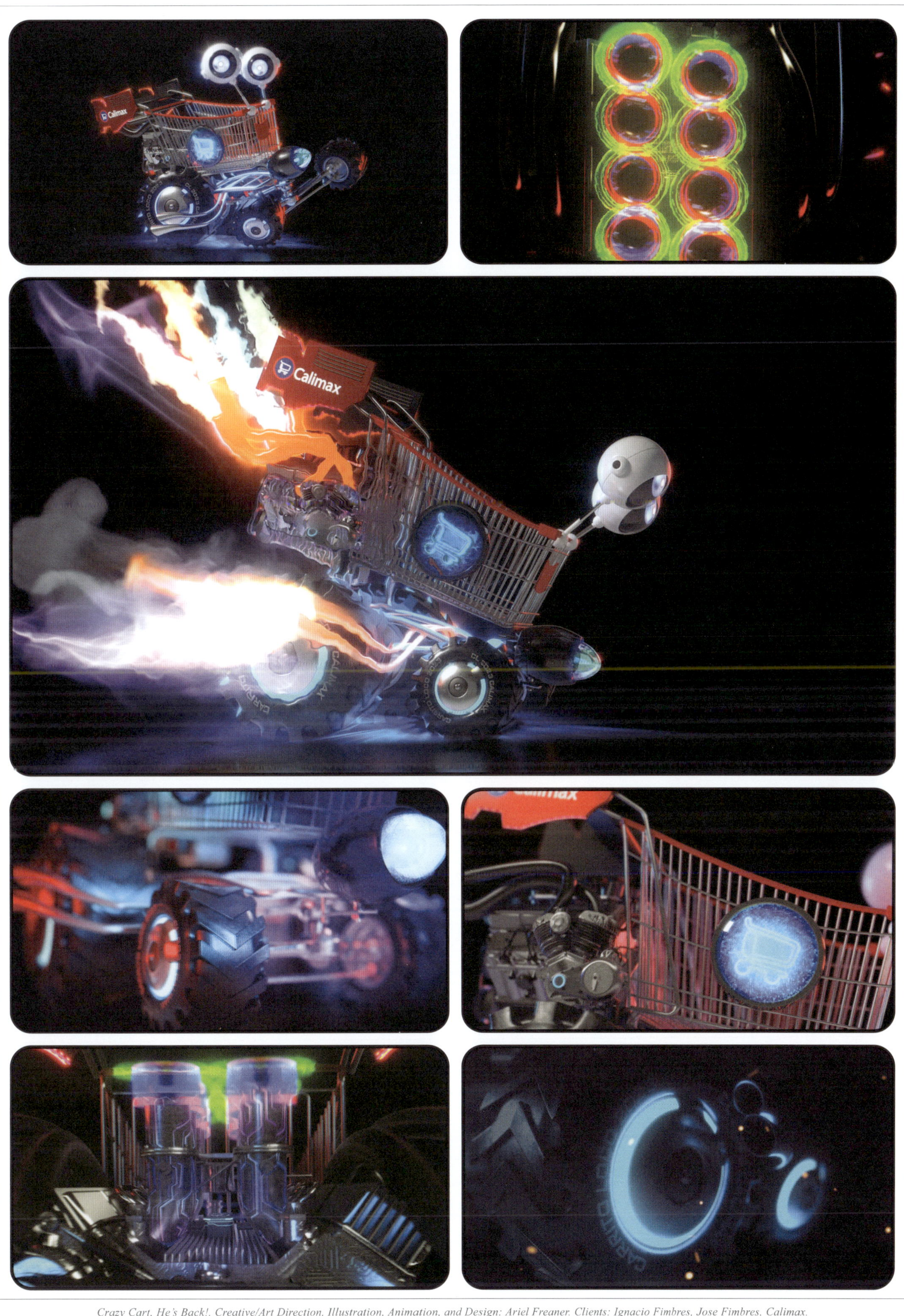

*Crazy Cart, He's Back!. Creative/Art Direction, Illustration, Animation, and Design: Ariel Freaner. Clients: Ignacio Fimbres, Jose Fimbres, Calimax.*

*What is your work philosophy?*
When I was 19 years old and living in Mexico, I had the opportunity to come to the US to work under a special visa for individuals who possess extraordinary abilities in the sciences, arts, education, business, or athletics or who have a demonstrated record of exceptional achievement in the motion picture or television industry and have been recognized nationally or internationally for those achievements. I didn't want to waste this opportunity, and I dedicated myself to working hard, studying, learning, improving daily, and developing a strong work ethic. I would tell anyone who wants a career as a creative to have a strong work ethic. It is incredibly valuable these days. Provide a service, be professional, honest, accessible, and courteous, and consistently deliver your best.

*Who is or was your greatest mentor?*
Jesús Blancornelas, the owner and director of a weekly newspaper named *ZETA* in Tijuana, Baja California. I was in college when he allowed me to work at his office. While he was not a designer, he respected and admired my work. Mr. Blancornelas allowed me to explore the world of graphic and editorial design, provided me with books, and even offered me a scholarship to continue my studies. He bought me a Macintosh IIFX, one of the first Mac computers to do digital design work. I worked with Digital Darkroom, PageMaker, the first Illustrator, TypeStyler, and other applications. It was fun!

As important as graphic design was for me back then, I also had some exciting and extraordinary experiences while working at *ZETA*. It was a time of turmoil in Mexico and Tijuana. There was an intense fight for democracy, and the anti-corruption movement was at its peak. Mr. Blancornelas led that movement with press freedom in northern Mexico, and *ZETA* became the barometer of Mexico's democracy and status. At the boiling point of this movement, while working at *ZETA*, I experienced the horrific assassinations of my coworkers, an assassination attempt against Mr. Blancornelas, drive-by shootings at the *ZETA* offices, home threats, and many more dangerous experiences. It's important to remember that this was long before social media, smartphones, or any of the digital advances we have today.

As horrific as that was, I also experienced the first fruits of democracy in Mexico. Thanks to Mr. Blancornelas' and *ZETA*'s support and efforts, the first mayor from the opposition party was elected in Ensenada, and years later, he became governor of Baja California. Other things happened during that critical period, like revealing another governor's corruption and forcing him to step down. It was powerful because this was one of the most corrupt governments in that region's history.

It was a great "hard knocks" school, and it inspired me to be a better person, have good ethics, and be a good designer. Putting all the drama aside, I designed the whole newspaper and earned *ZETA* multiple awards from Graphis, SND, and others. After several years, *ZETA* became one of my best clients, and when Mr. Blancornelas passed away, my relationship with *ZETA* slowly ended.

*What is it about advertising that you are most passionate about?*
The creativity and evolution of traditional applications for advertising thoroughly absorb me. For example, I learned to compose my designs utilizing a photo enlarger (or stats camera for some), Letraset transfer sheets, an airbrush, inks, Leroy pens, etc. Today, we use Photoshop and Illustrator, among many other applications. However, most concepts and technical names, such as posterization, halftones, and duotones, are still the same; they are just digital and live inside a menu in Photoshop.

Advertising itself is evolving: We used to have (and still do) billboards with static 3D images, like some French fries reaching beyond the edges. Now, we see the same concept with an animated digital billboard showing the French fries coming at the viewer in a stereoscopic or anaglyphic 3D fashion. Being a part of this evolution is humbling. While some designers see the ongoing digital evolution as a threat (first, the computer, then the Internet, and now AI), I see it as an exciting opportunity to produce and create more advanced, creative, and fascinating work. In a way, I live by this Edna Mode quote from *The Incredibles*: "I never look back, darling. It distracts from the now."

*What is the most difficult challenge you've overcome to reach your current position?*
Honestly, my biggest challenge has been financial. I started with nothing, so I needed to support myself from a very young age. I saved every penny to get the best education available, from buying books and supplies to supporting myself through college. Then there are the usual challenges: competition, bad experiences, dishonest and unscrupulous people, gossip, envy, etc. However, I believe in learning from your mistakes, leaving the past behind, and always looking and moving forward.

*Who have some of your greatest influences been?*
There have been so many creative people I've learned from. Still, my key influences have been designers, writers, and creatives such as Milton Glaser, Roger Black, Mario García, David Carson, Armin Hofmann, Saul Bass, John Dykstra, Ridley Scott, Mary Blair, George Lucas, Steven Spielberg, Michael Crichton, Brian Johnson, Joaquín Salvador Lavado Tejón (Quino), Charles Shulz, Jim Davis, Berkeley Breathed, and José Palomo.

*Who among your contemporaries today do you most admire?*
I am a bit old school, but I have been following some of the work of more contemporary graphic designers and design studios. I love Pentagram's cutting-edge design and how they're always at the forefront of whatever is new in this industry, the unexpected experimental typographic designs of David Carson and Paula Scher, the work of the now extinct *Emigre* magazine, Ray Johnson's collages, and the fantastic paintings of Remedios Varo. There's so much incredible and advanced work available today that I always take some time to get lost in Behance, Pinterest, and other sites, as well as some design and motion art accounts on Facebook and Instagram.

*What would be your dream assignment?*
My dream has always been to create special effects for Industrial Light & Magic, a cover for *Time* magazine, or a complex multi-page pop-up annual report utilizing unlimited printing techniques such as die cuts, metallic inks, UV spotting, foiling, embossing, and much more.

*Who have been some of your favorite colleagues or clients?*
I have no favorite colleagues, but I do have clients I appreciate working with. They include Jesús Blancornelas at *ZETA*, the County of San Diego, the Navy, Bill Melendez Productions, Fujitsu, the San Diego DA's Office, Calimax, and the Red Cross of Tijuana with Jorge Astiazarán. These individuals and organizations have inspired me both in my work and because of their community contributions.

*What are the top things you need from a client to do successful work for them?*
First, I always ask them to provide as much information as possible about what they want to help me assess and research

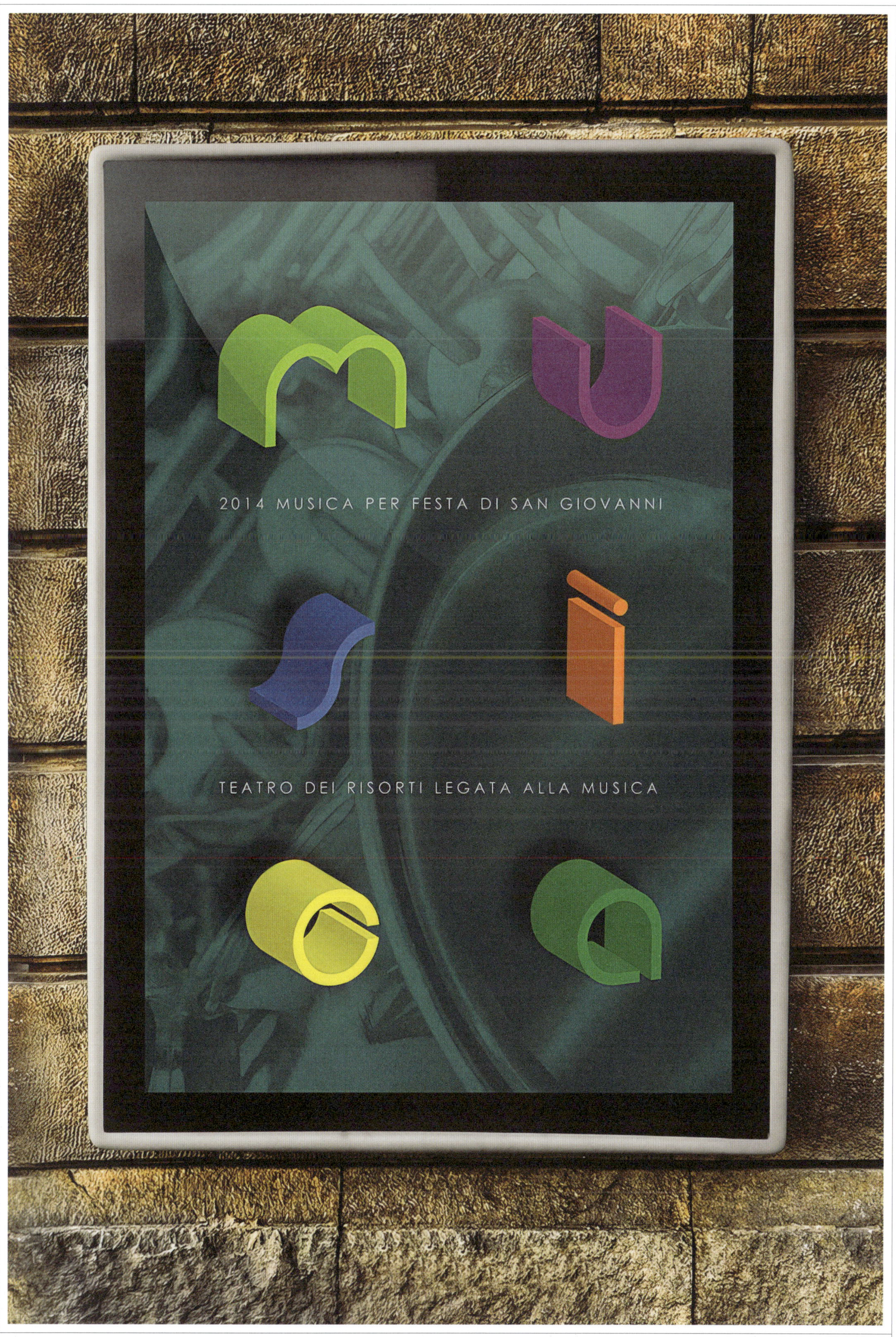


*MUSIC Poster, Radicondoli, Italy. Creative/Art Direction, Illustration, Graphic Design: Ariel Freaner. Client: City of Radicondoli, Italy.*

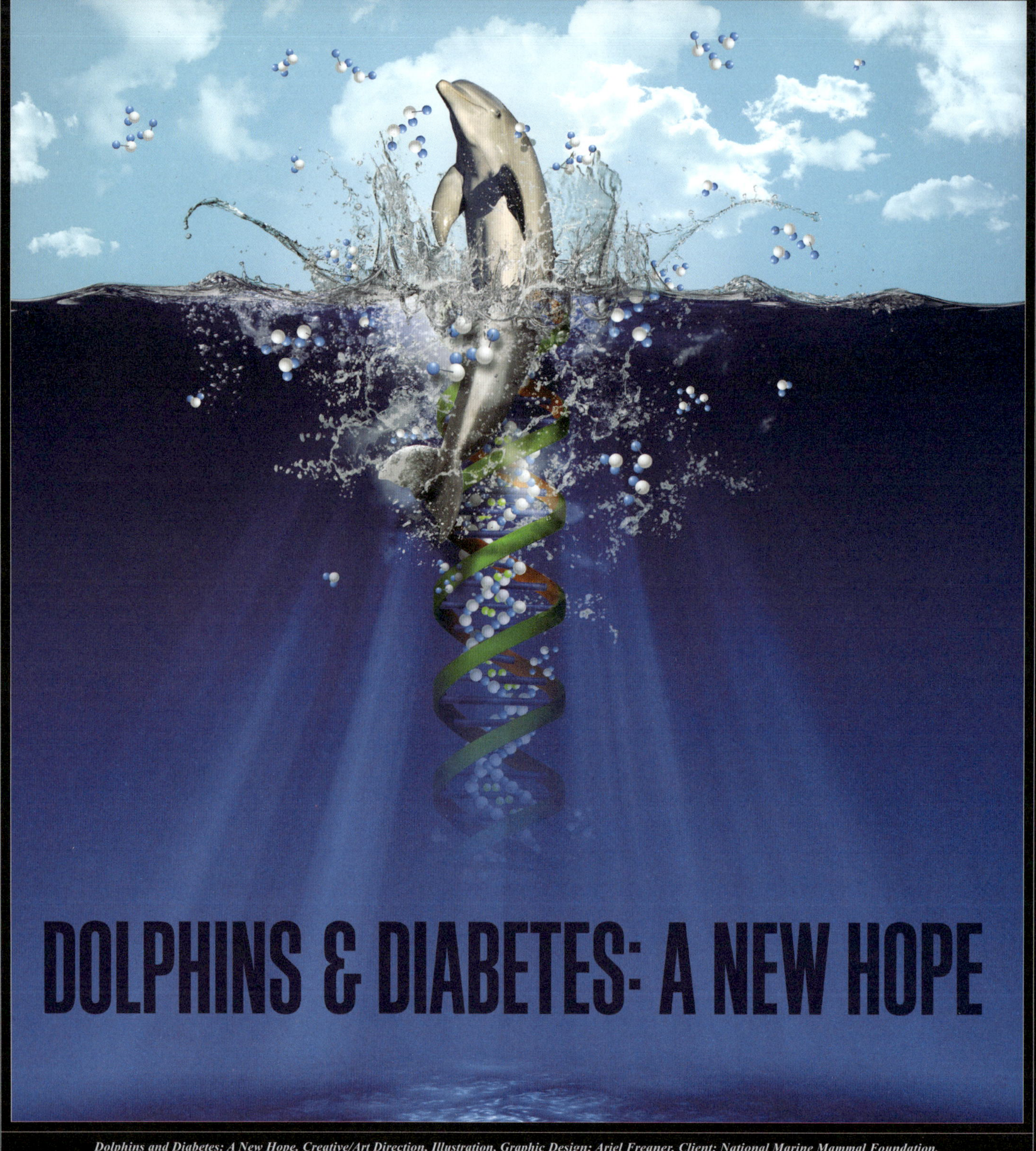


*Dolphins and Diabetes: A New Hope. Creative/Art Direction, Illustration, Graphic Design: Ariel Freaner. Client: National Marine Mammal Foundation.*

WE ARE PROUD TO HAVE WORKED WITH ARIEL FREANER, WHOSE DESIGNS BEAUTIFULLY CAPTURE OUR COMMITMENT TO SUSTAINABILITY, QUALITY, AND INNOVATION, LEAVING A LASTING IMPRESSION ON CUSTOMERS AND PARTNERS WORLDWIDE.

**Mayra Velazquez de León,** *President & CEO, Organics Unlimited*

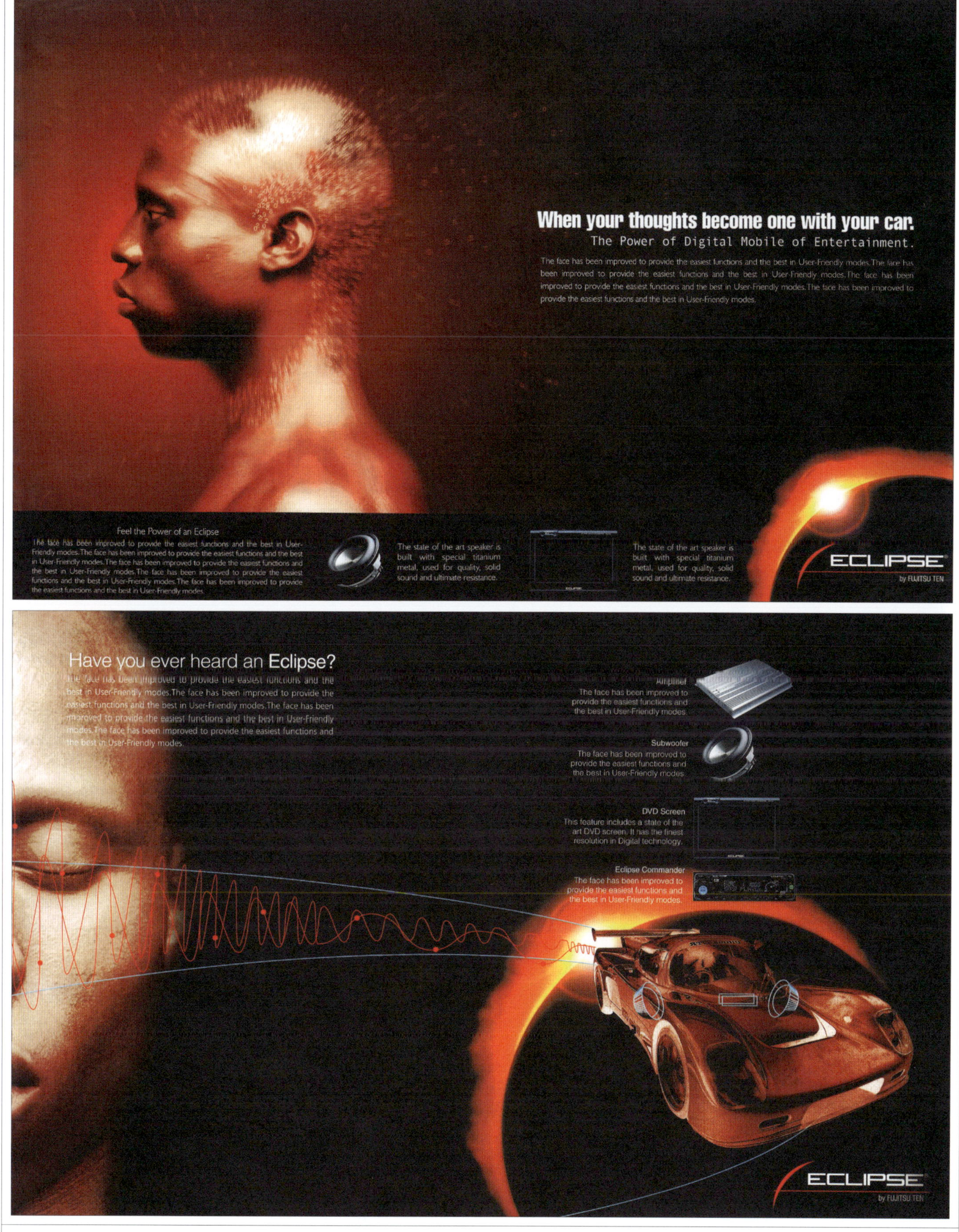


*ECLIPSE Mobile Entertainment Campaign. Creative/Art Direction: Ariel Freaner. Client: ECLIPSE by Fujitsu Ten.*

the right creative and design solution. Secondly, I ask the client to respect and trust our expertise and let us work! It is essential that the client who hires our design firm trusts our approach and enables us to do what we do best. The moment the client starts designing (which differs from making changes), the nightmare begins, and the process goes downhill. Lastly, of course, we ask clients to please pay their bills.

***What do you consider your most outstanding professional achievement so far?***

We love everything we do. Big or small, we put our heart into it. That said, we are very proud of a couple of projects: the Calimax Crazy Cart, Beto, the Red Cross mascot, the County of San Diego's Agriculture, Weights & Measures Crop Report, the LUEG Budget infographics website, the San Diego

District Attorney's Office designs, and the Fujitsu ECLIPSE mobile entertainment campaign.

*Is there a specific award you've won that is the most memorable to you?*
I received an award in my early teens for a character I designed for the Hermosillo Sonora Red Cross. It was my first professional award, and they even sent an ambulance to pick me up at my high school to take me to the conference where the award was being presented. It was a fantastic experience. I felt so important.

The first award I received in the United States was from *Print* magazine in 1992 for two logo designs. I was amazed when I received my first US award certificate. Following that, we received some award of excellence certificates from the Society of News Design, but I never got a trophy.

Then, I received my first trophies from Graphis. They were gold and silver and came in a neat, beautifully packed box along with the hardcover books with the award publications. That was a great moment!

While the studio grew in different areas, such as animation and visual effects, we also had a great memorable event when we won our first few Emmys for visual effects, art direction, audio, and motion graphics, which included nominations for my daughter and son.

*What about your work gives you the greatest satisfaction?*
That's the thing: I have never felt that I go to work. I delight in being creative for a living every day. I get excited every morning just walking into my studio, passing by my shelves, and seeing my colored pencils, markers, books (including Graphis), Pantone guides, drafting tablet, papers, brushes, and watercolor station—all well-organized and ready to be used. Oh, I can go on and on!

*What part of your work do you find the most demanding?*
Accounting and administration. A business can only run well with sound accounting and administration. Thank God I have the perfect partner: my beautiful wife, Yolanda. Oh, she's so good with numbers, administration, and forecasting. She's responsible and down-to-earth, but better yet, she is more beautiful than anything.

*What professional goals do you still have for yourself?*
God permitting, studying! I am planning and getting organized to start a new career in new media here in San Diego. I want to expand my knowledge in all interactive media and aspects of digital and visual design, user experience design, interaction, motion graphics, and technology.

*Besides advertising, you also work as a career advisor for schools and other educational organizations. How did that start, and what do you like about it?*
I get invited sporadically to be a career advisor for schools and other educational organizations, such as Cuyamaca College, the Advertising Arts College, and City College here in San Diego. I have also spoken in Tijuana, Mexico City, and Guadalajara. I have found it very rewarding, and it keeps me up to date.

*What advice would you give students starting out today?*
Keep studying, always stay up to date, practice, and respect your career and profession. I have met people who think careers in the visual arts fields are not "real" careers. Do not let anyone make you feel less; I know several lawyers, doctors, and engineers who are anything but successful in their fields.

*What do you value most in life?*
My family and the time I spend with them. Even though design, animation, special effects, and other visual arts are my passions, being with my loved ones is what I cherish most. It's the most valuable time you can ever have.

*What interests do you have outside of work?*
I like traveling, reading, eating, photography, working on my comic strip, and collecting toys.

*What would you change if you had to do it all over again?*
I would not change anything. We all have personal missteps, but that's part of growing up. Sometimes, we forget who we are today is due to everything we have lived through. I believe in learning from the past and living in the present to build a better future.

*Where do you find inspiration?*
Everywhere: looking at the scenery, seeing locations, traveling, researching, movies, TV shows, the Internet, and listening to music. Sometimes, I connect my brain to the rhythm of music while working: I transform beats, rhythms, melodies, and musical notes into design elements that play with each other and ultimately create great designs.

*How do you define success?*
I am happy when I am with my family, at work, and in everything else I do. In the business sense, I am also pleased when my clients are happy with my work and services. Recognition is excellent and essential for self-growth; however, I believe success is being happy with everything you do.

*Where do you see yourself in the future?*
God willing, I will be with my beautiful wife and family, sitting at my drafting table doing design experiments, cartooning, and working on my comic strip. I may do illustrations occasionally, but I will mostly enjoy life with my loved ones. I have three things I would love to do on my bucket list: take a course at ArtCenter, visit Antarctica with my family, and travel to space if possible.

*How do you balance your work with your personal life if there is a distinction between the two for you?*
There's a distinction for me. My personal life is about my family. When I'm with them, I try to avoid talking about mundane, daily work things so I can focus on being with them. One of the reasons I don't work at home and have a studio is to separate my work from my personal life. Yes, there's a time when both merge, such as when we celebrate an achievement, an award, or another event worth sharing, but I don't want to mix personal time with everyday work.

*In what ways do you see your field changing over the years?*
I see a new digital world offering multiple opportunities to today's design studios and future designers. Rather than being some evil competition or a threat, I believe the Internet and AI are opportunity generators with the potential to provide expert assistance. As an example, we work so much faster today with AI. We can use it to help remove backgrounds, create algorithms for batch processing, suggest faster HTML and CSS codes as well as program production routes, and finish designs based on our original prompts. The more the digital world expands, the more visually original it must be to compete in today's global arena. Other than Edna Mode, I also live by Walt Disney's famous phrase, "It's kind of fun to do the impossible."
**Freaner Creative & Design** www.freaner.com

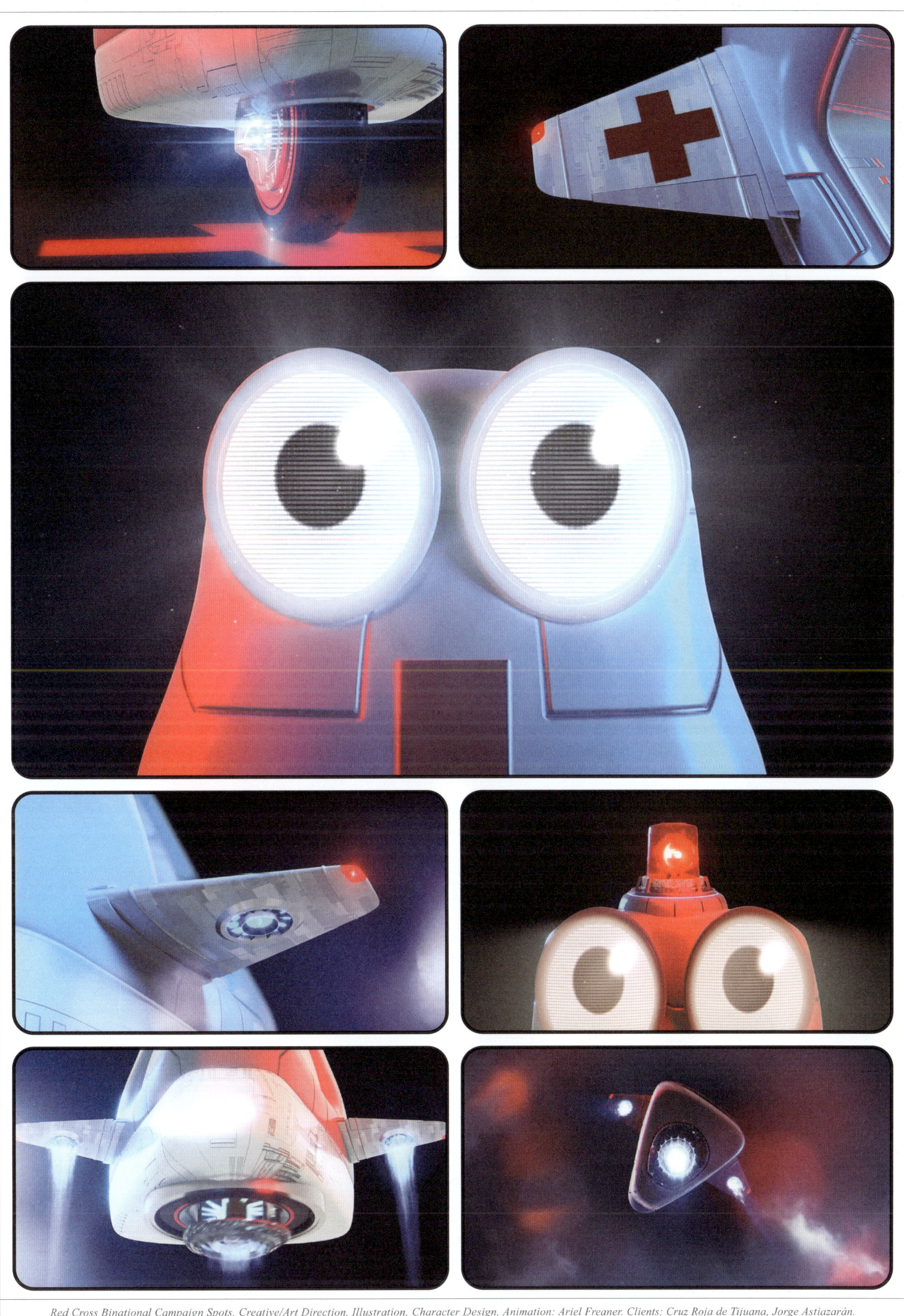

*Red Cross Binational Campaign Spots. Creative/Art Direction, Illustration, Character Design, Animation: Ariel Freaner. Clients: Cruz Roja de Tijuana, Jorge Astiazarán.*

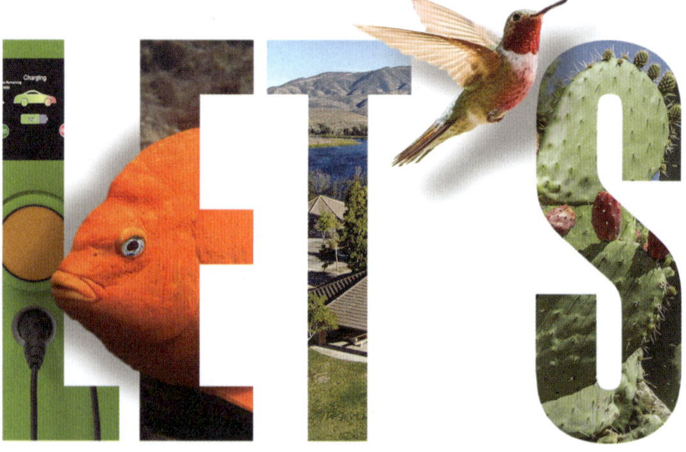
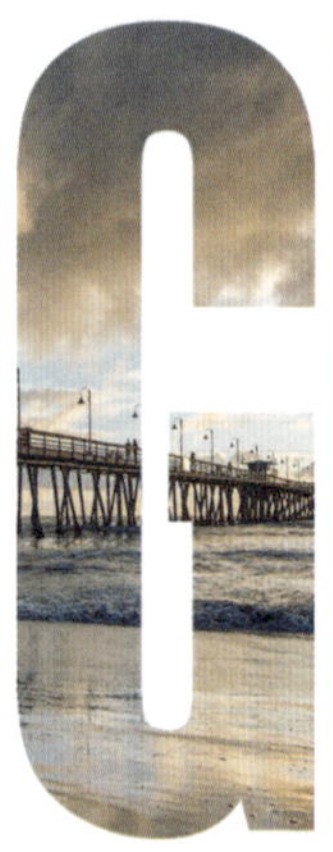
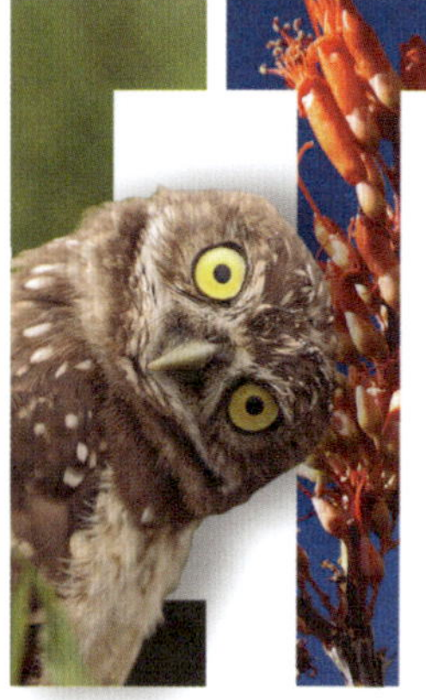
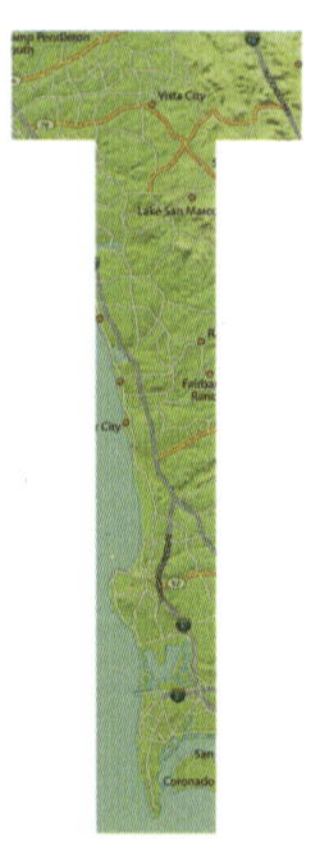
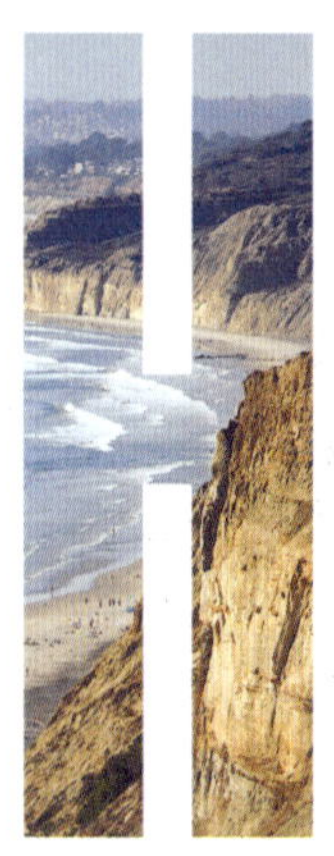
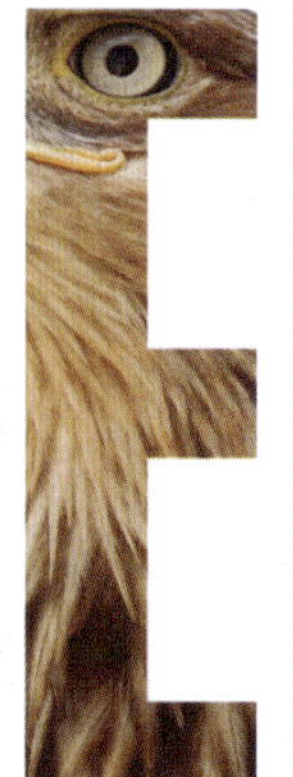
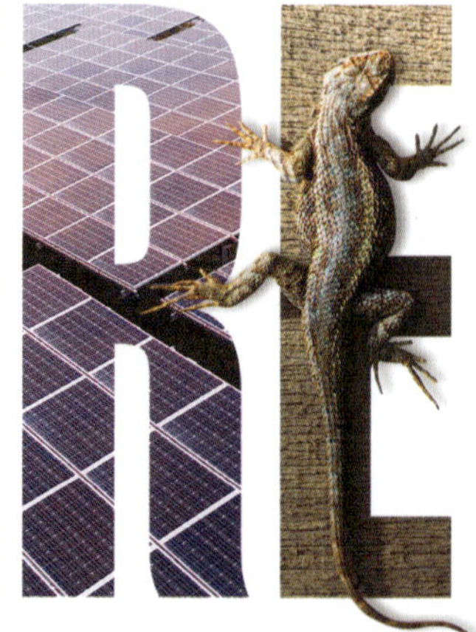

# LET'S GET THERE

## A GUIDE FOR COLLECTIVE CLIMATE ACTION ACROSS OUR REGION

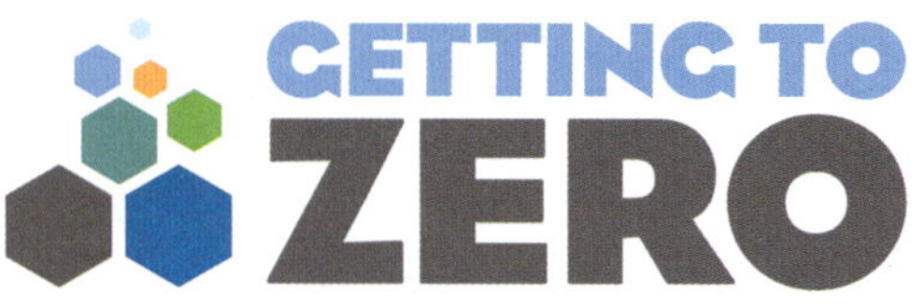

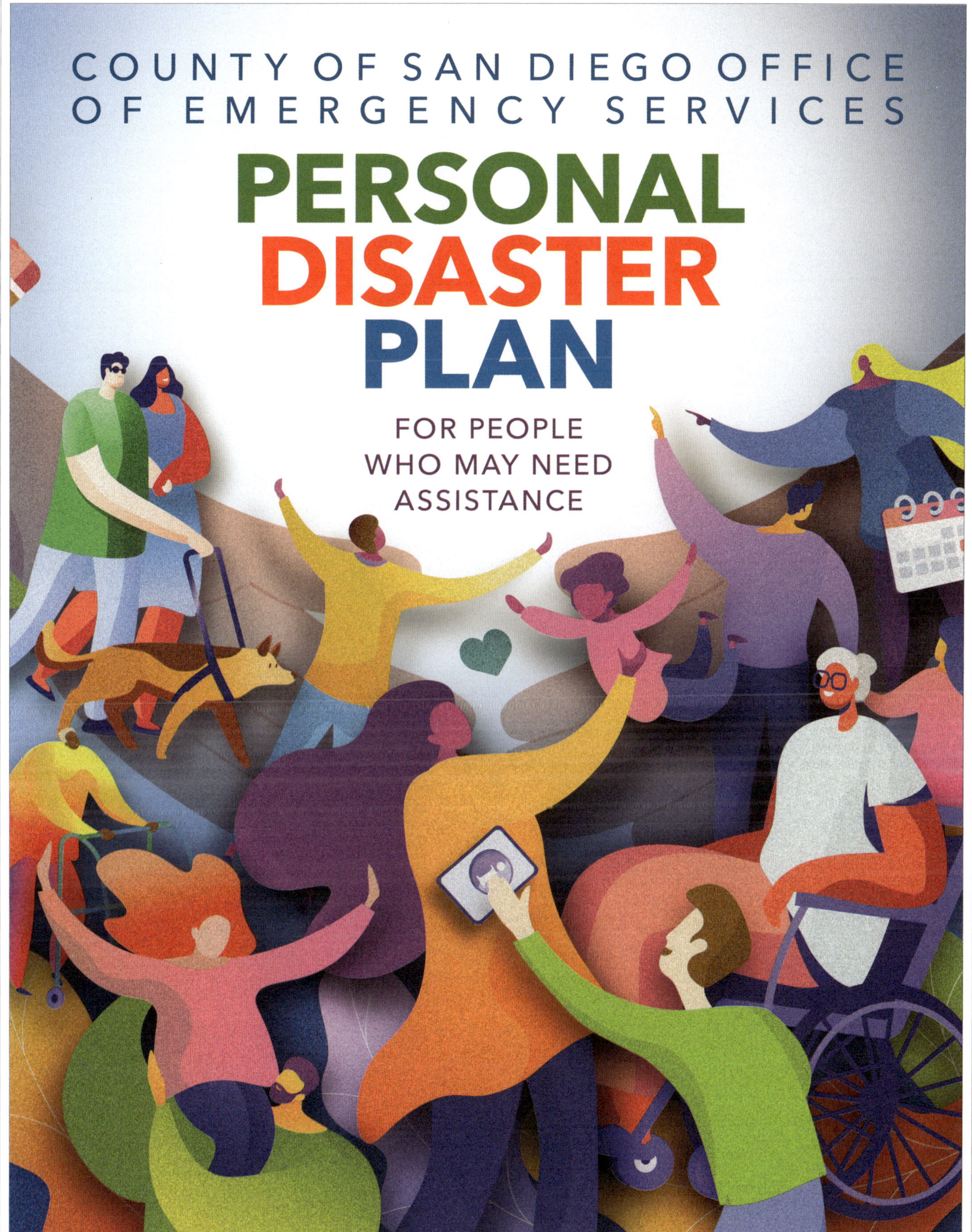


*Personal Disaster Plan. Creative/Art Direction, Illustration, Editorial Design, Infographics: Ariel Freaner.*
*Client: OES | County of San Diego Office of Emergency Services, Daniel Vasquez.*

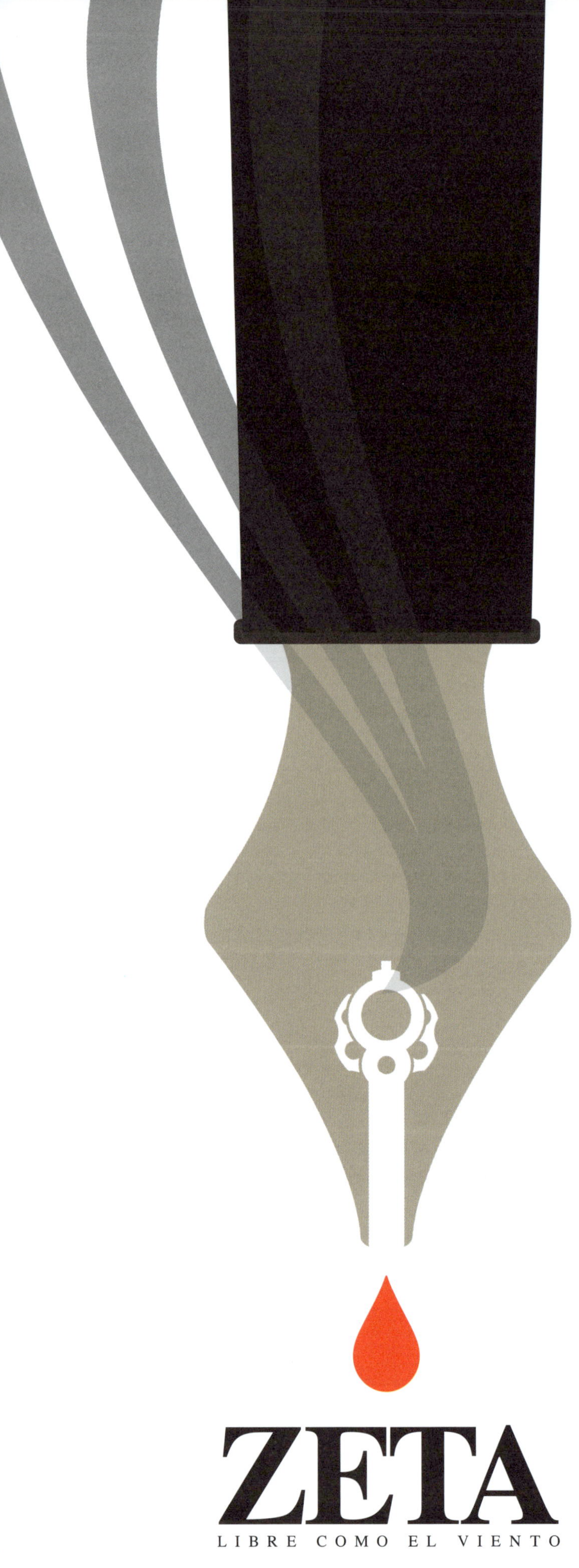

ZETA
LIBRE COMO EL VIENTO

*Honoring Our Fallen Heroes. Creative/Art Direction, Illustration, Graphic Design: Ariel Freaner.*
*Client: Silver Star Magazine, David Leonhardi, Rachel Parrot, Melanie Perry.*

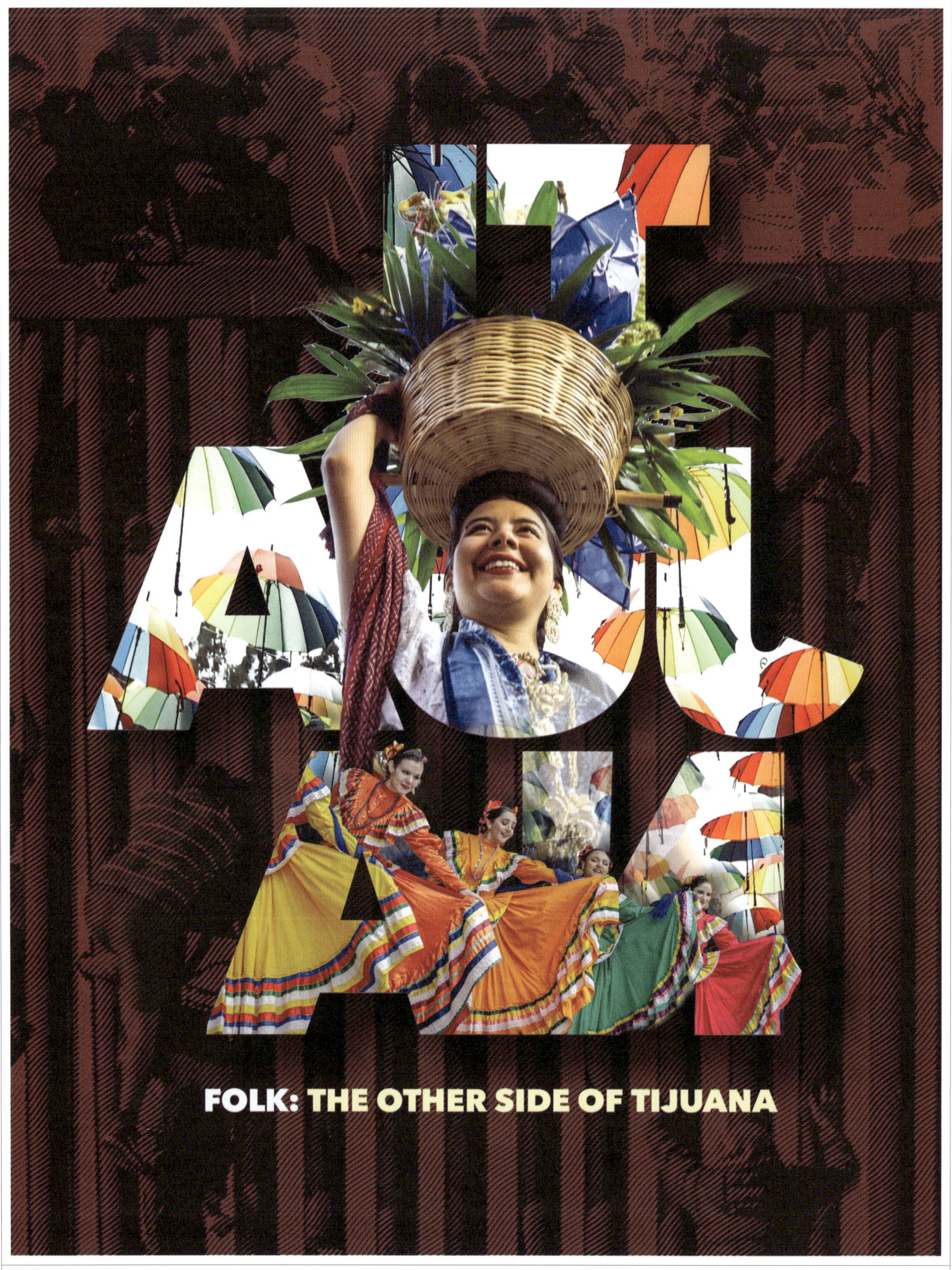


*The Other Side of Tijuana - Culture. Creative/Art Direction, Illustration, Graphic Design: Ariel Freaner. Client: City of Tijuana, Jorge Astiazarán.*

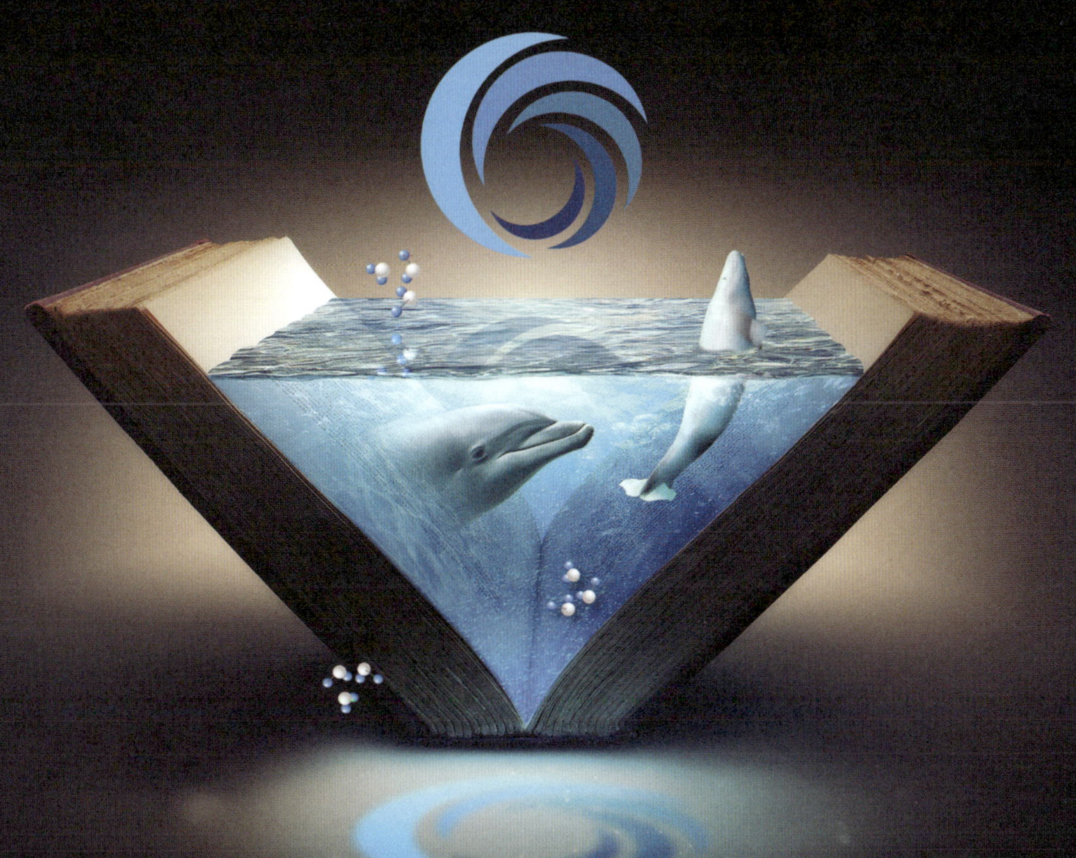


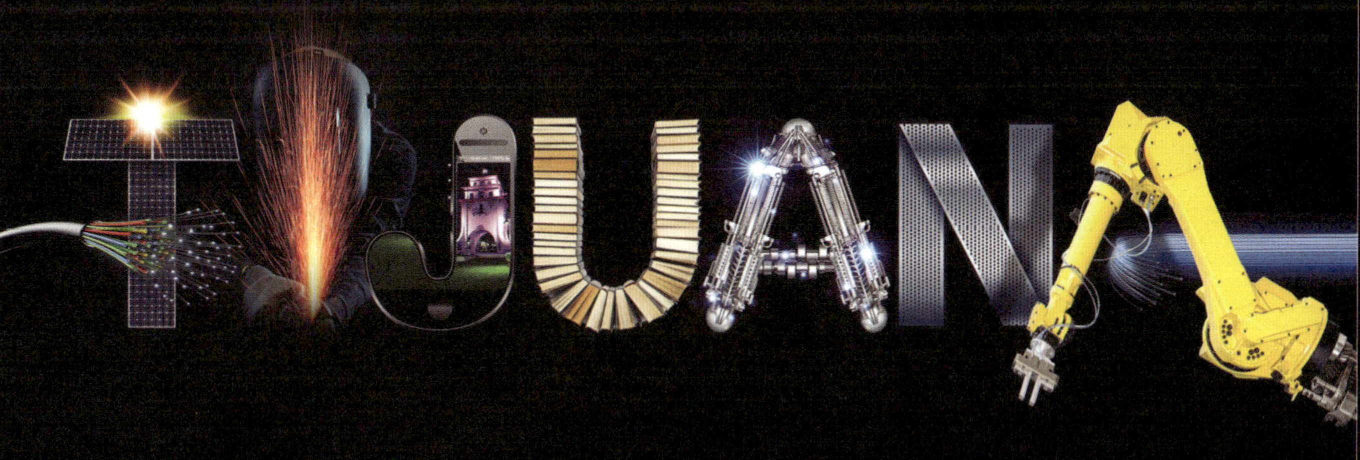

*(Top) Research. Innovation. Discovery. Creative/Art Direction, Digital Collage Illustration, Graphic Design: Ariel Freaner.*
*Client: National Marine Mammal Foundation.*
*(Bottom) TIJUANA City Brand. Creative/Art Direction, Digital Illustration, Graphic Design: Ariel Freaner. Client: City of Tijuana, Jorge Astiazarán.*

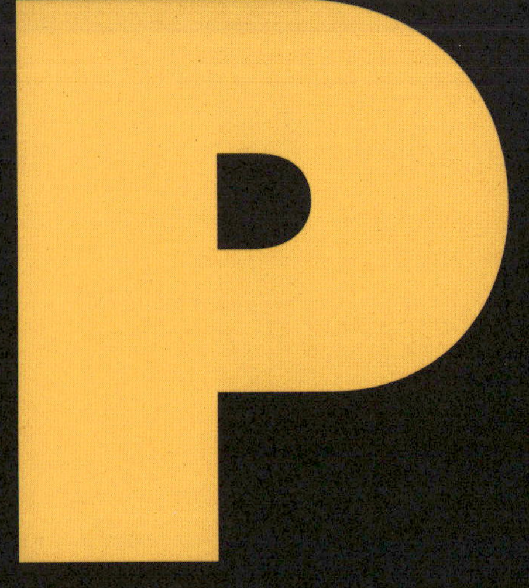

# P

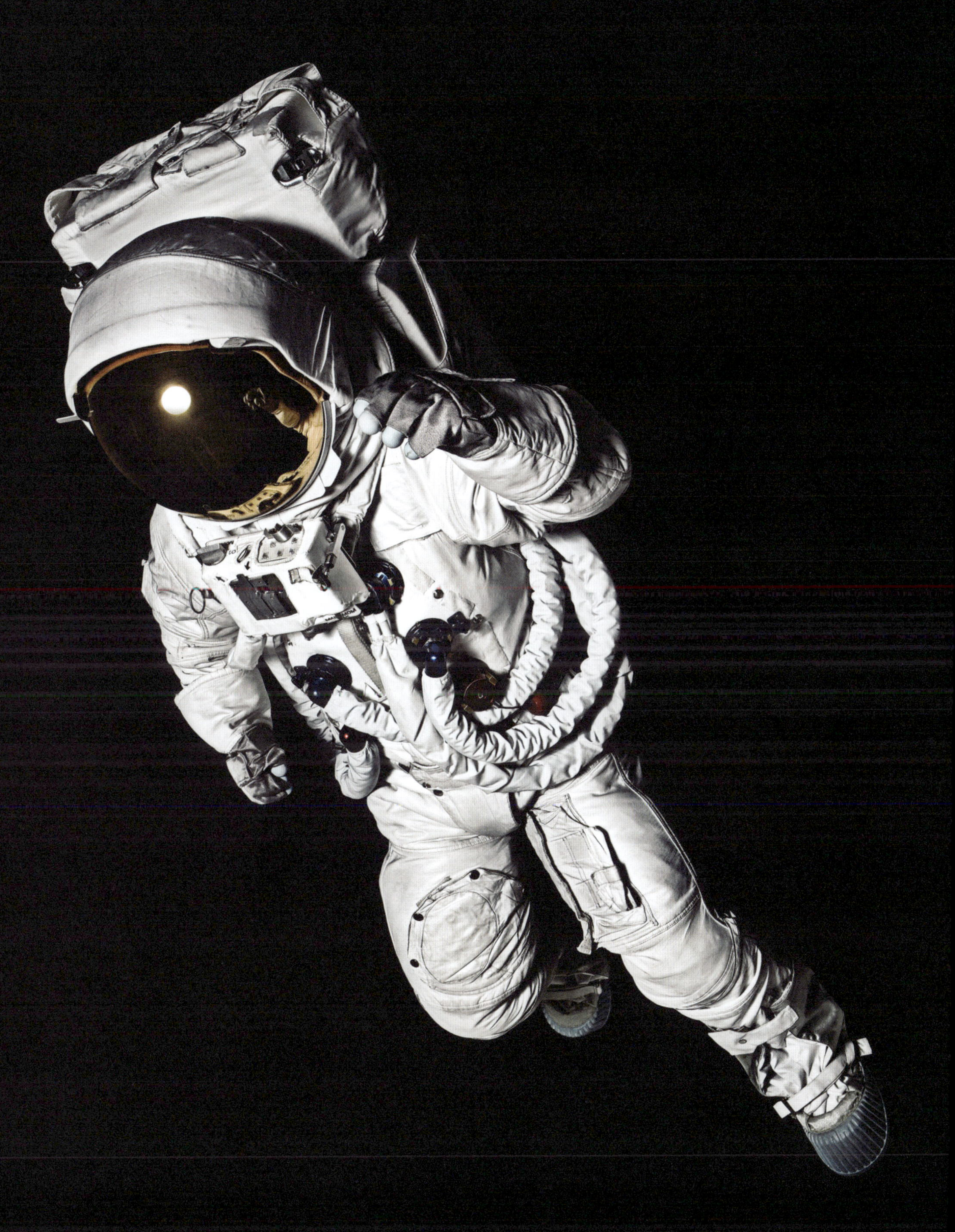

STAN HAS A UNIQUE WAY OF IDEALIZING AND HUMANIZING HIS SUBJECTS AT THE SAME TIME.

**RJ Muna,** *Photographer, RJ Muna Pictures*

STAN MUSILEK IS A VERSATILE PHOTOGRAPHIC MASTER WHO MOVES EFFORTLESSLY BETWEEN BEAUTY, NUDES, AND STILL LIFE WITHOUT THE RISK OF COMPROMISING ANY CHANGE.

**Torkil Gudnason,** *Photographer, Torkil Gudnason Studio*

STAN'S WORK IS BOLD AND GRAPHIC, WITH AN IMPECCABLE SENSE OF COMPOSITIONAL BALANCE AND, OFTEN, A SHOCKING USE OF COLOR. WHEN I AM LOOKING FOR INSPIRATION FOR MY OWN WORK, I NEVER FORGET TO CHECK IN ON WHAT STAN IS WORKING ON.

**Robert Tardio,** *Photographer, Robert Tardio Photography Ltd*

HIS IMAGES ARE THRILLING, SEXY, SEXUAL, AND POWERFUL. ASIDE FROM HIS SKILLED TECHNICAL MASTERY AND REVELATORY LIGHTING, HIS EYE HOLDS FAST THROUGHOUT ALL HIS WORK.

**Howard Schatz,** *Photographer, Howard Schatz Photography*

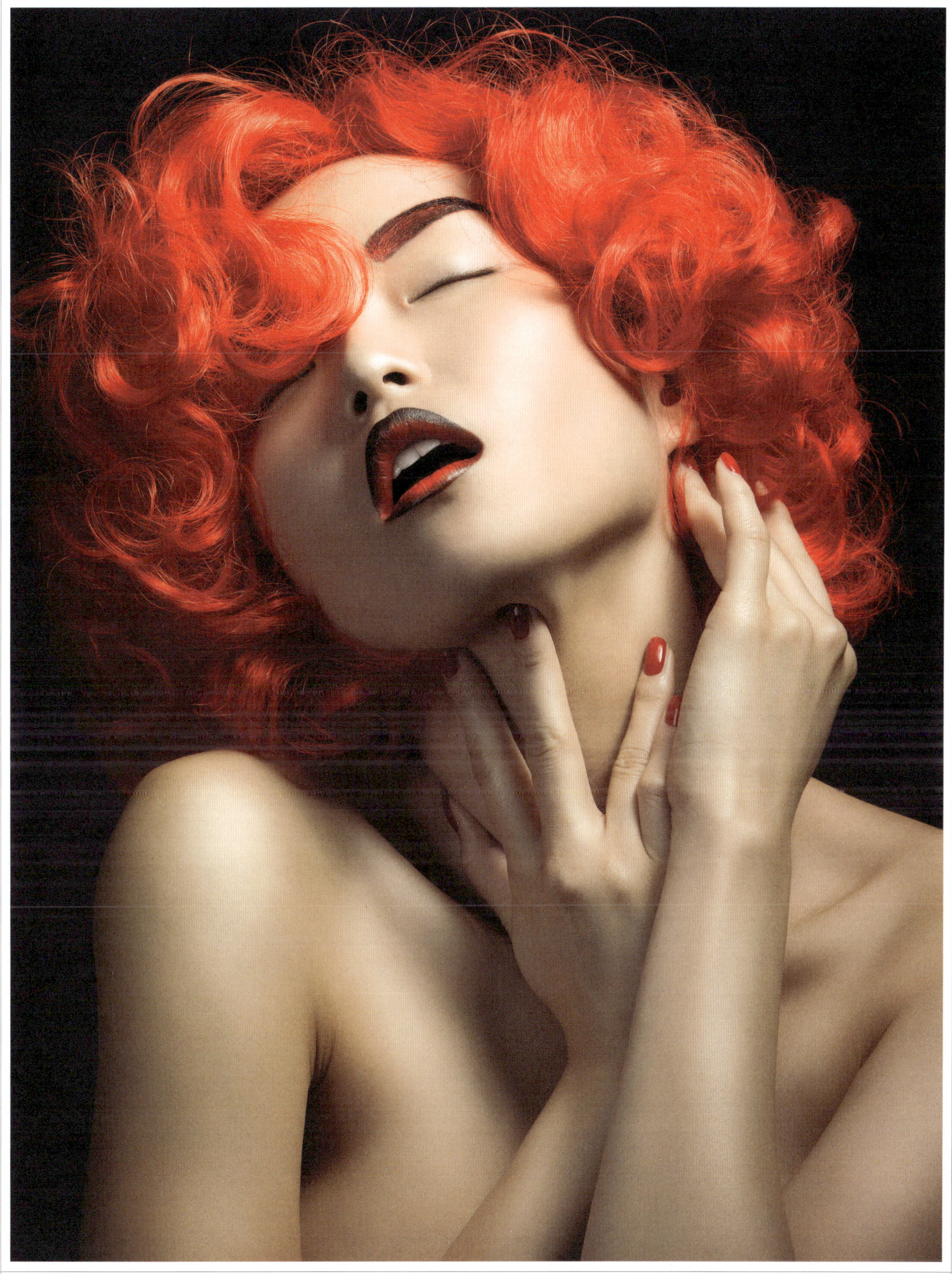

*Moon*

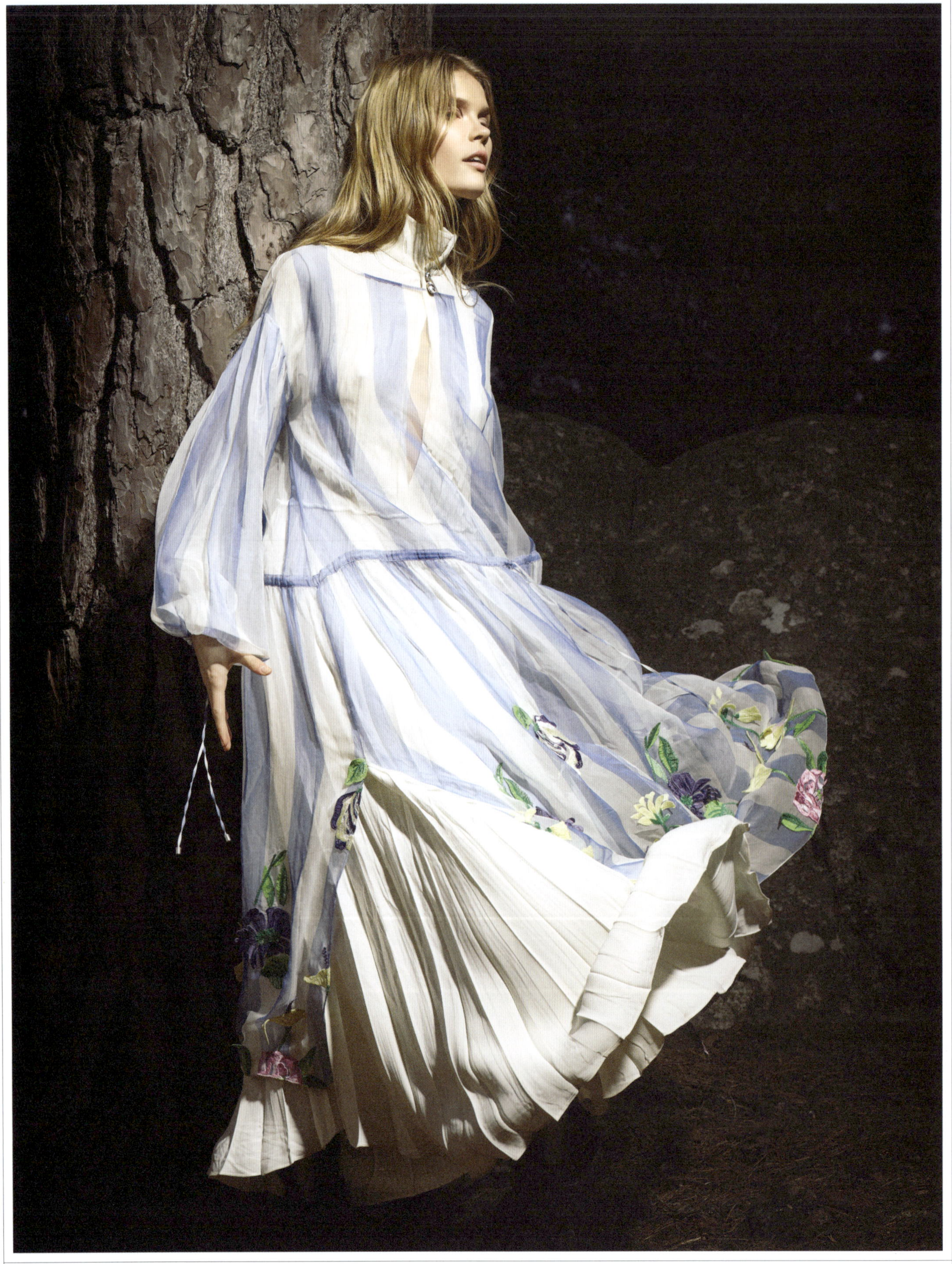

*Barbizon*

**Introduction by Patti Judd** *Creative Director & Founder, Judd Brand Media*

Through the lens of Stan Musilek, beauty is both a philosophy and a pursuit. As the founder of Musilek Studios, with spaces in San Francisco and Paris, he has spent decades capturing images that challenge and celebrate the feminine form. His work, marked by a thoughtful yet dictatorial process, has earned him both artistic acclaim and commercial success—a rare combination in an industry where compromise often feels inevitable. In this candid conversation, Stan reflects on a career shaped by the influences of photography legends like Helmut Newton and Guy Bourdin while maintaining his distinctive vision. With characteristic dry wit and European sensibility, he discusses everything from his disdain for influencer culture to his simple secret for success: "Think first, shoot later." Whether orchestrating high-stakes commercial shoots or pursuing personal projects, Stan's enduring drive remains the same—to create something that tops the last shot.

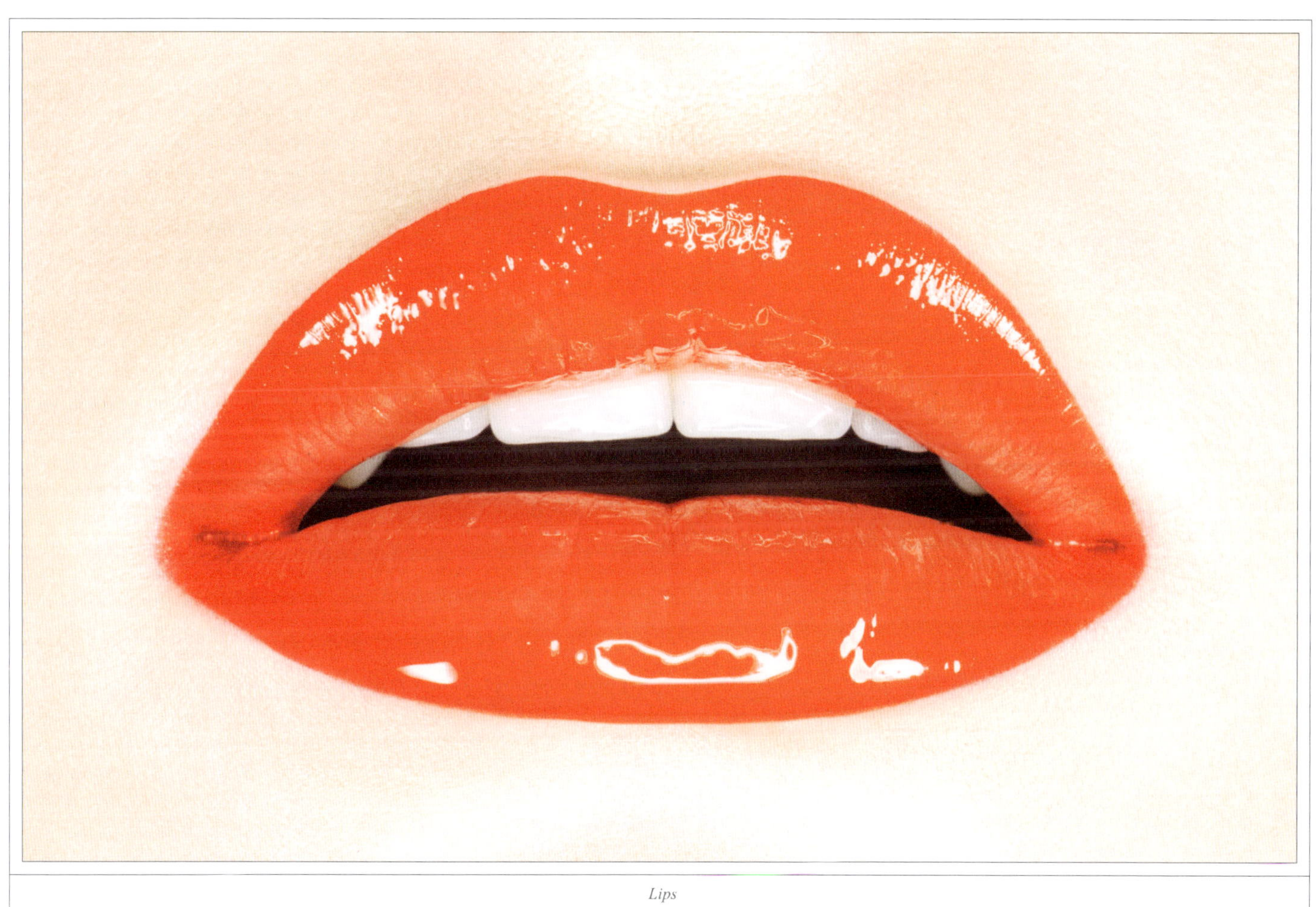

*Lips*

# THERE IS ALWAYS THE MOTIVATION TO CREATE SOMETHING THAT TOPS THE LAST SHOT.

**Stan Musilek,** *Photographer & Founder, Musilek Studios*

*What inspired or motivated you in your career?*
Women.

*What is your work philosophy?*
Think first, shoot later.

*Where do you seek inspiration?*
Memories and experiences.

*What aspect of photography do you most enjoy?*
It fluctuates. Currently, I'm really enjoying printing large format prints of my personal work.

*How would you describe your process?*
Thought out, streamlined, and dictatorial.

*Who is or was your greatest mentor?*
No mentor per se.

*Who were some of your greatest past influences?*
Helmut Newton, Chris von Wangenheim, and Guy Bourdin.

*What is your most outstanding professional achievement?*
Maybe becoming independently wealthy by taking pictures and doing something I would do anyway.

*Who among your contemporaries today do you most admire?*
I've seen some interesting images shot by Johnny Dufort and Nadia Cohen.

*Who have been some of your favorite people or clients you have worked with?*
I have made many friends through my work and have been fortunate in that aspect, with the exception of one or two "trouble clients." I'm not one to start name-dropping; it feels too much like a thank-you speech at the Oscars. I think I hear the music getting louder.

*What are the most important ingredients you require from a client to work successfully?*
A realistic budget in the context of the planned visuals and the courage to be a bit irreverent.

*Can you talk about the collaboration process with your models?*
There used to be a natural progression of meeting on a commercial shoot and then collaborating on personal or editorial projects. It's a little more challenging these days, particularly due to my intense dislike of influencer culture.

*How is nude photography a unique challenge when compared to traditional portraiture?*
There's a different kind of small talk on set. ;)

*You were born in Europe before moving to the USA. How has your time here differed from your days in Europe? Were you able to access a new variety of clients or collaborators?*
Yes, my work was well-received; the studio ended up being very successful commercially.

*What is the greatest satisfaction you get from your work?*
It depends on whether it is commercial or personal. Commercially, the satisfaction comes from producing something that goes beyond the client's initial expectation. In my personal work, it is more of an ongoing satisfaction; there is always the motivation to create something that tops the last shot. Happy accidents, curiosity, what ifs...?

*What advice would you give to young photographers starting out today?*
That is a difficult question. The process of establishing yourself has changed dramatically in recent years. I was happy to see, for decades, that all of my first assistants who survived the Stan Musilek "boot camp" went on to have careers of their own. It was based on their exposure to advertising agencies and design firms we shot for and the visuals we created. The world no longer exists in that form.

*What interests do you have outside of your work?*
You mean besides philatélie and heraldry?

*How do you balance your time between your two studios in San Francisco and Paris?*
It is pretty much 50-50, but I'm always trying to be in California in winter. ;)

*How do you define success?*
Working with fun people on inspired shoots for good money.

*What would you change if you had to do it all over again?*
I would outlaw conference calls on speakerphone.

*Where do you see yourself in the future?*
As far away as possible from Elon Musk.

**Musilek Studios** www.musilek.com
*See his Graphis Master Portfolio at graphis.com.*

# SATISFACTION COMES FROM PRODUCING SOMETHING THAT GOES BEYOND THE CLIENT'S INITIAL EXPECTATIONS.

**Stan Musilek,** *Photographer & Founder, Musilek Studios*

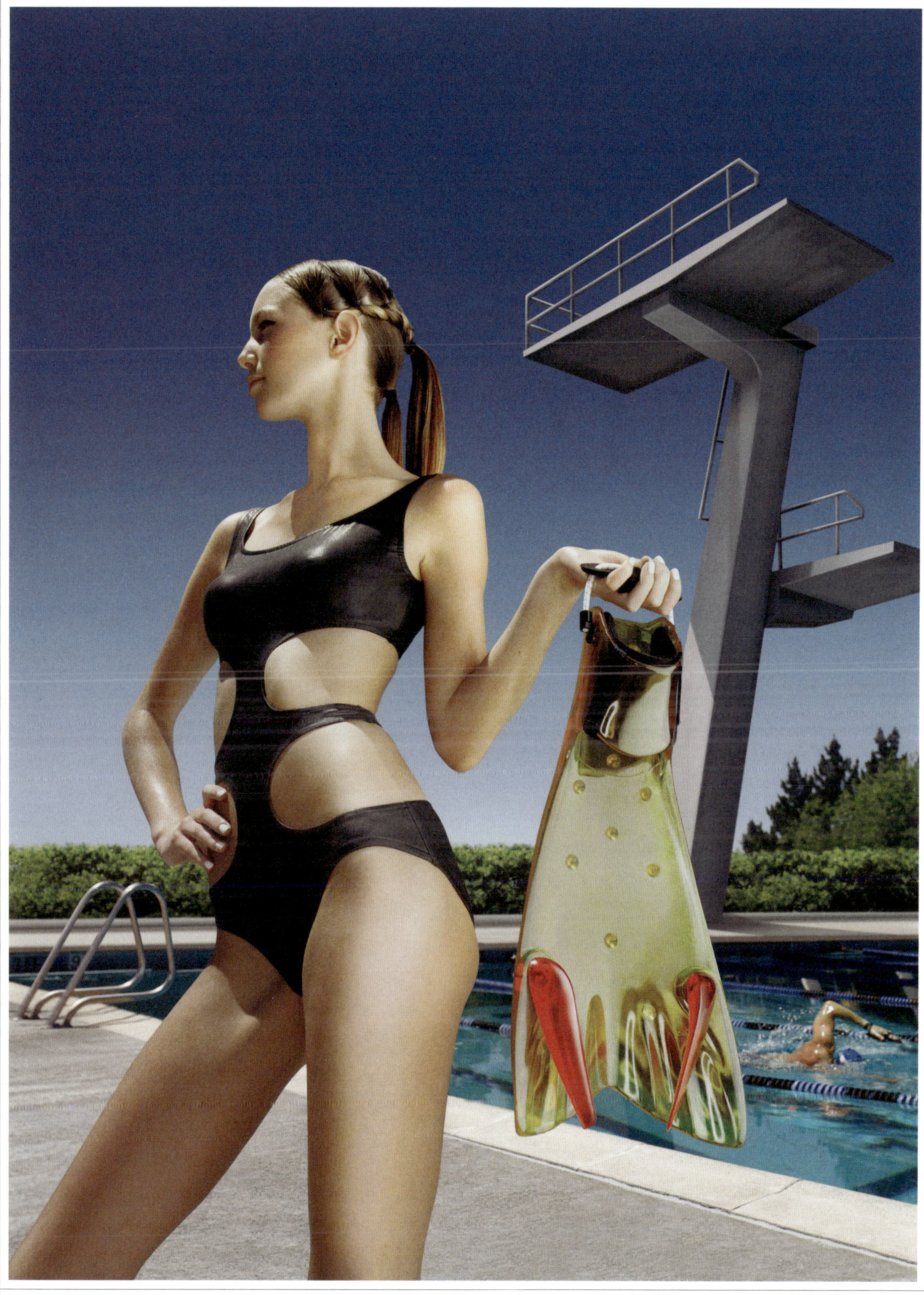

*Pool Girl*

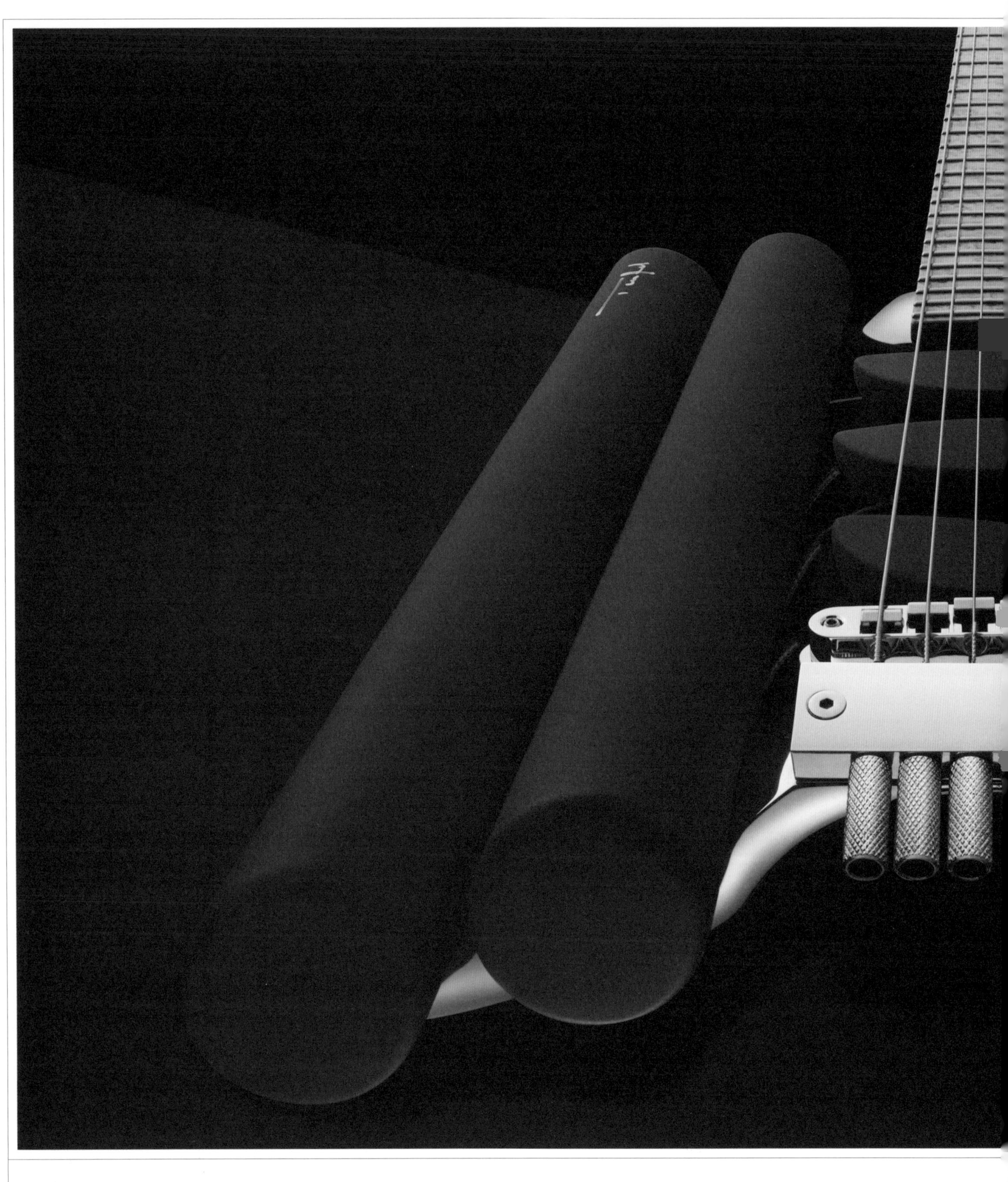

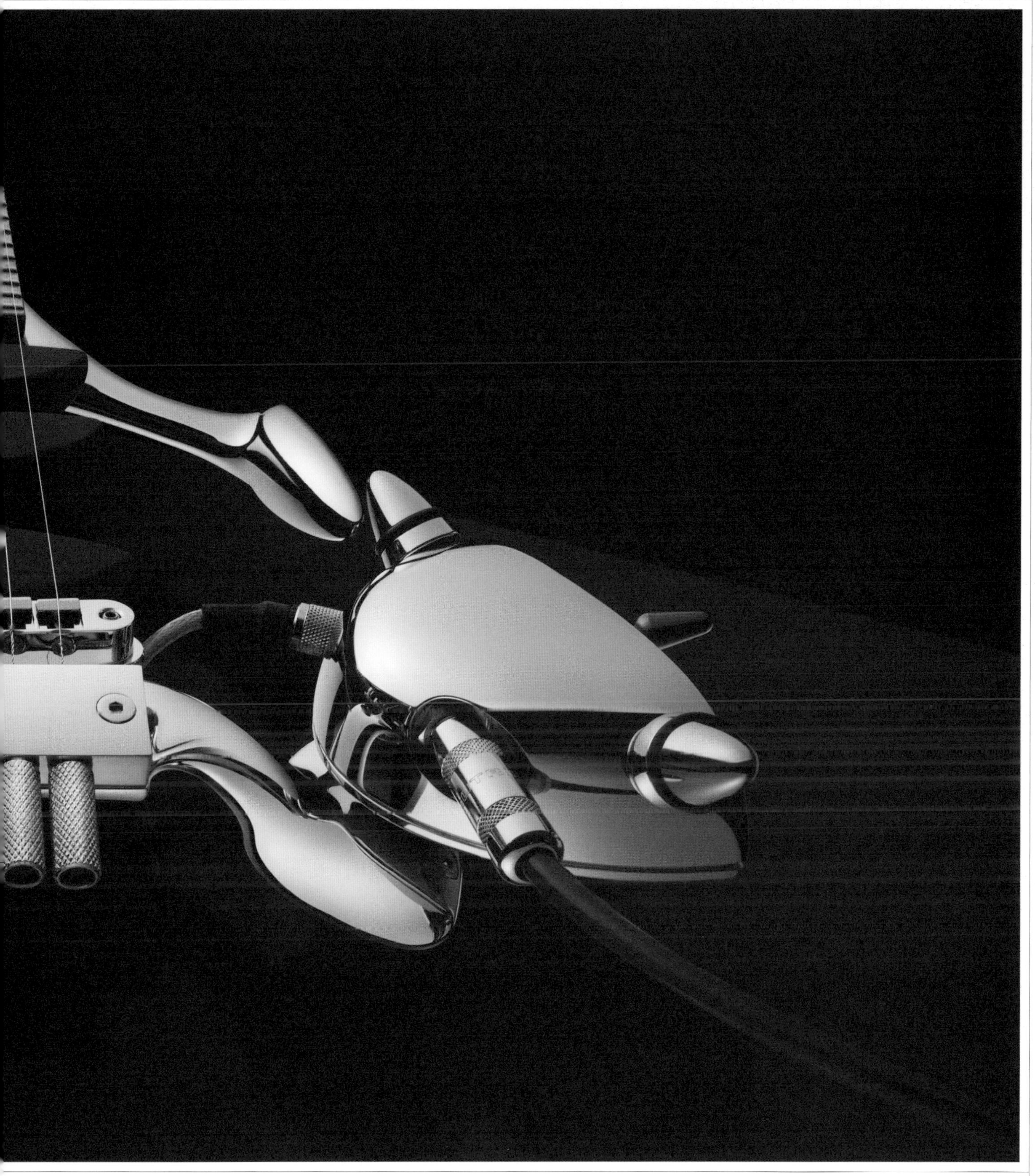

*Teuffel*

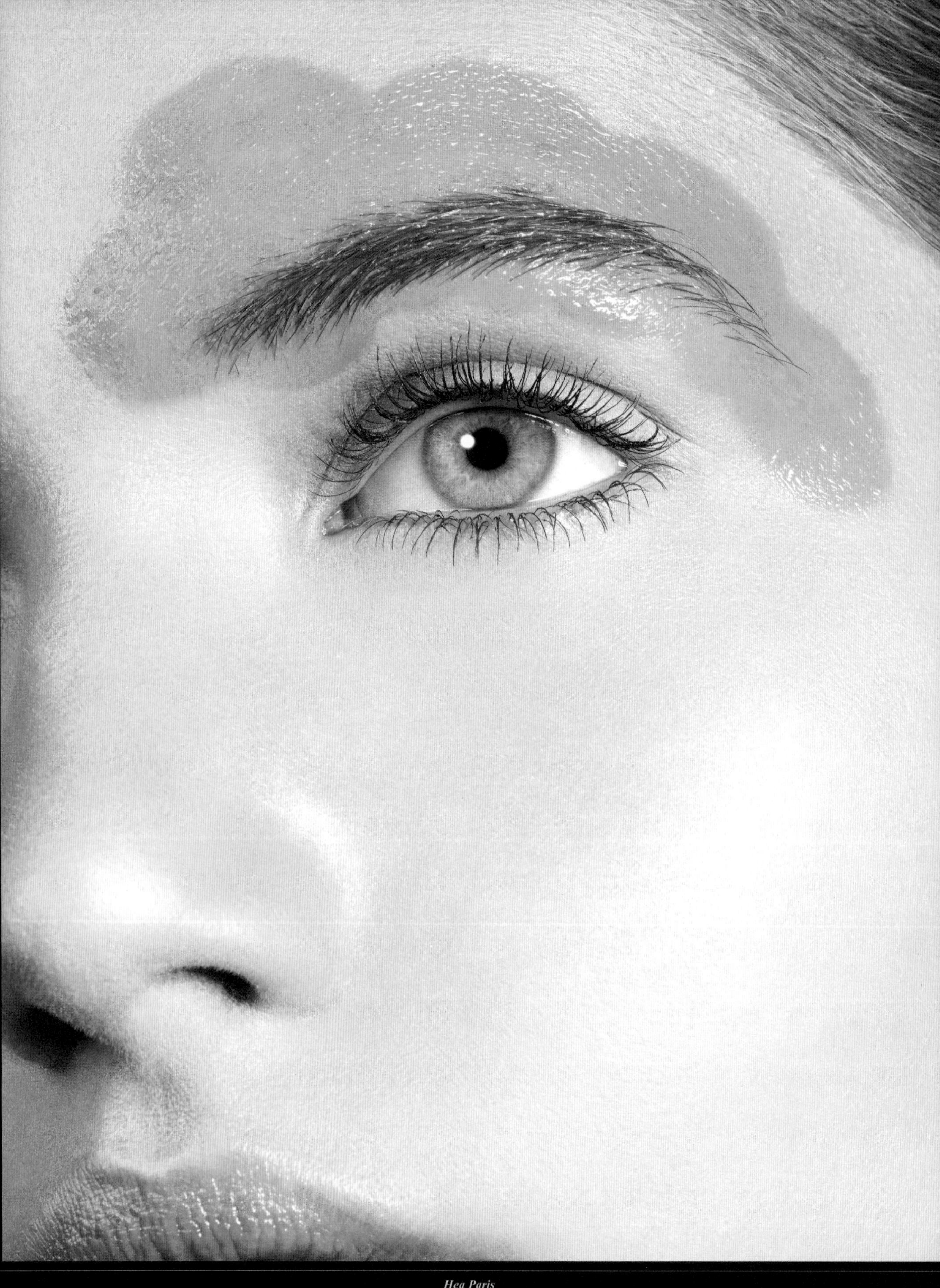

Hea Paris

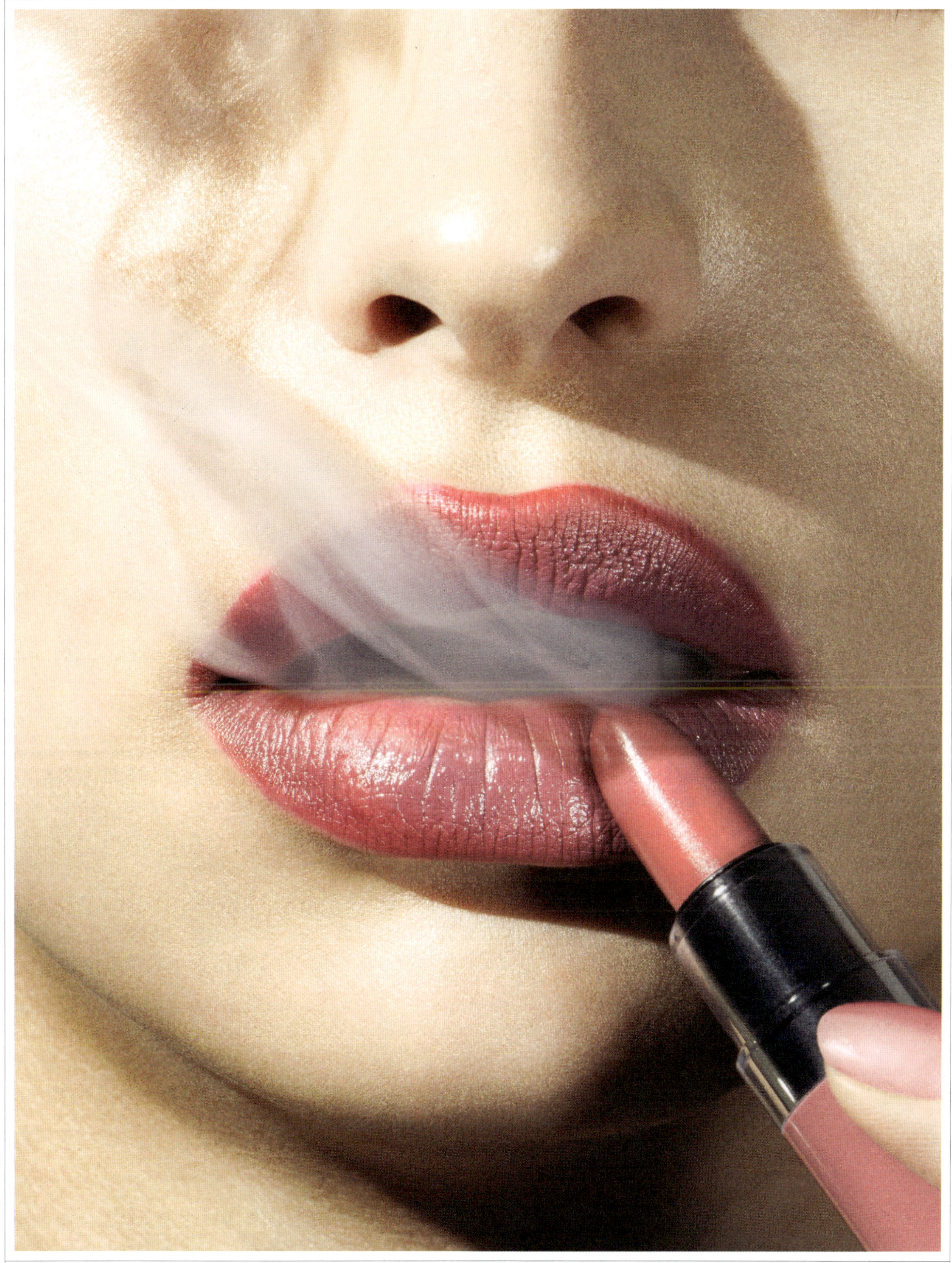

*Abla*

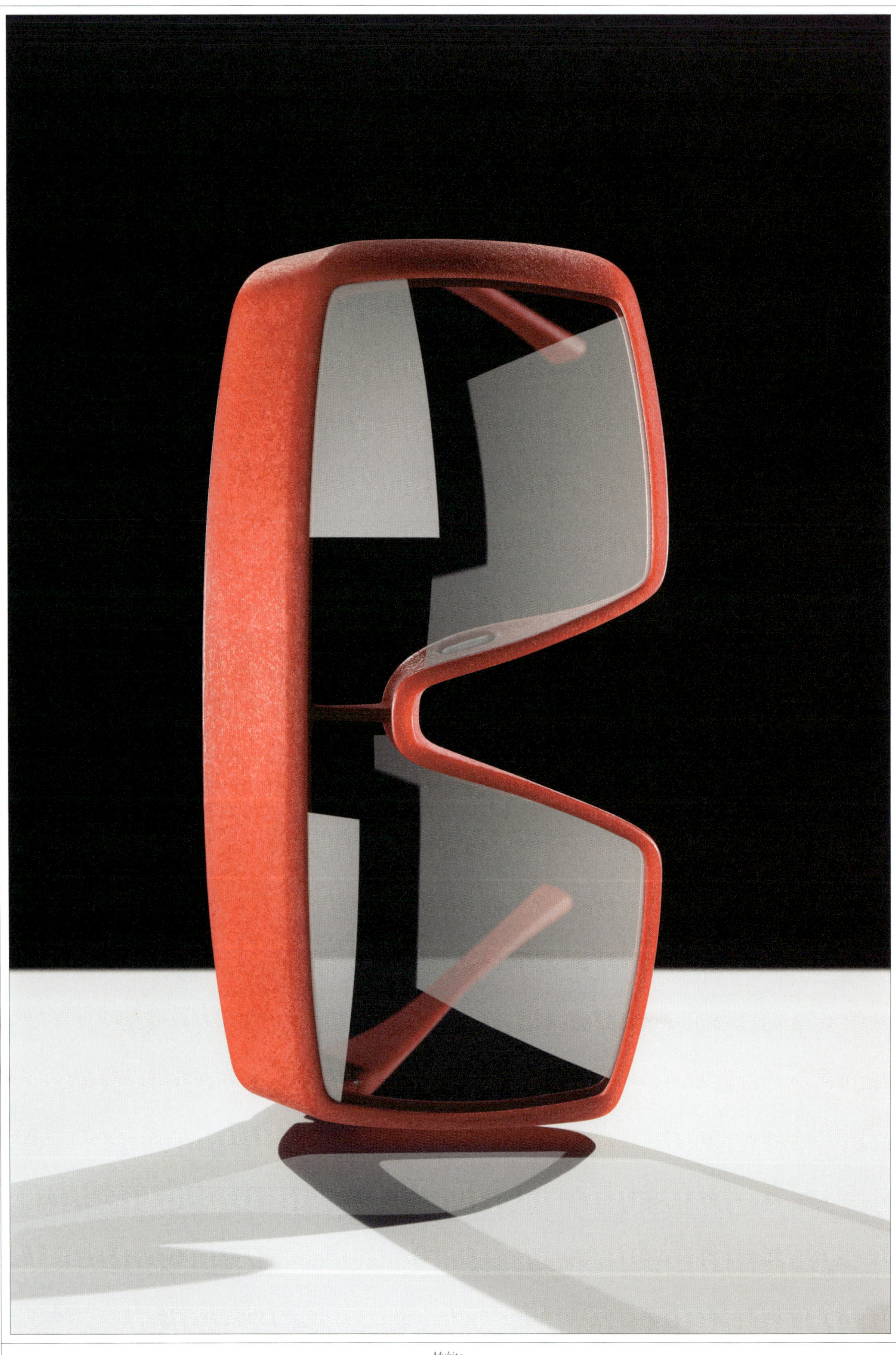

*Mykita*

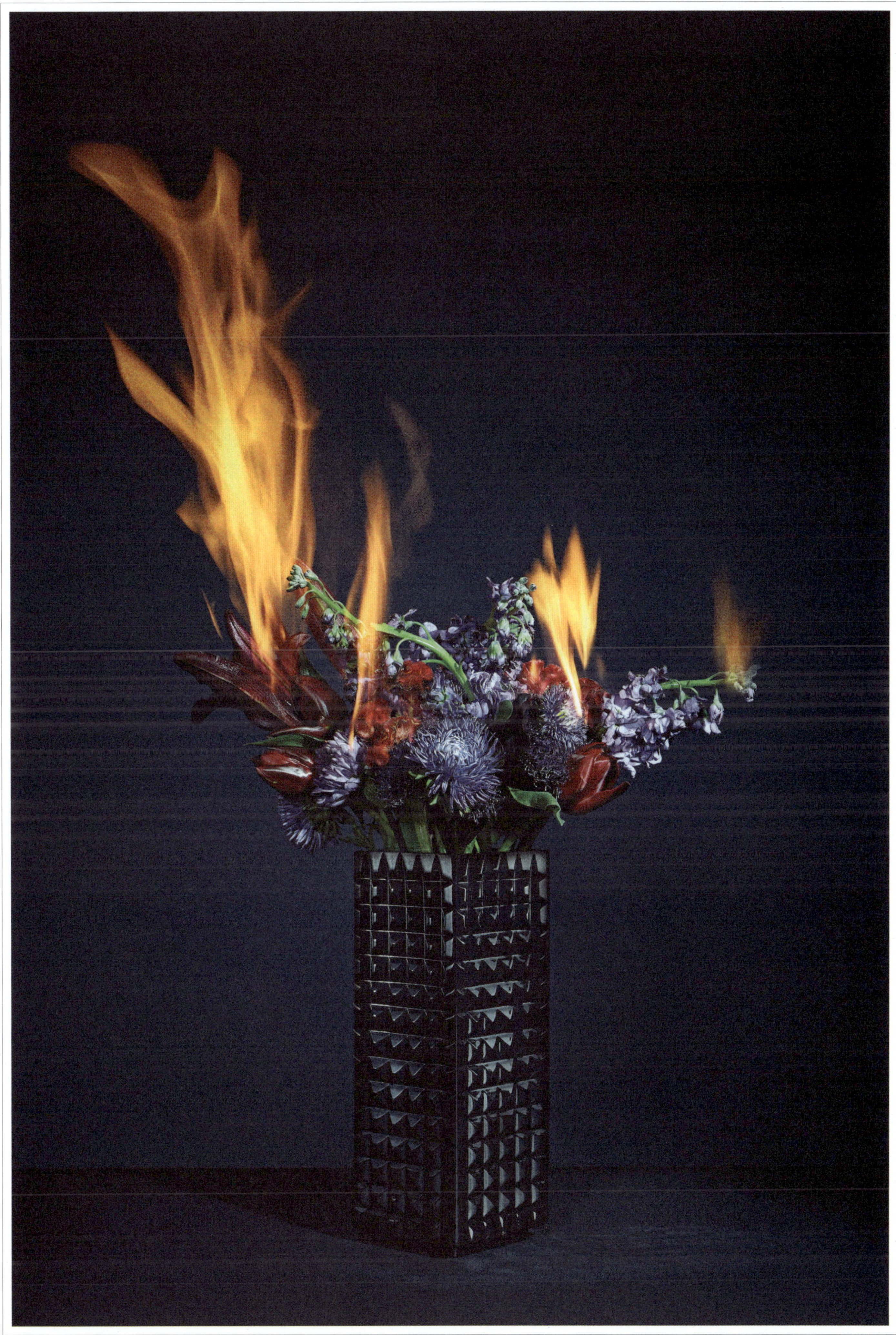

*Burning Flowers*

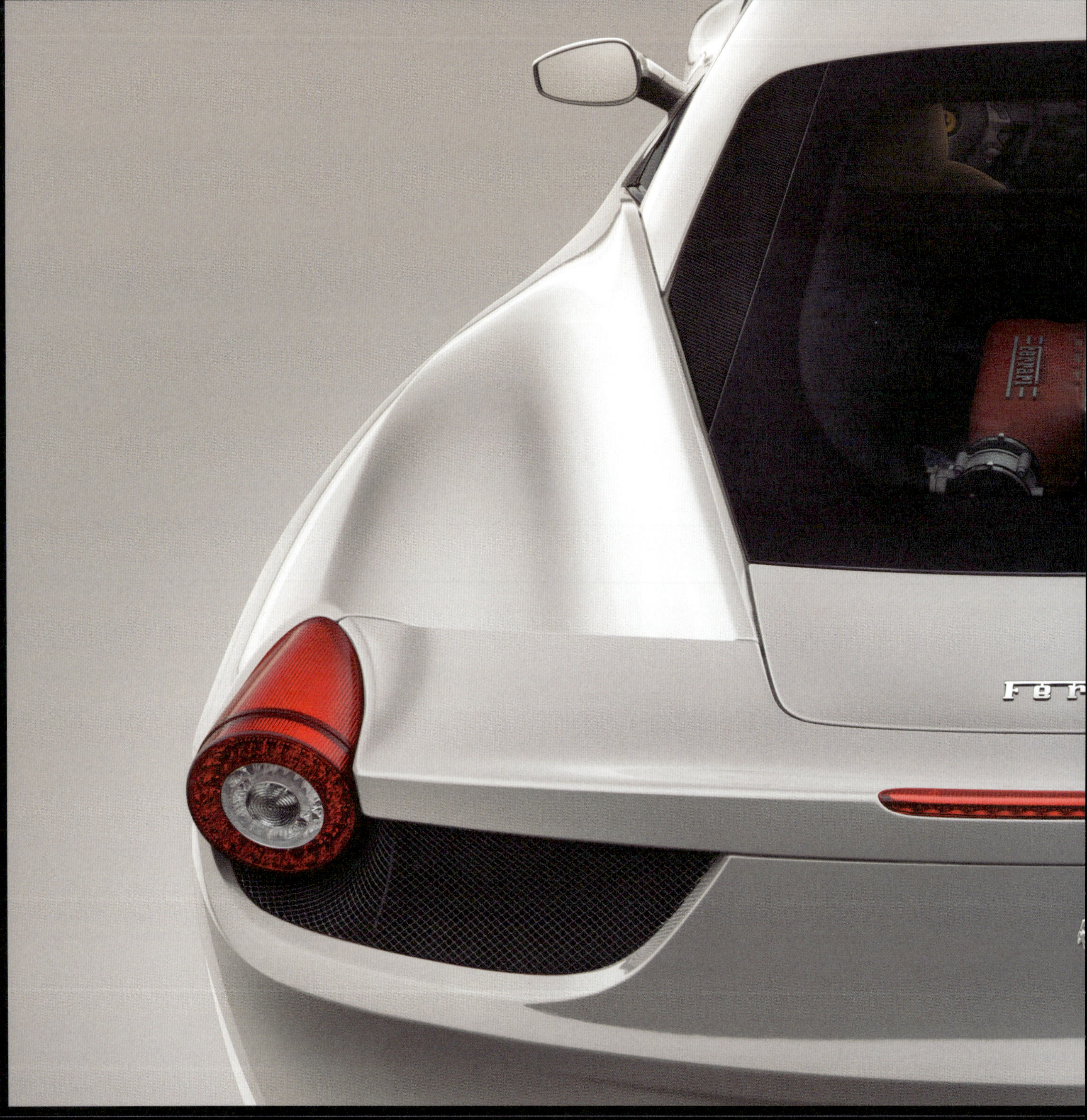

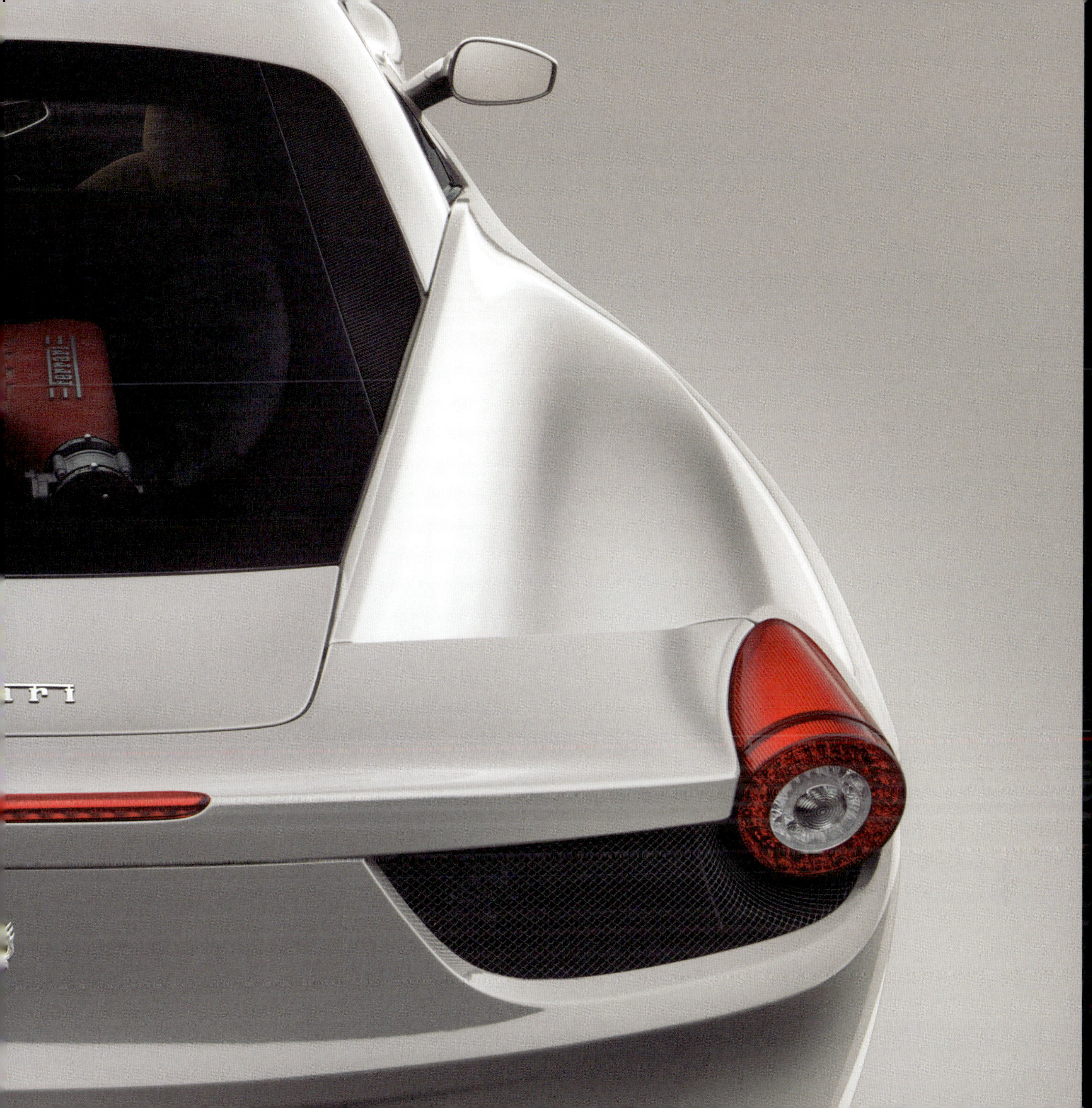

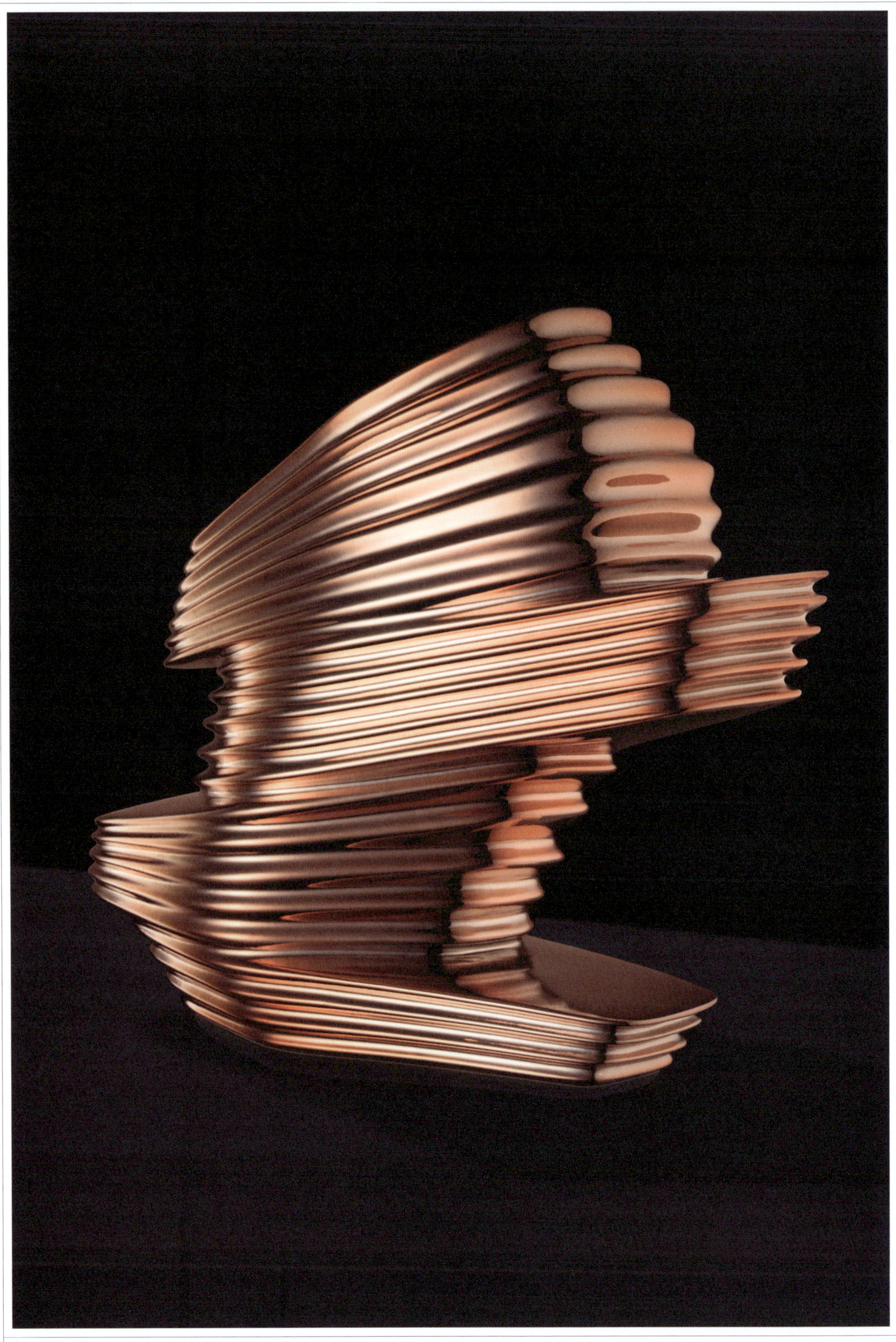

Nude

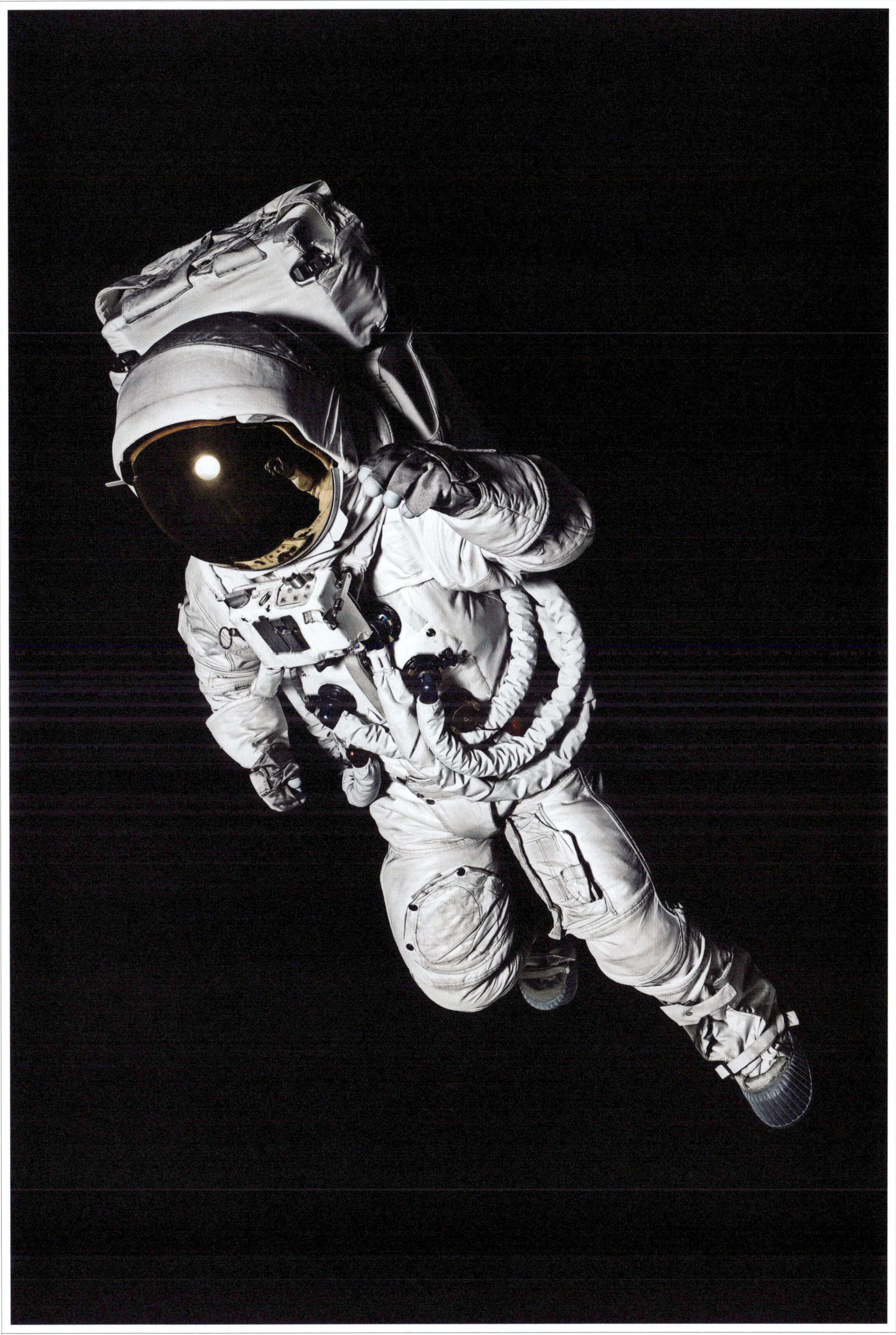

*Astronaut*

# Eric Melzer: Saying Something Authentic

I HAVE WORKED WITH ERIC ON FOUR CONTINENTS, AND WHAT STANDS OUT IS NOT ONLY THE EXCELLENCE OF HIS PHOTOGRAPHY, HIS EYE FOR DETAIL, AND IMPECCABLE TIMING, BUT HIS ABILITY TO CONNECT WITH ANYONE HE MEETS. ANYONE.

**Thomas Fuller,** *Page One Correspondent, The New York Times*

ERIC SEES THINGS OTHERS DO NOT. IT'S AS SIMPLE AND AS COMPLEX AS THAT. HE'S YOUR FAVORITE DOCUMENTARIAN'S FAVORITE DOCUMENTARIAN.

**Kate O'Reilly,** *Writer, Brand Strategist, & Consultant, Clever Kate*

ERIC MELZER'S STUNNING PHOTOGRAPHY HAS BEEN INSTRUMENTAL IN CAPTURING THE BREATHTAKING BEAUTY OF GLACIER NATIONAL PARK, INSPIRING COUNTLESS PEOPLE TO CONNECT WITH AND CARE ABOUT THIS NATIONAL TREASURE.

**Becca Wheeler,** *Creative Lead, Glacier National Park Conservancy*

DECADES OF STORYTELLING EXPERIENCE ARE BAKED INTO HIS EXCEPTIONAL, AWARD-WINNING WORK. HIS FIERY PASSION, HUMANITY, GENIUS PERSPECTIVES, AND IDEAS ARE THE DRIVING FORCES BEHIND HIS WORLD-CLASS, UNIQUE VISUALS.

**Per Breiehagen,** *Photographer, Per Breiehagen Photography*

ERIC IS THE COMPLETE PACKAGE: ABLE TO PRODUCE A WIDE VARIETY OF COMMERCIAL WORK ON DEMAND BUT ALSO ABLE TO DIVE DEEP INTO A PERSONAL PROJECT THAT WINS AWARDS AND DISTINGUISHES HIM AS A TRUE ARTIST.

**Christopher Bickford,** *Freelance Photographer & Writer*

*(Opposite page) 'Hoopin' was shot as a part of 'The Play Project.' In this image, Kenny digs into warm-ups before a pickup game at the Peavey Park basketball courts in Minneapolis.*

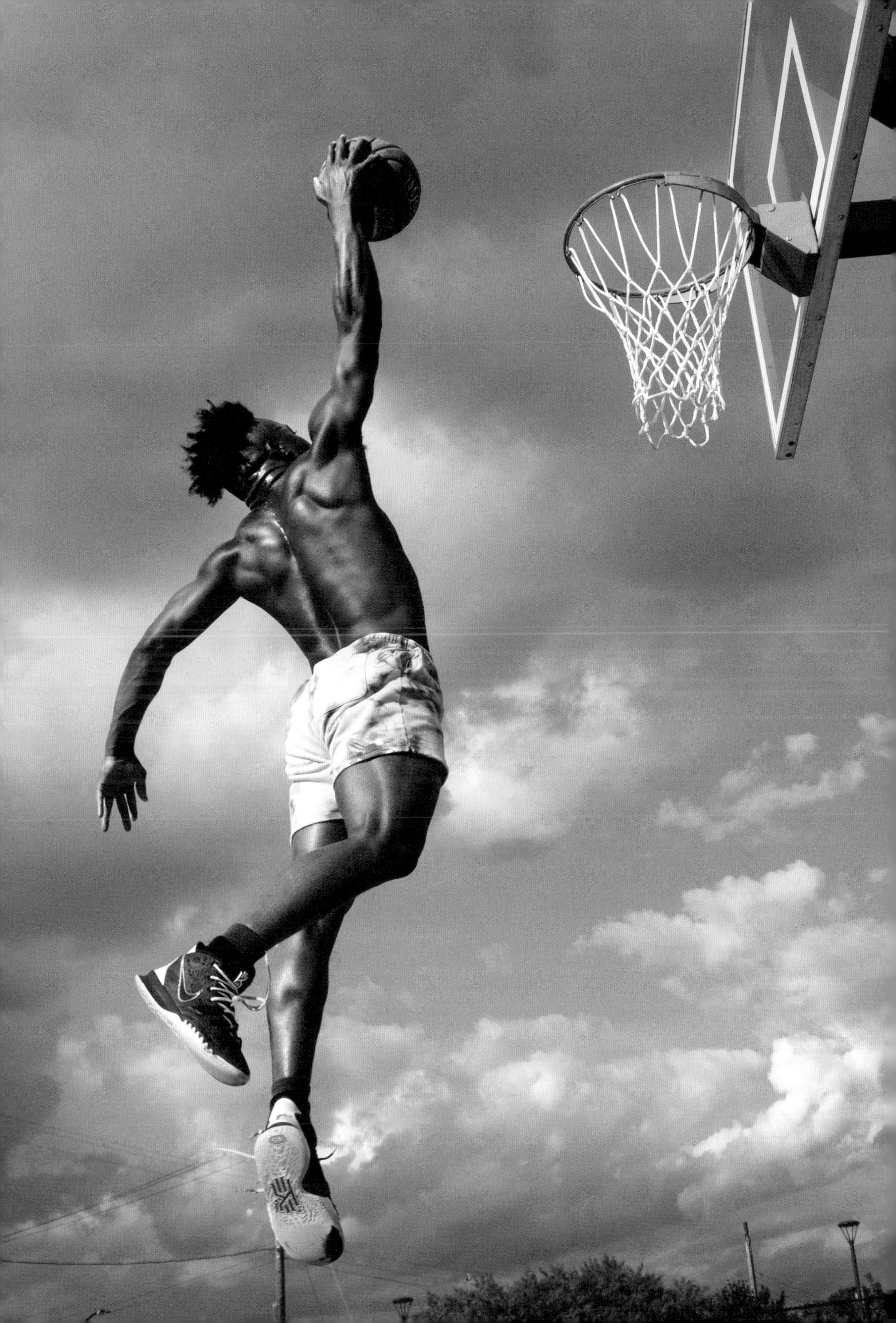

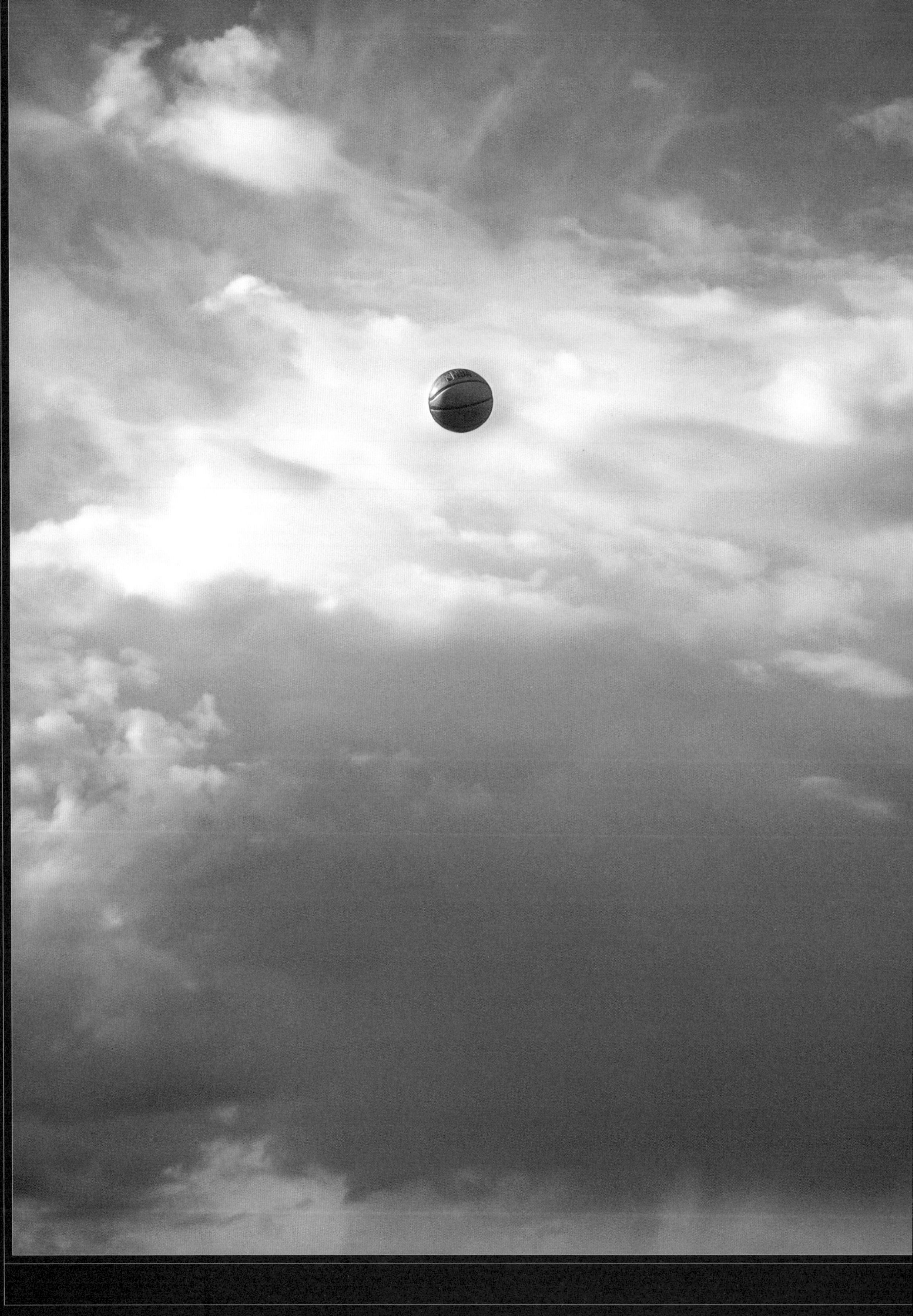

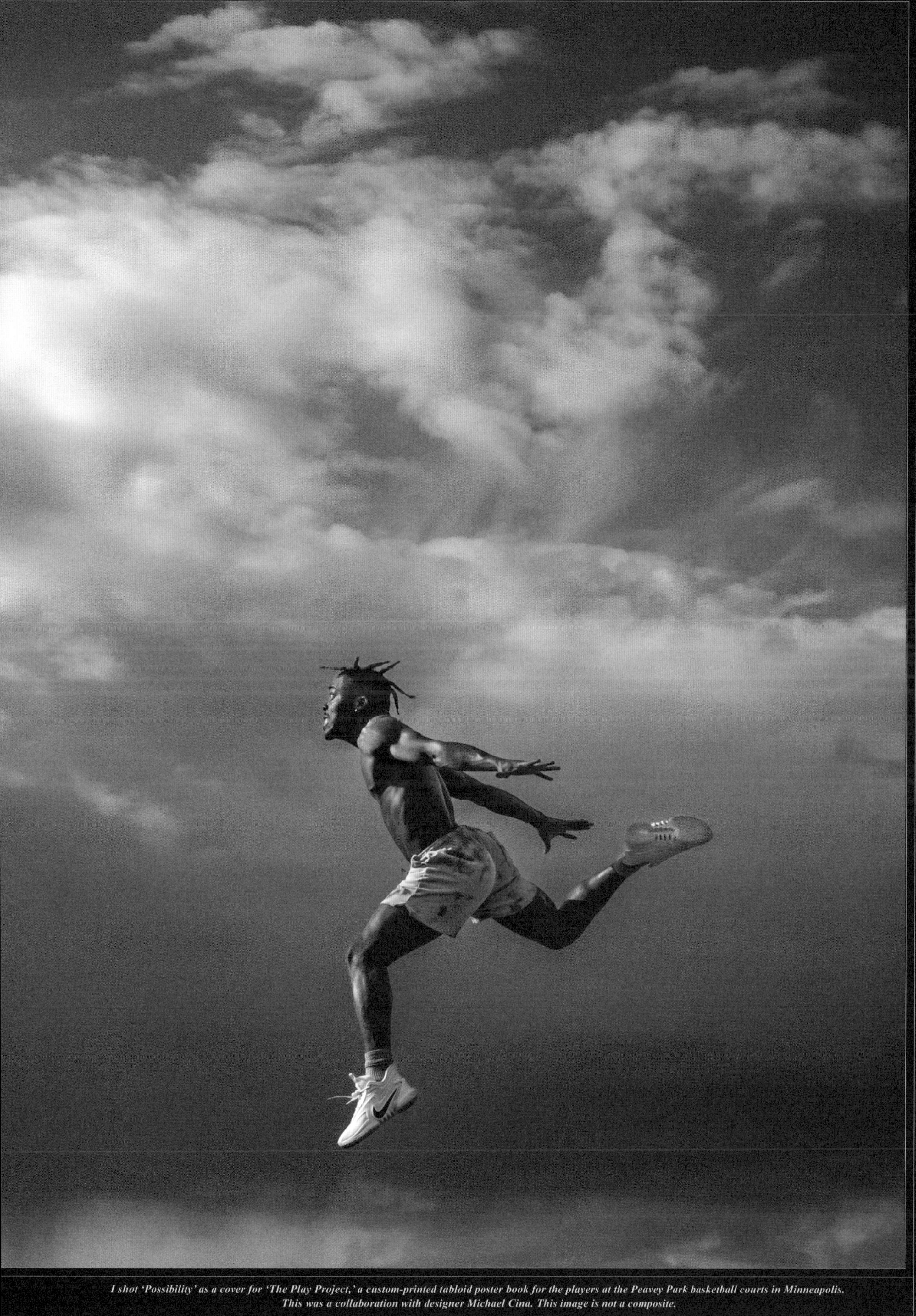

*I shot 'Possibility' as a cover for 'The Play Project,' a custom-printed tabloid poster book for the players at the Peavey Park basketball courts in Minneapolis.
This was a collaboration with designer Michael Cina. This image is not a composite.*

Eric Melzer is a deeply gifted photographer whose work transcends aesthetics, blending thoughtful mastery with emotional depth. I first met Eric over a decade ago and immediately recognized his talent. I have pitched his work on several projects and got the chance to collaborate last year on "The Play Project." By then, he had already dedicated hundreds of hours, showcasing his unwavering commitment and passion. Eric's creativity, combined with his deep care for community, amplifies the stories he captures, making his photography not just visually striking but also profoundly meaningful and enduring.

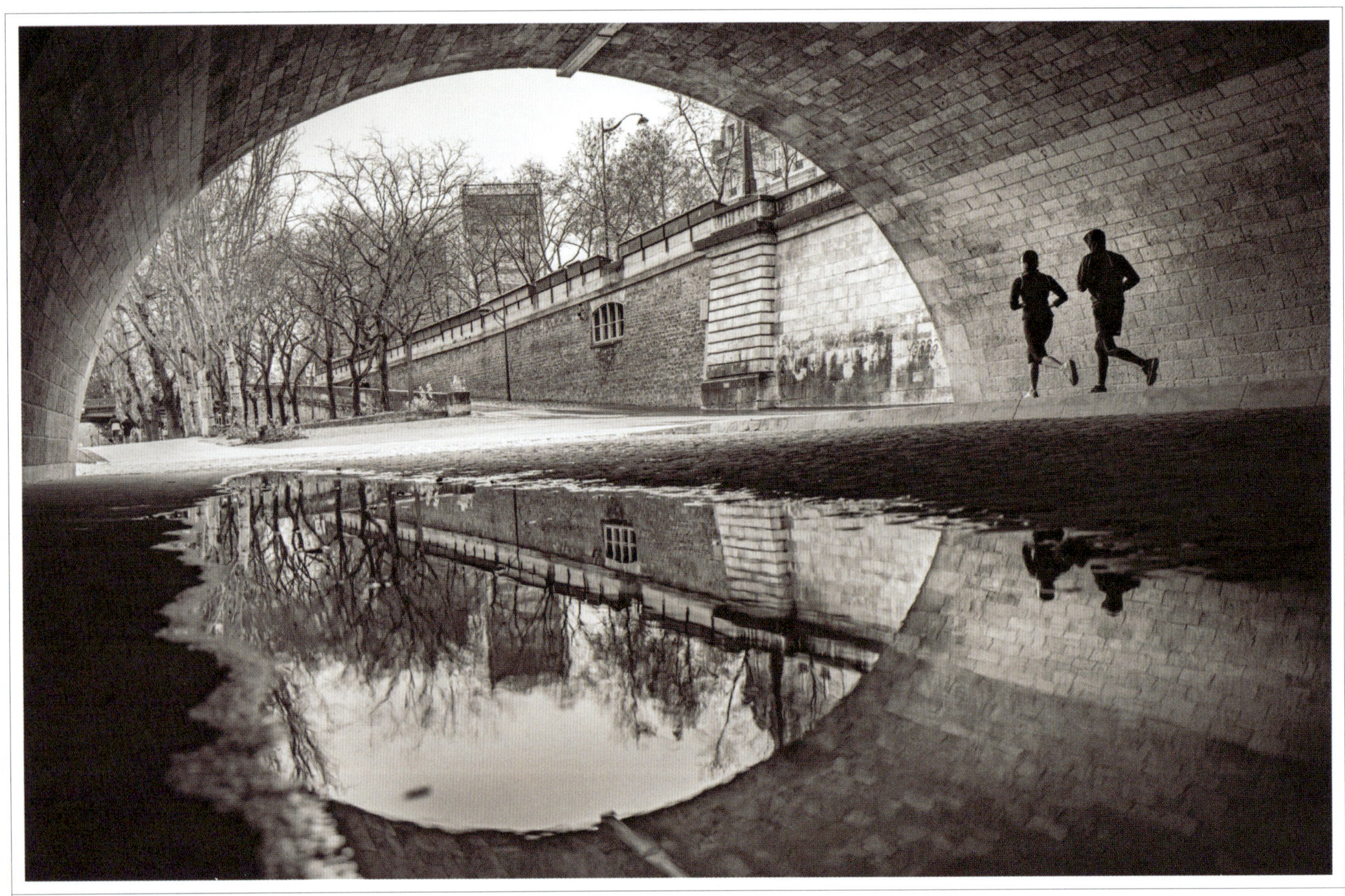

*Friends clear their heads along the Seine in Paris, France.*

## Q&A: Eric Melzer

*What inspired or motivated you to have a career in photography?*
*National Geographic*, Jacques Cousteau, and Yvon Chouinard. They all lit my imagination about the world. I grew up in a small city in Wisconsin, and their work deeply inspired me to see other cultures and places. In particular, the *National Geographic* photographers drove me to explore. Now that I've traveled, worked, and lived in many locations worldwide, I feel more instinctive about what I say.

*What is your work philosophy?*
Listen keenly, keep making, and do your best not to let your opinions of yourself and those of others get in the way of keeping on.

*What is the most difficult challenge you've overcome to reach your current position?*
Probably overcoming impostor syndrome. But I had an "A-ha!" moment once: I was walking down the street with one of the world's most accomplished violinists after she'd earned a standing ovation in a concert hall, and she said, "I wonder if they'll ever figure out I don't know what I'm doing?" Turns out, everyone has to push through self-doubt. Nervousness is just your body getting you ready to do big things. Now, I try to use nervous energy. If I know I have the trust of the people around me, I crush it every time because I just get excited.

*Who were some of your greatest past influences?*
Elliott Erwitt for his wit and humor, Sebastião Salgado for his vision, William Allard for his poetic imagery, and Monty Python for turning it all on its head.

*Who is or was your greatest mentor?*
My best friend, Erik. I lost him in an accident about 25 years ago. He never let a minute burn by that he wasn't plugged into. He taught me to lean in hard but not take it all too seriously.

*What is it about photography that you are most passionate about?*
Finding the bravery to say something authentic. If we work from a personal enough place, we say something universal. If they're successful, works like these can change societies.

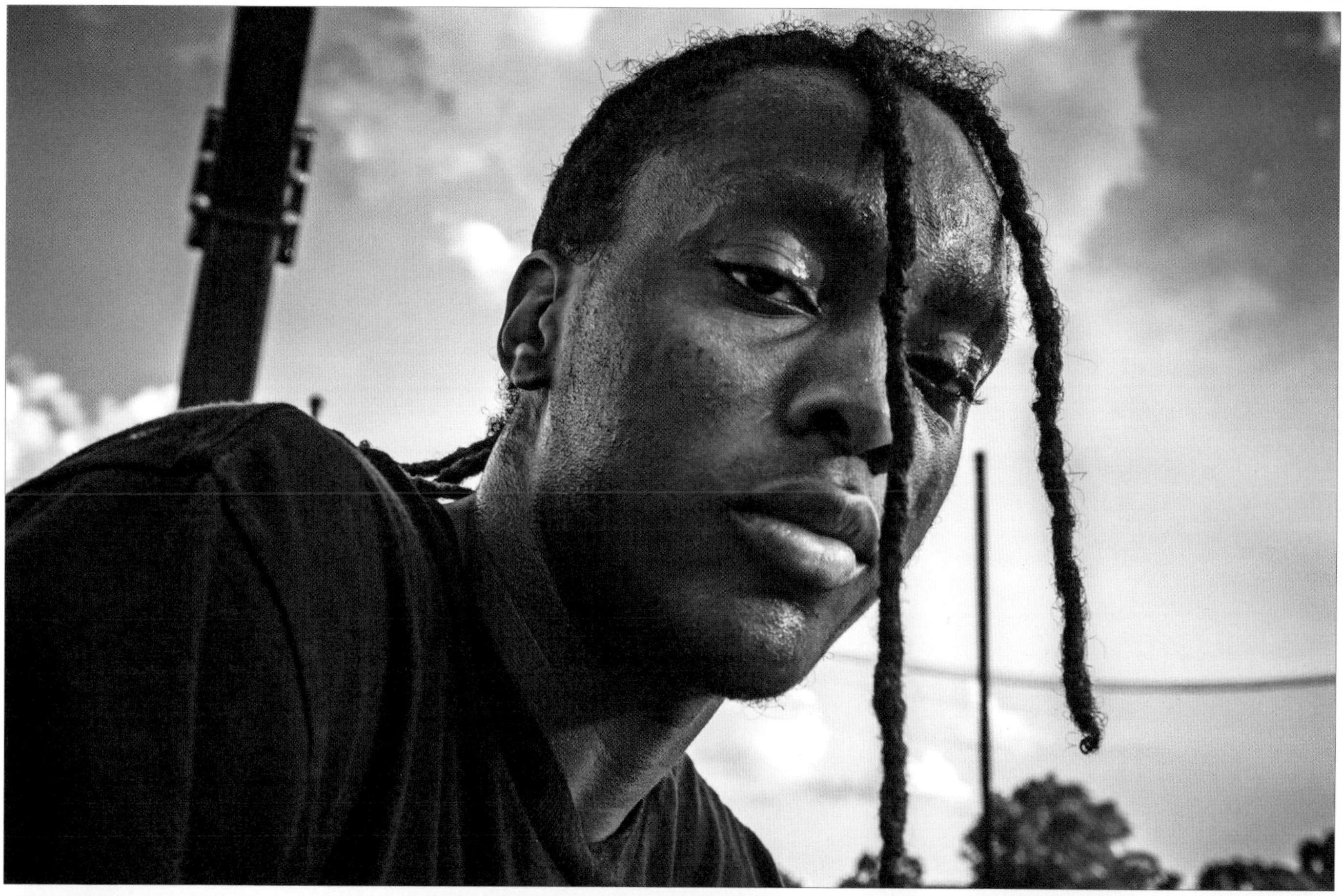

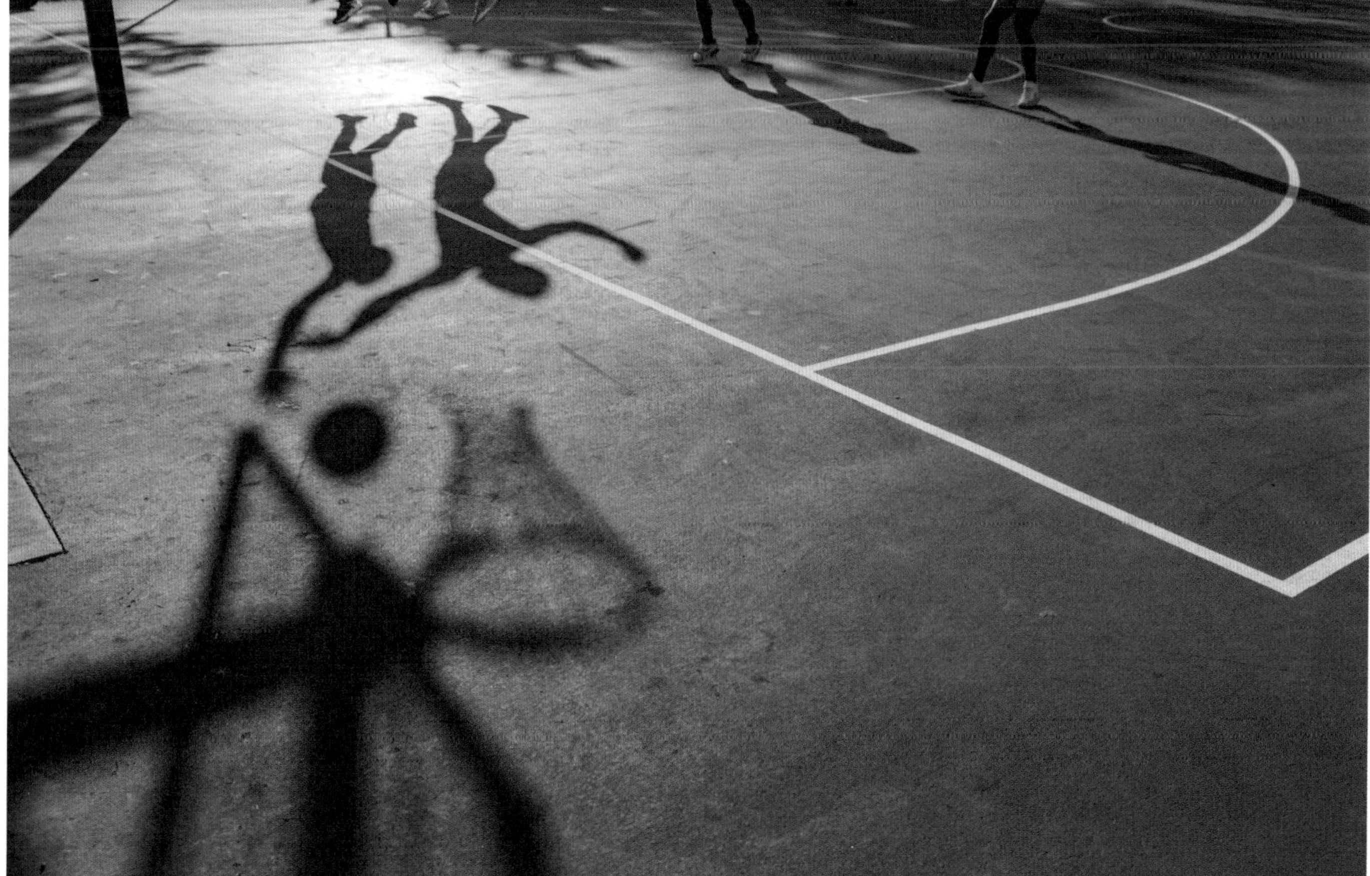

(Top) 'Jabari,' shot as a part of 'The Play Project.' / (Bottom) The visual vocabulary of 'The Play Project' is based on the tension between sunny summer clouds and shadow—between positive and negative thoughts. 'Shadow Ball' illustrates the internal struggle we all have during times of social and climate crisis.

**Who among your contemporaries today do you most admire?**
Chris Bickford for his photographic artistry and observations. Thomas Fuller for his craft, tenacity, and keen eye for a compelling story. Per Breiehagen for his mastery and continuous drive to explore new ways of image-making. Image Studios' president Donna Gehl for her intrepid business savvy, and Michael Cina for his incredible design vision.

**What would be your dream assignment?**
I currently have two passions. One is community play, and the other is climate change mitigation. So, I have two dream assignments:
   1. I would love to be paid to travel to communities world-

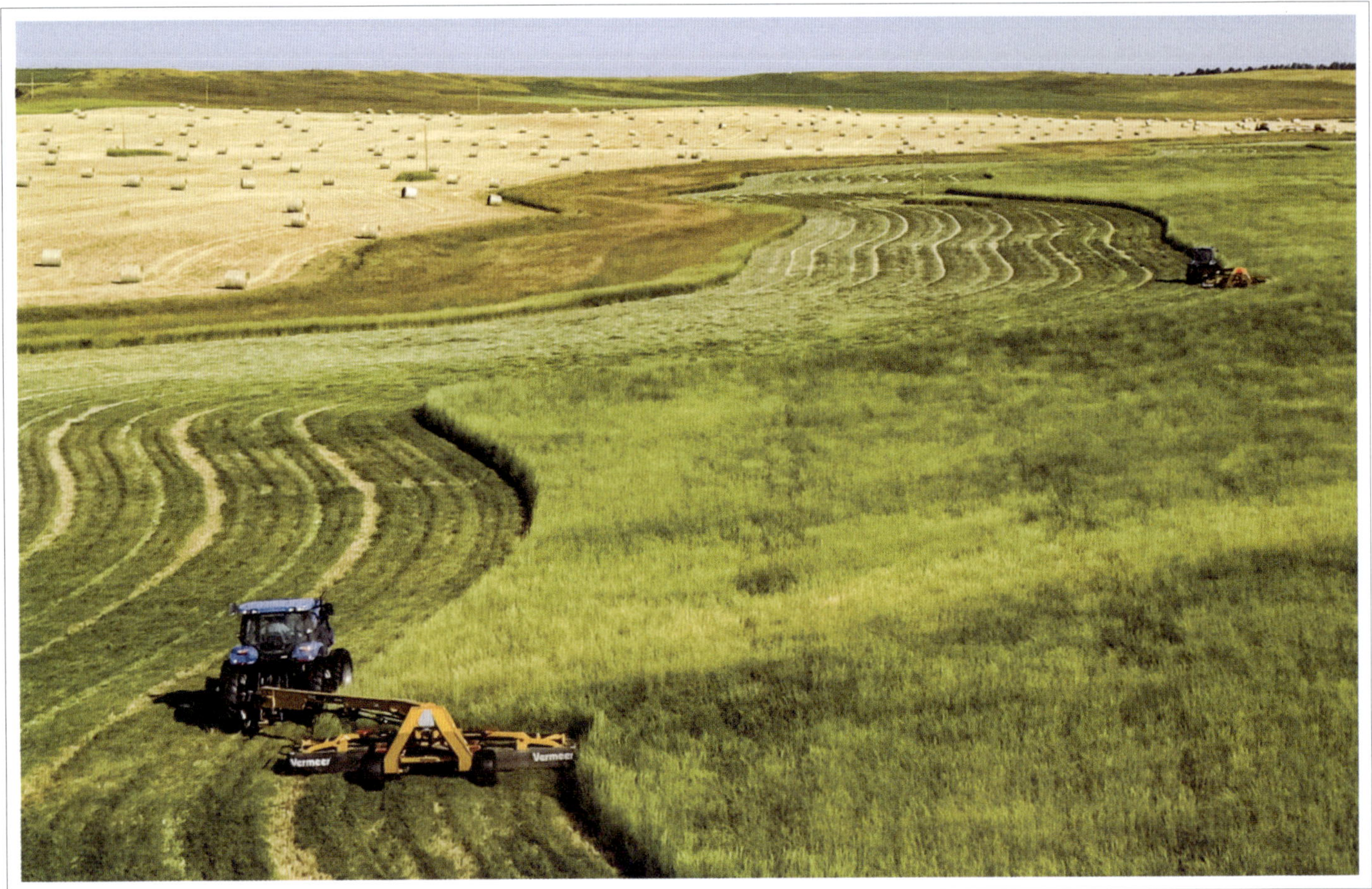

*Tractors harvest hay for a regenerative ranching operation on the Bruski ranch outside Ekalaka, Montana. Producer/Art Director: Todd Melby.*

wide to document and celebrate local pickup sports.

2. On the climate front, I would love the opportunity to tell the stories of climate change's unsung heroes—regenerative terrestrial and ocean farmers, conservationists, and scientists who can push and shape technology to help us catch up to the deadline that's already past us.

### What equipment do you primarily use and why?

That's, of course, very project-specific, but the kit I always have packed has a Sony A-1, two cards, four batteries, ND filters, a Peak Designs tripod, and 16-35 f2.8, 24-105 f4, and 70-200 f2.8 lenses. I'll rent primes, other bodies/systems, etc., as projects and crews call for it. Oh, and Ricola. A little hard candy goes a long way during a long day on set.

### Who have been some of your favorite people or clients you have worked with?

On the professional front, *New York Times* correspondent Thomas Fuller, communications consultant Meredith Moore, Kristin Russell of Flex, Mark Hayes of NRG Energy, and Drs. Joe Meisel and Catherine Woodward of The Ceiba Foundation for Tropical Conservation. In my personal work, all of the pickup basketball players from the Peavey Park basketball courts in Minneapolis, Minnesota.

### Much of your photography focuses on people and companies working on sustainability and solving the climate crisis. How did this become an important subject matter for you?

I was on an assignment for the *International Herald Tribune* in the Andaman Sea, and I dove into the water to snorkel and photograph the reef we were over. The entire coral reef had bleached. It was vast. And dead. I used to work as a photo-journalist in Southeast Asia and was based out of Bangkok, so I'd seen nearby reefs teeming with life. I was shocked and compelled to act. Imagery is the best tool to educate the public and change policy about climate change. It drives awareness

for that change. Let people know what they stand to lose, and they might take action. Otherwise, they may just not get it, and it'll be gone. I work and hang out with some very bright Ph.D scientists, and they all believe the climate deadline is past us. If it's all just management now, imagery is truly critical to shaping long-term outcomes.

### What are the most important ingredients you require from a client to work successfully?

Trust. Trust converts nerves into creative momentum. The best art and creative directors foster a kind of flow state with trust. All creatives are just agents of the muse, so the best results come when we're allowed (e.g., steered but not microman-aged) to find a state of mind where we get out of our own way and just let the work come down the antenna.

### You also do film work. How did that start, and how does it influence your photography and vice versa?

I'm most interested in the moment when an idea or a creative impulse arrives because it's a record of instinct. That's why still photography is the purest photographic creation, in my opinion. In my experience so far, motion is way more likely to bleed that moment of artistic weight. Bigger crew. More prep. By the time "Action!" is called, the interesting part has most likely left the room. I've recently (finally) fallen in love with motion image sequencing, though, and I will continue to lean in hard to explore that and push boundaries.

The sad part about our current culture is that we no longer seem to have time to really consider (and reconsider) art anymore. We forget that images don't have to move, flash, and explode to be compelling. Speed bleeds meaning. We're apparently too busy scrolling or something. We need to slow down. AI is showing us that. AGAIN.

### What is your greatest professional achievement?

Earning awards from Graphis, CA, and IPA in the same year.

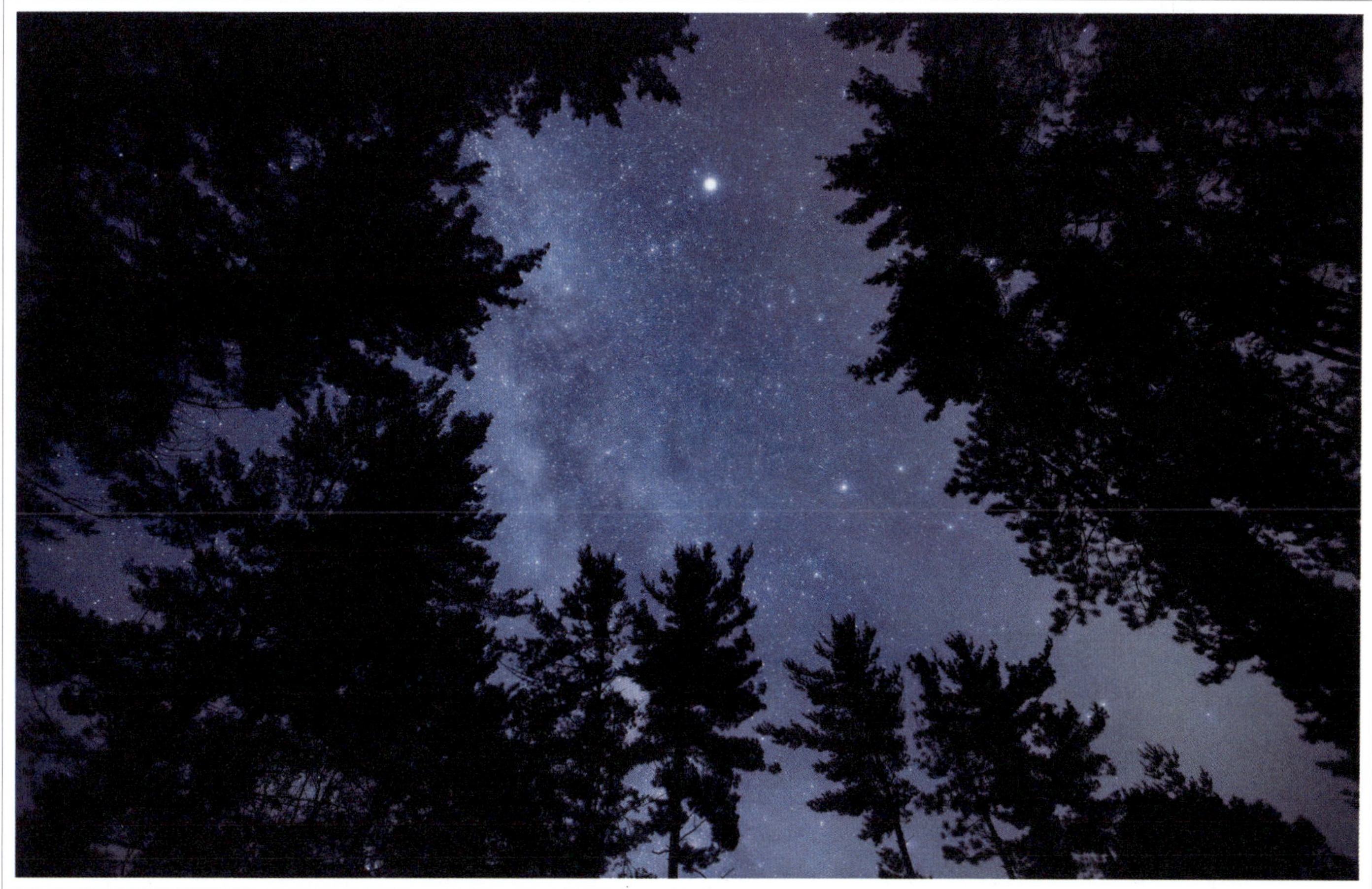

*I shot this starscape at Wildcat Mountain State Park in Wisconsin's Driftless Area, one of Wisconsin's darkest places.*

### What is the greatest satisfaction you get from your work?

Being in the moment. When I take the time to really consider what's in front of me, I appreciate what I have instead of wanting what I don't.

### What part of your work is most demanding, considering your position?

Unfortunately for me, my wiring is too Midwestern to enjoy shouting my name from the rooftops. So, selling is very demanding and taxing. It feels like dentistry. I just want to make pictures because I love composition and visual serendipity. That part's pure joy because it's fun waiting for that moment.

### What professional goals do you still have for yourself?

I'd like to shoot underwater work to document reefs before they're gone and explore abstract visual motion design to imagine new worlds and ways of expressing myself visually. They're both completely new to me, and I like that because it keeps me open.

### What advice would you give students starting out today?

I would tell students three things:

1. What you will create is both deeply profound… and entirely meaningless. So, lean in and work hard, but don't take yourself too seriously. To drive this point home, I'd tell them to Google "Pale Blue Dot still image" and suggest looking at it every time they get too self-involved. It's best to keep it all in perspective whether you're being berated or celebrated.

2. Good clients beget good clients, and bad clients beget bad clients, so be careful whose money you take.

3. Be sure to see your work series and ideas through to their end so your bodies of work are complete. That said, try not to worry too much about fitting into society's boxes. Everyone has many interests because humans are complicated. Just shoot and show what you love, and let curiosity and enthusiasm fuel the ride.

### What interests do you have outside of your work?

Anything outside, really. I like water sports and mountain biking, and I'm an avid skate skier (for the uninitiated, that's like cross-country skiing, except it's fast and fun). I also love to travel, cook, eat, and drink with friends.

### What do you value most?

Friends, family, and making. Oh, and chocolate. I value that deeply.

### What would you change if you had to do it all over again?

If I had a choice, I would've been born a little earlier. The era from the early '60s to the '90s was a great window into the photographic profession. It was interesting for its history, creativity, access, and cultural inspiration. Plus, if you bought a Leica, Hasselblad, or 4x5 in that era, it was likely the only camera system you would have ever needed. Even though digital photography and all that comes with it is amazing, planned obsolescence and new tech burn a lot of our money and creative time now.

### Where do you seek inspiration?

Iggy Pop, Joseph Campbell, Elliott Erwitt, and Dave Chapelle.

### How do you define success?

I think money is really tricky because it tends to warp the best of people. So, success, to me, is having a life where money is invisible: I don't have so much money that it runs my life, and I don't have so little money that it runs my life.

### Where do you see yourself in the future?

I'll continue to be small and agile… as uncomplicated as possible. I'll be listening and observing carefully because with AI coming for us all like a freight train, I'm afraid I don't have a compass for the map.

**Eric Melzer Photography** www.ericmelzer.com

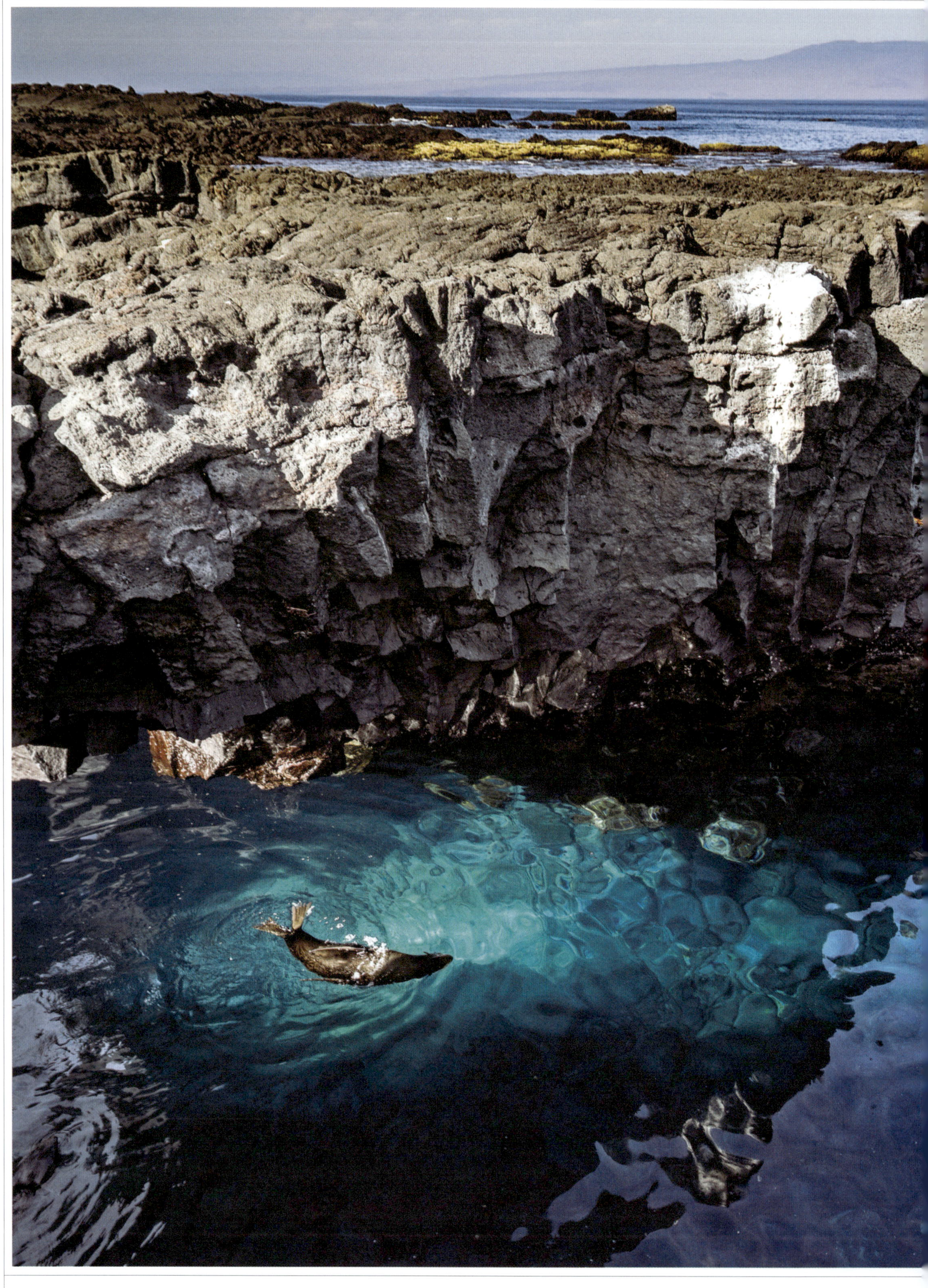

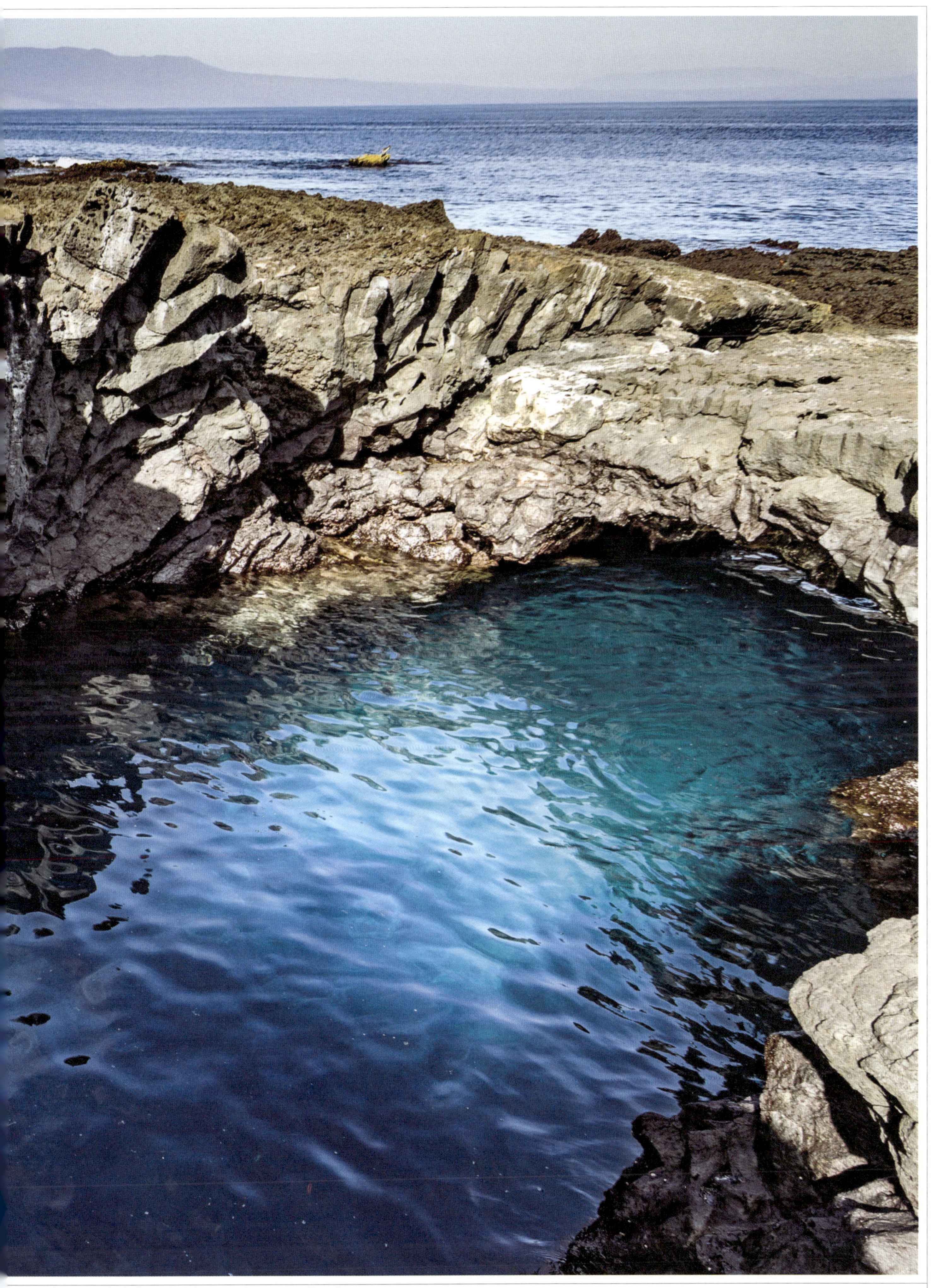

*A sea lion finds the spotlight in Puerto Egas, Santiago Island, Galápagos Islands, Ecuador.*

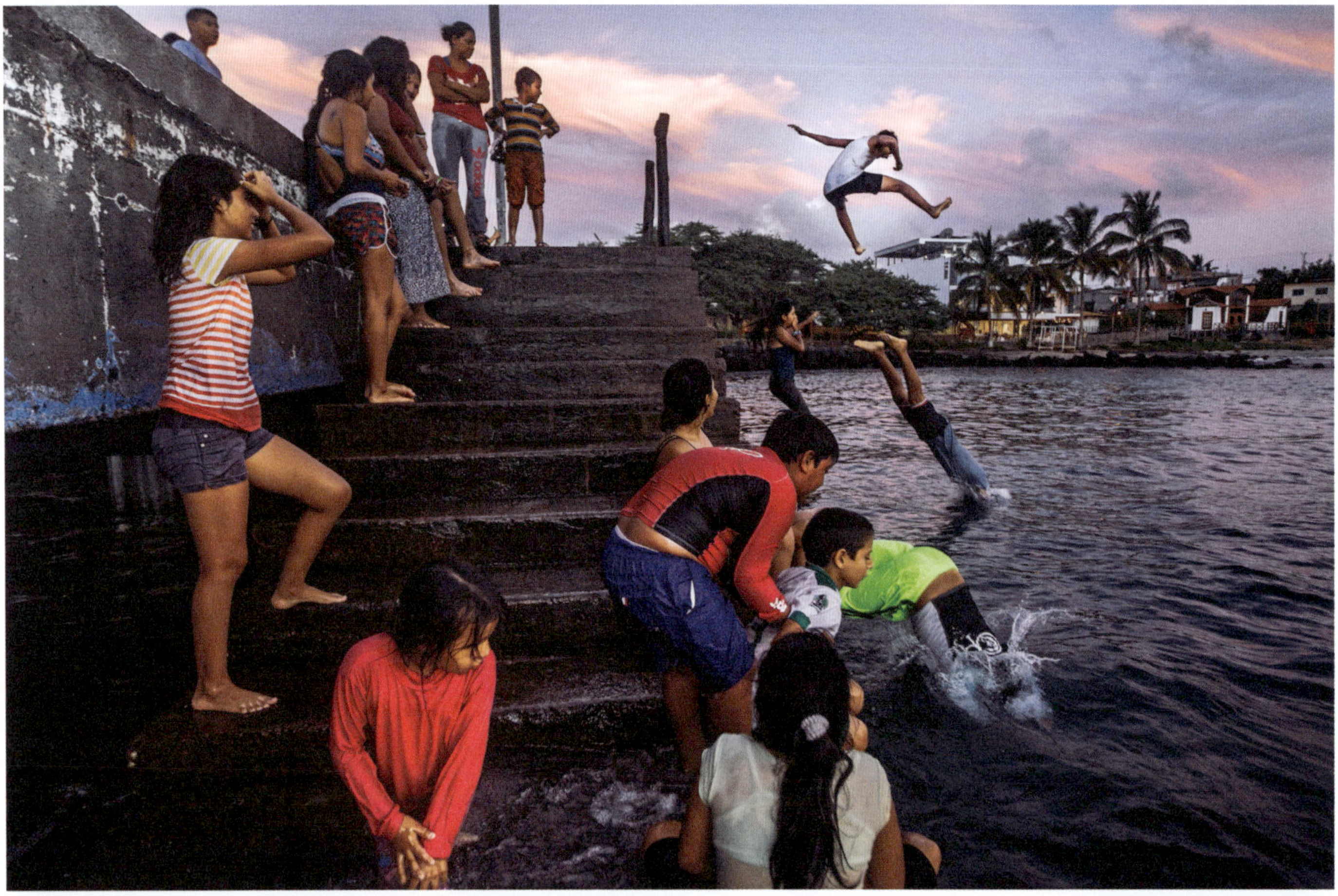

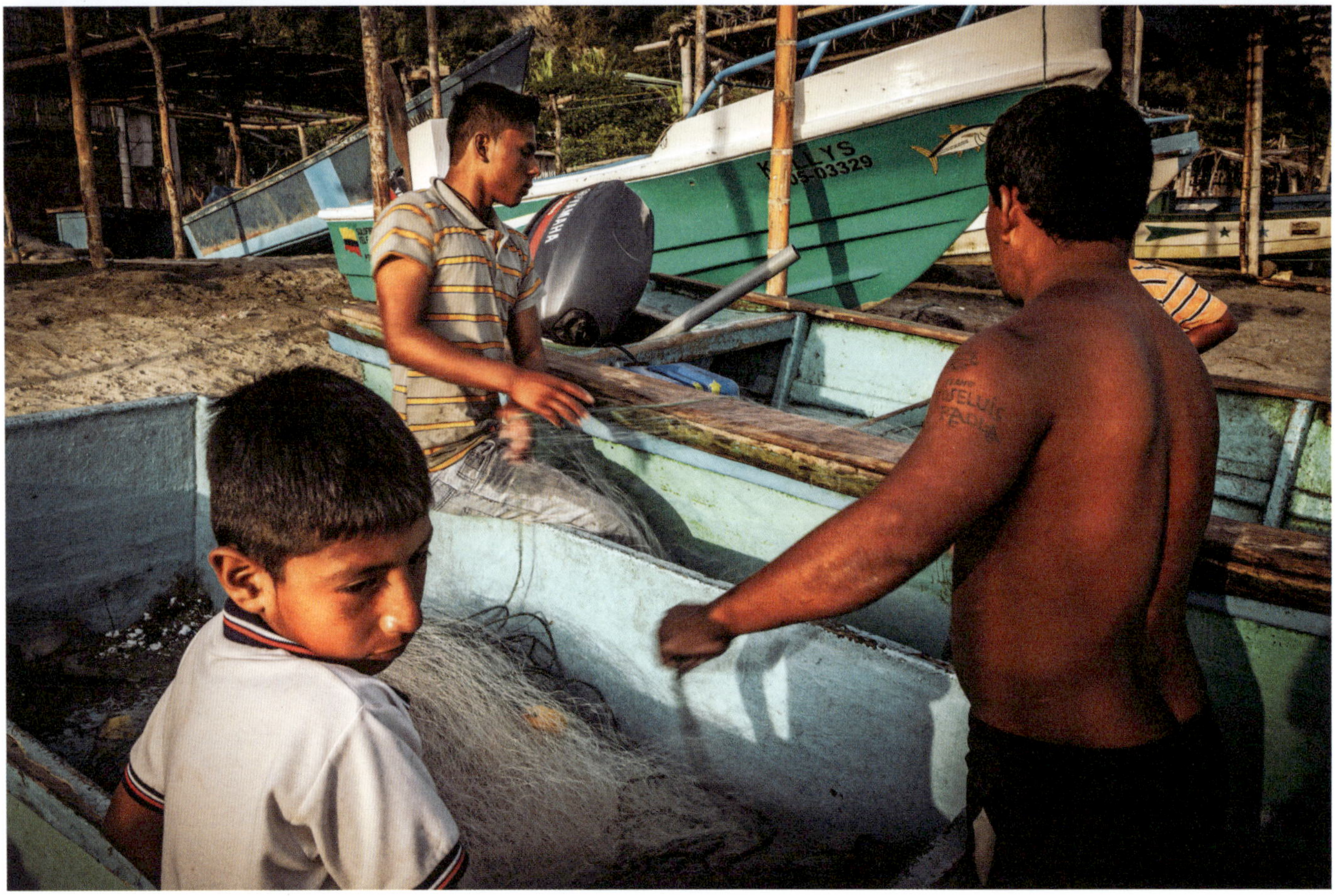

*(Top) Sunset play happened each night during my time at the harbor on San Cristóbal Island, Galápagos Islands, Ecuador.*
*(Bottom) Fishermen mend nets during last light in the village of Don Juan in Manabí Province, Ecuador.*

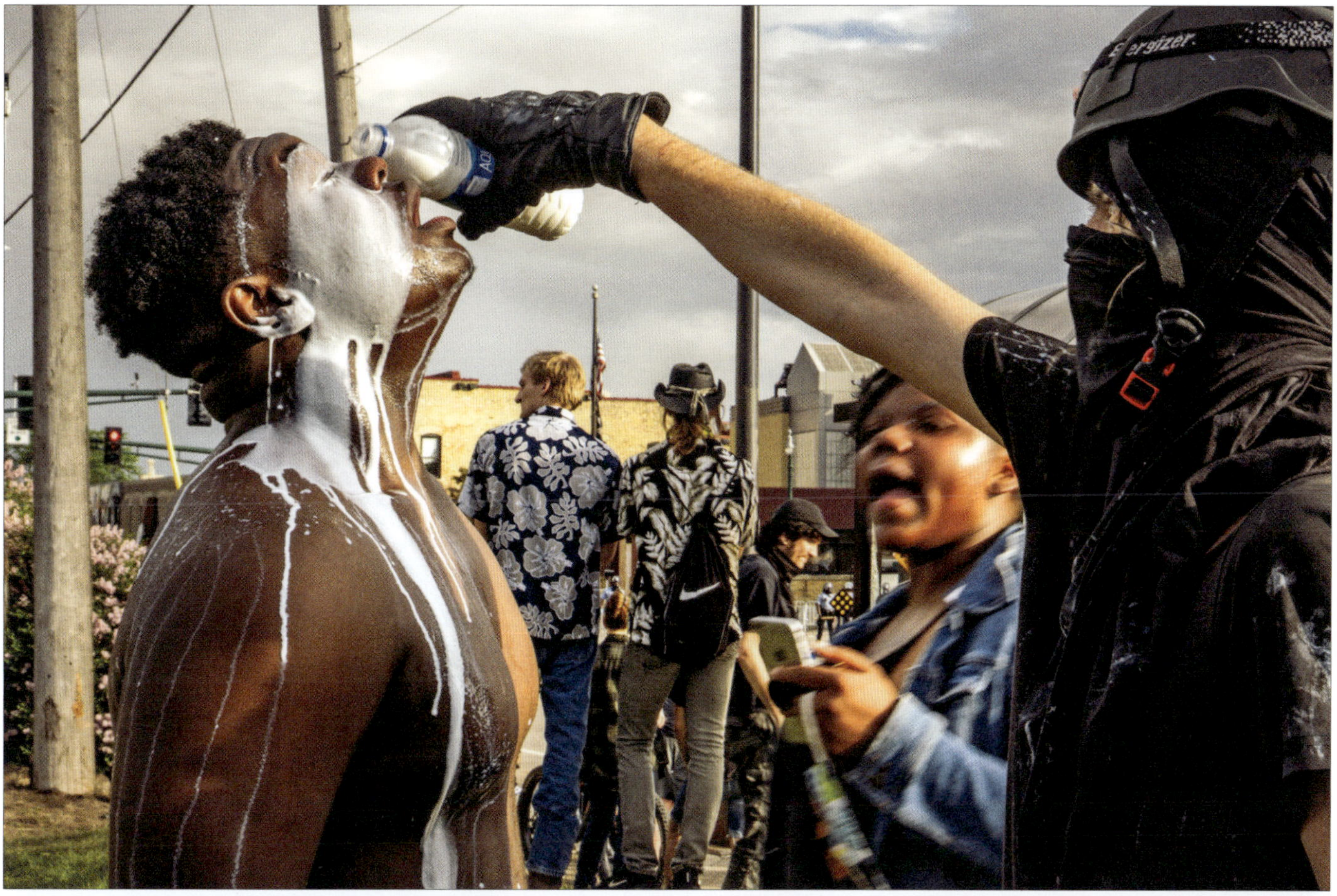

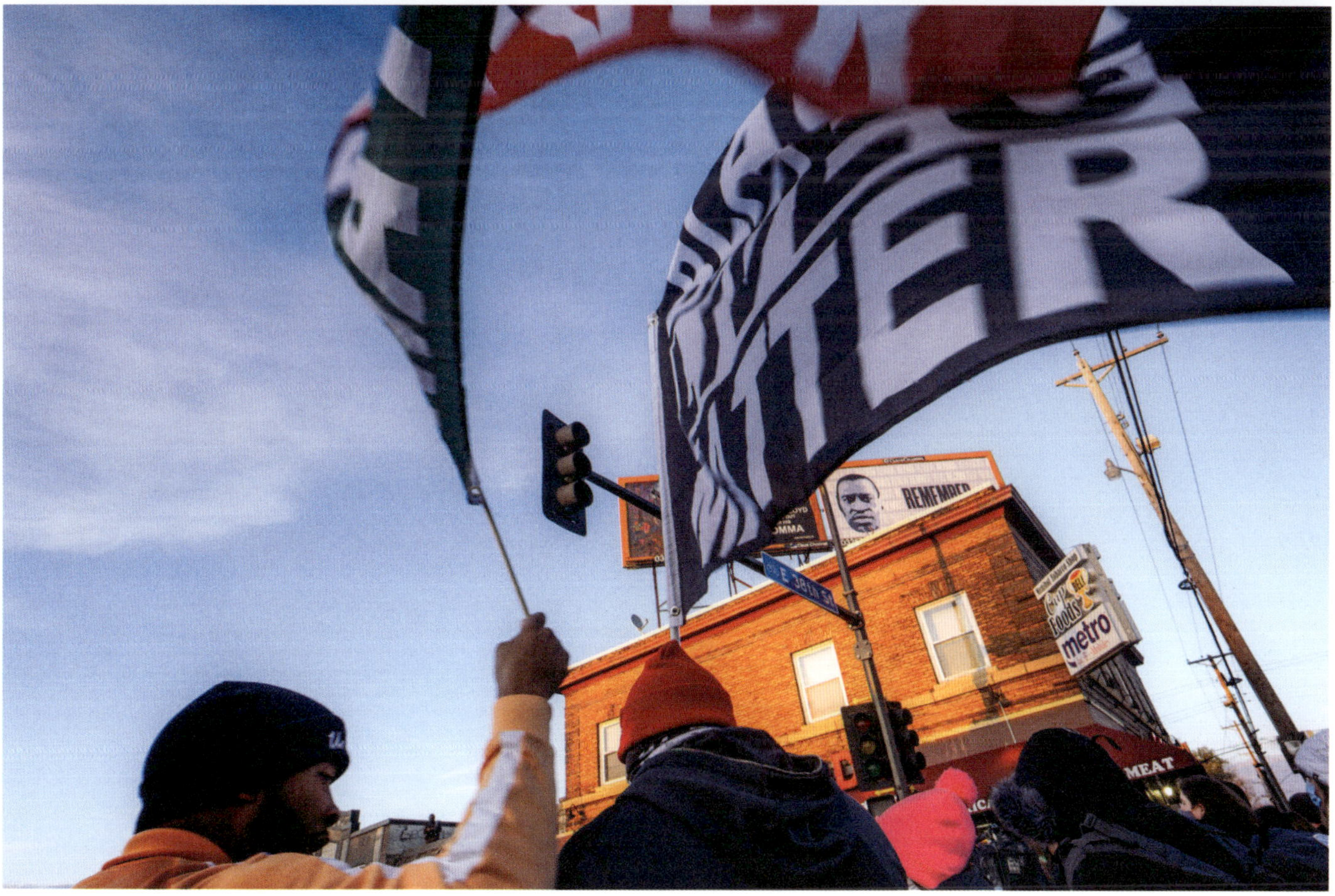

(Top) Across from the 3rd Precinct in Minneapolis, Minnesota, a protestor pours milk on the face of another to alleviate the burn from tear gas fired by Minneapolis police the day after George Floyd was murdered.
(Bottom) Protestors gather outside Cup Foods at the site of George Floyd's murder in Minneapolis, Minnesota, after the sentencing of Minneapolis police officer Derek Chauvin.

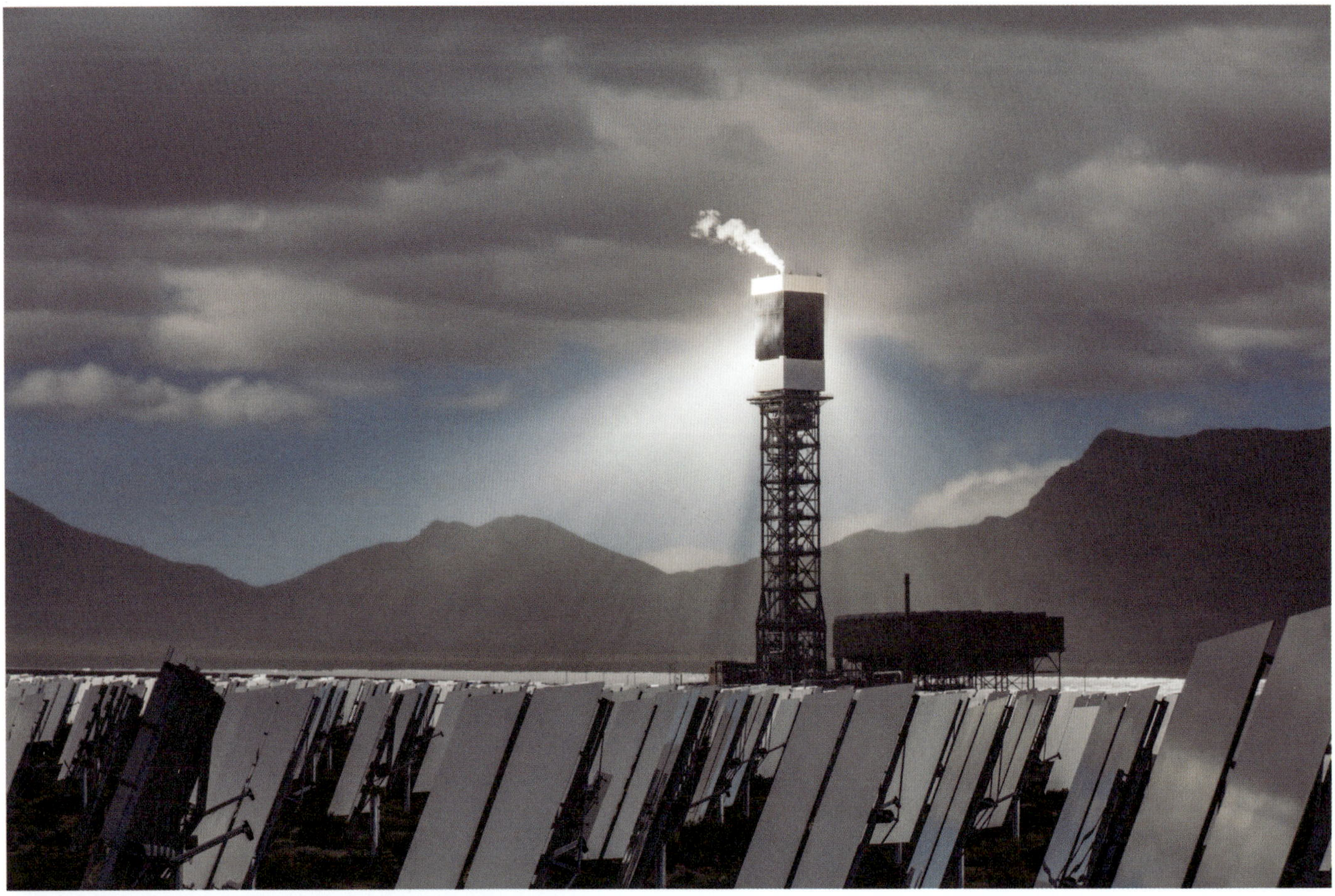

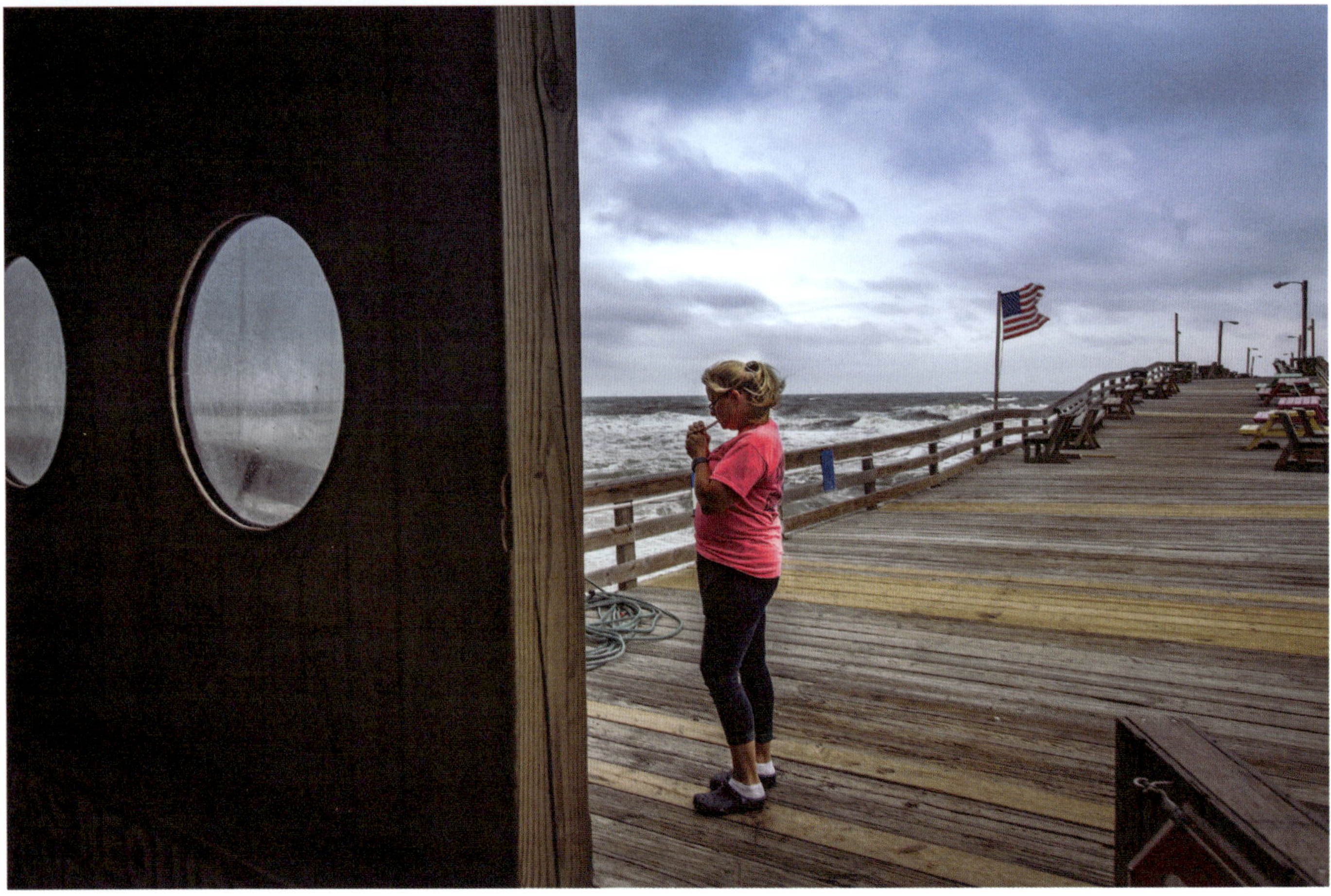

*(Top) Heliostat mirrors reflect light onto a thermal solar tower at the Ivanpah power generation station outside Las Vegas, Nevada.*
*(Bottom) A server at the Nag's Head Pier House Restaurant takes a smoke break during a nor'easter in Nag's Head, North Carolina. Storms along America's East Coast are becoming more severe every year as ocean temperatures rise.*

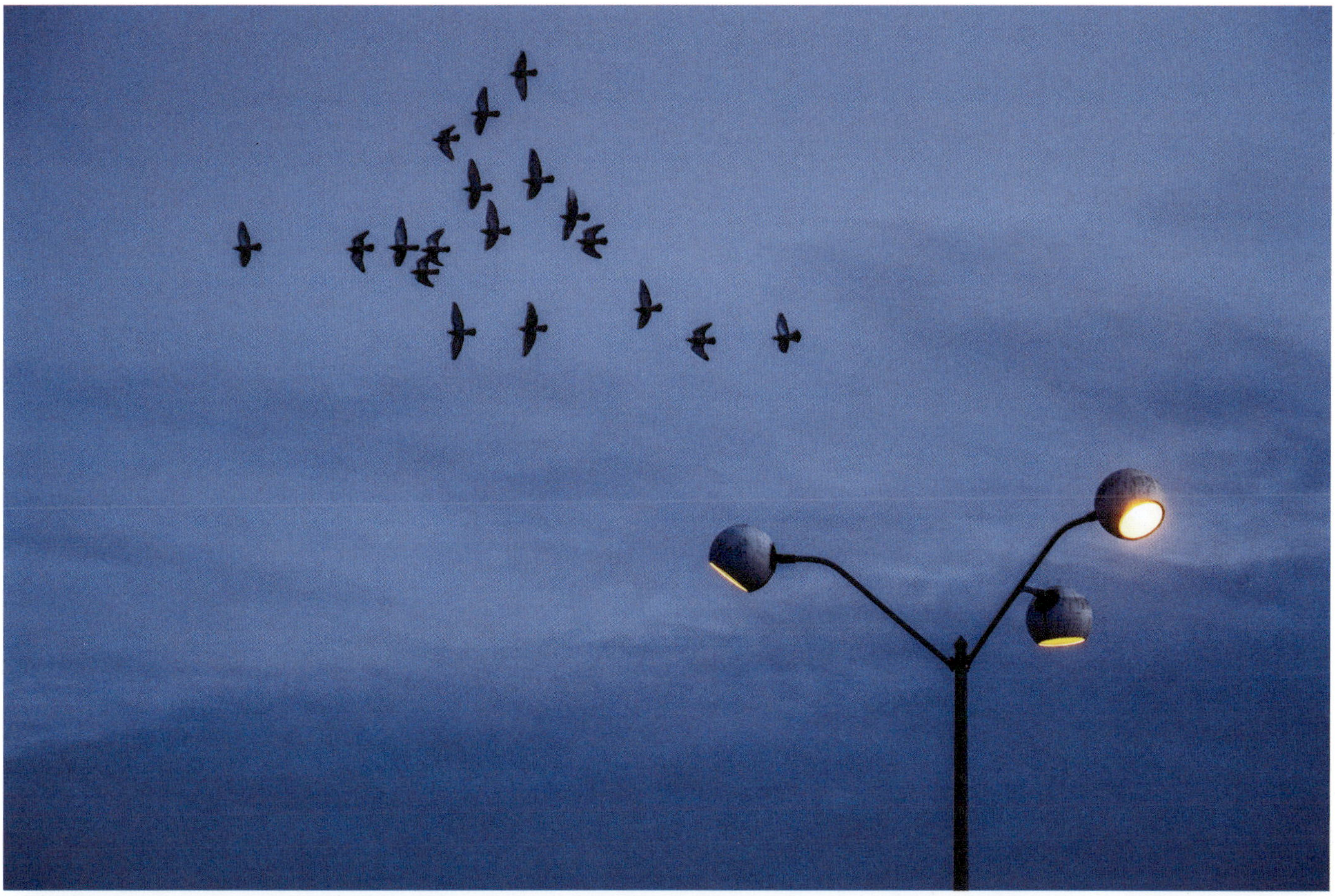

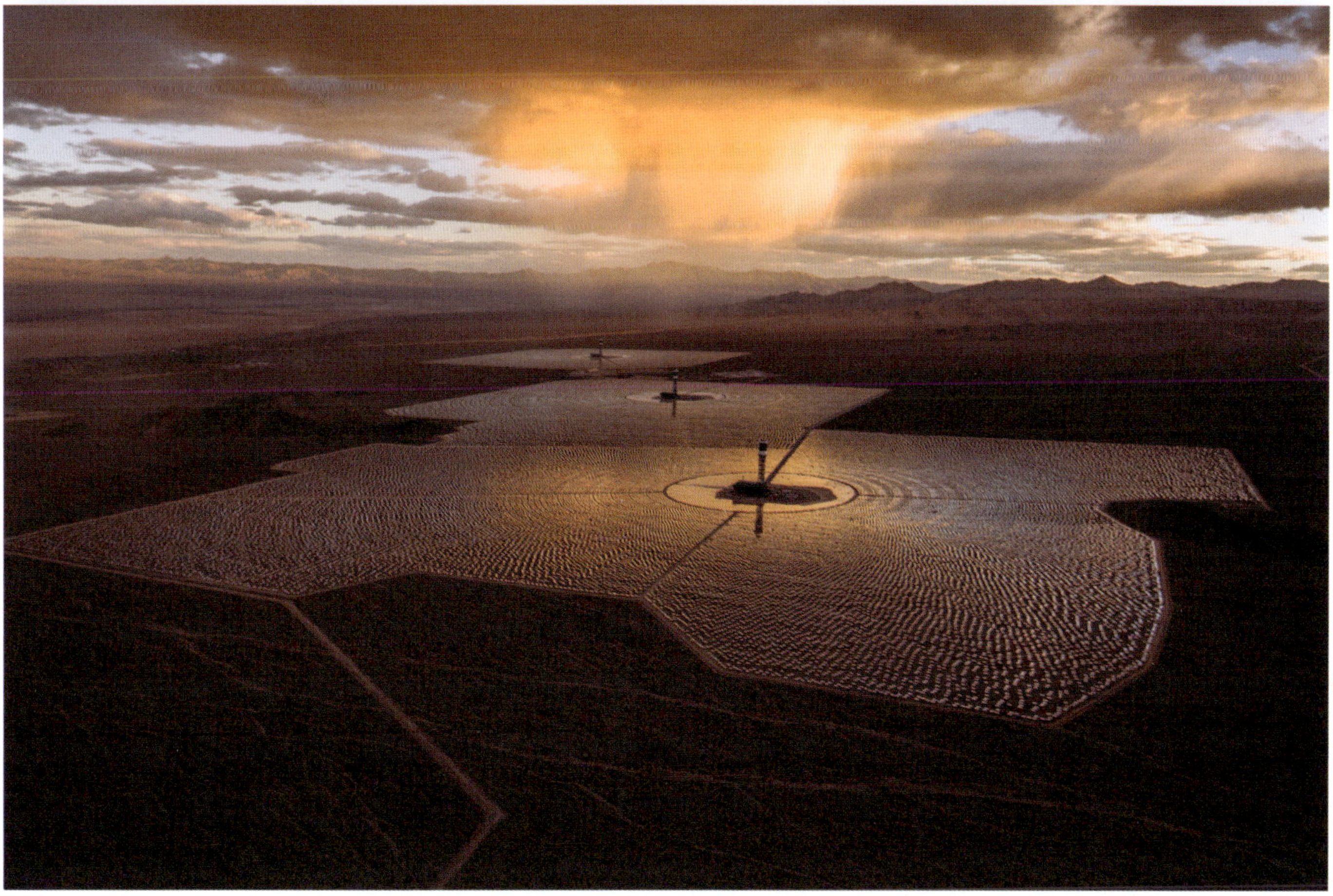

*(Top) Startled pigeons circle retro parking lot lights in Minneapolis, Minnesota.*
*(Bottom) 173,500 mirrors reflect the day's last light onto three thermal solar towers at the Ivanpah power generation station outside Las Vegas, Nevada.*

# A

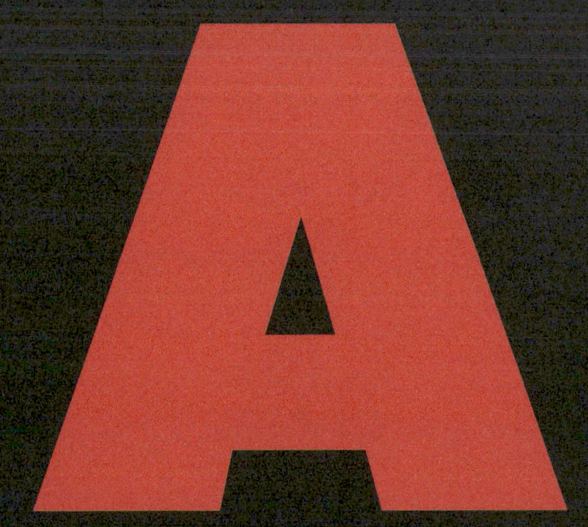

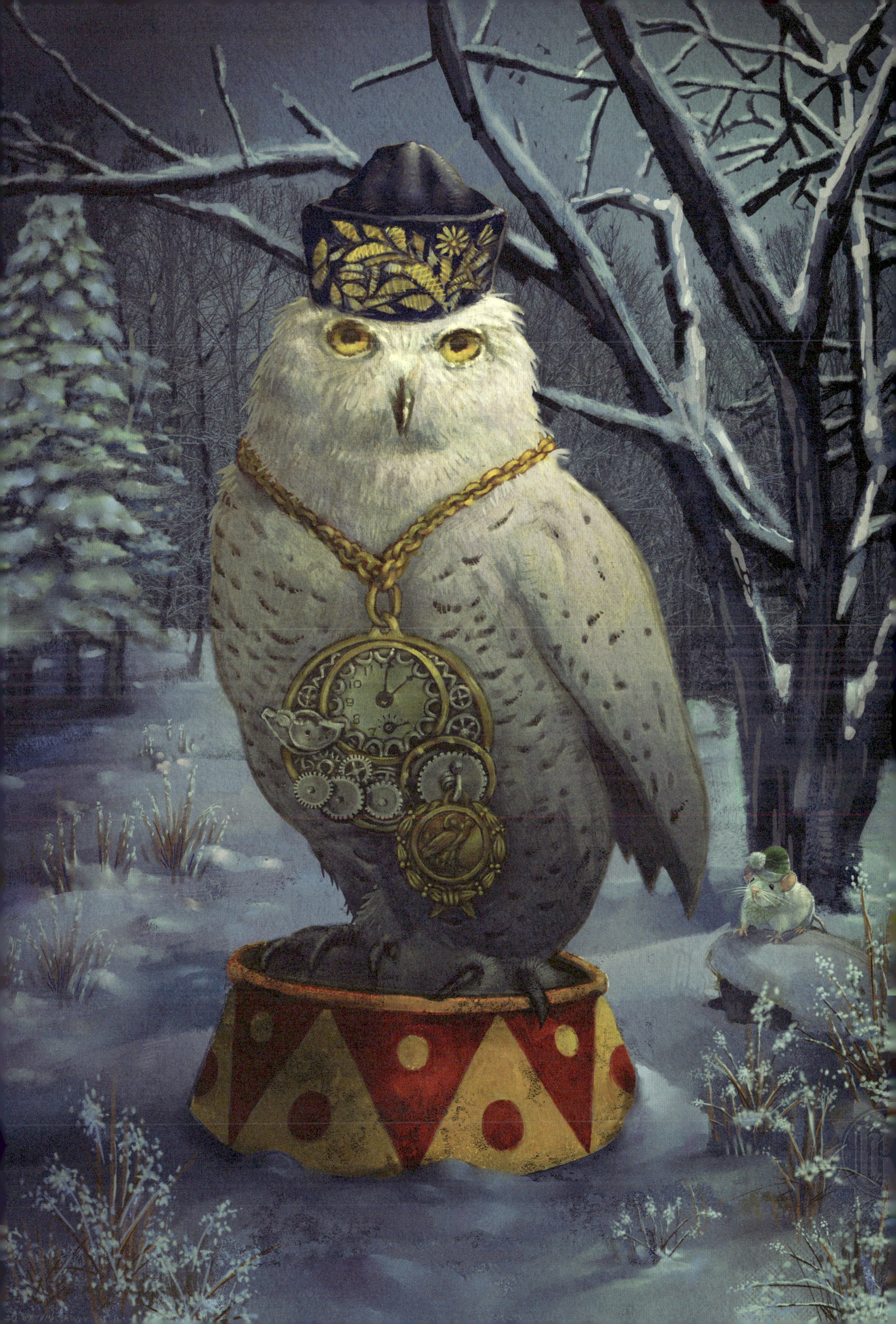

# **Mark Braught:** Creating Successful Creative Solutions

MARK'S IMAGES FOR MY PICTURE BOOK, *T IS FOR TOUCHDOWN*, BROUGHT THE GAME TO LIFE WHILE MAKING IT ACCESSIBLE TO KIDS OF DIFFERENT AGES. IT WASN'T EASY, BUT HE SCORED.

**Brad Herzog,** *Author & Writer*

MARK IS A PROLIFIC AND TALENTED ARTIST WHO NEVER MISSED A DEADLINE, WAS ALWAYS PROFESSIONAL, AND, MOST IMPORTANTLY, WAS A COMPLETE PLEASURE TO WORK WITH!

**Jennifer Bacheller,** *Creative Director, Sleeping Bear Press*

TAKE A BRIEF LOOK AT MARK'S PORTFOLIO, AND HIS TALENT IS QUICKLY APPARENT. LOOK LONGER, AND YOU THEN REALIZE HIS VERSATILITY. THAT IS MARK'S "SECRET SAUCE" — COMBINING HIS SKILL WITH A ROBUST VISUAL VOCABULARY.

**Tim Jessell,** *Illustrator, Tim Jessell Illustration*

AN ILLUSTRATOR OF INCREDIBLE TALENT, MARK IS KNOWN FOR HIS MASTERFULLY CRAFTED PASTEL WORK AND HIS IMAGINATION, WHICH IS NOTHING SHORT OF BRILLIANT.

**Bill Mayer,** *Illustrator, Bill Mayer Studio*

MARK IS SO INCREDIBLY VERSATILE! HE'S CONSTANTLY EVOLVING AS AN ARTIST, AND I LOVE THAT HE ISN'T AFRAID TO EXPERIMENT. HIS ILLUSTRATIONS ARE BEAUTIFULLY RENDERED, WELL-DESIGNED, AND CLEVER. I'M A FAN!

**Laura Freeman,** *Illustrator, LFreeman Illustration*

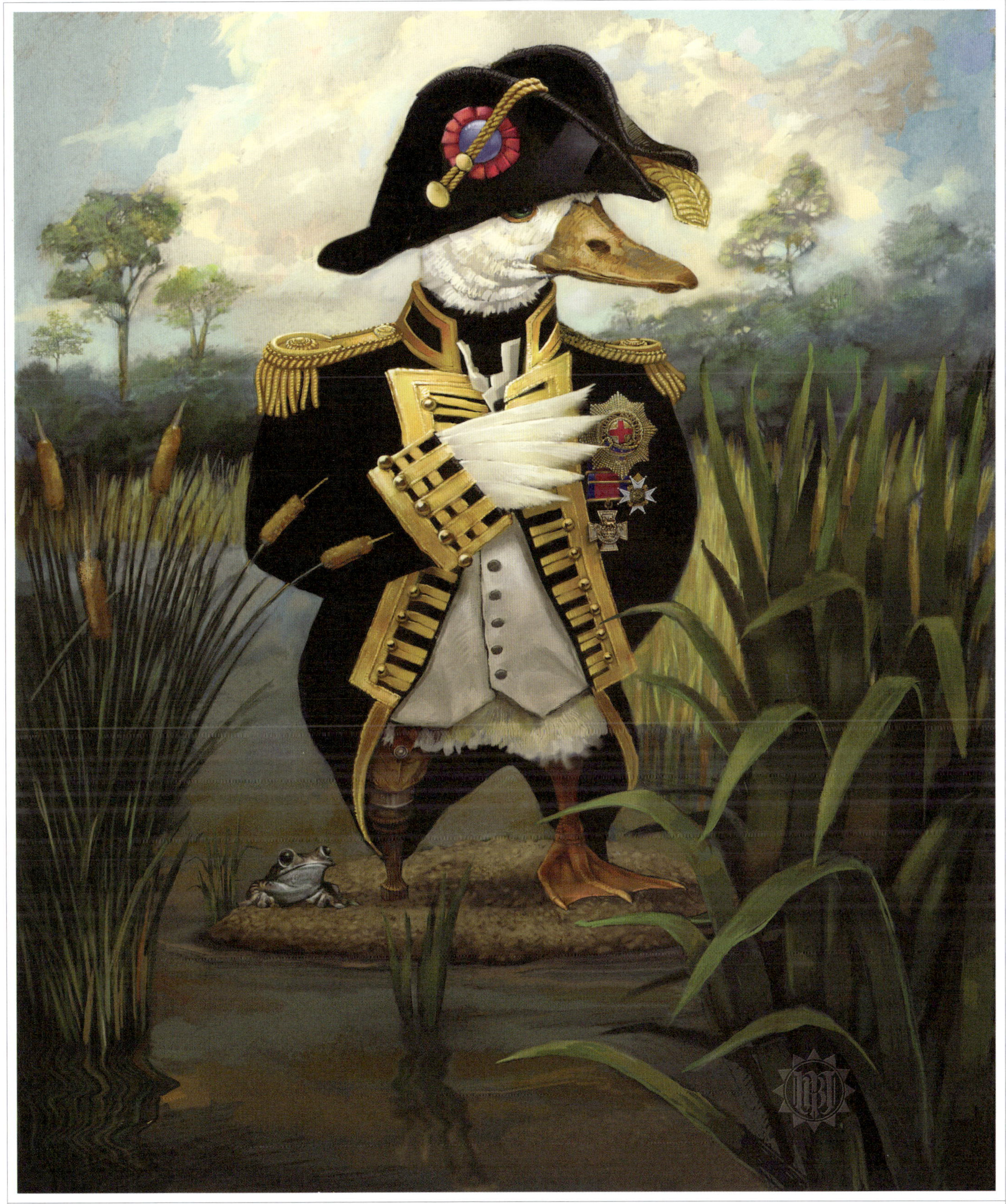

*(Page 93) Title: Another Year. AD: Roger Sawhill. Client: Up-Fun. Year: 2023. / (Above) Title: Primas Anatidea. AD: Kristen Robertson. Client: Strange Duck Brewery. Year: 2020.*

I know Mark Braught as an illustrator, designer, art director, type designer, teacher, friend, business partner, and distant cousin (something we learned by accident). He likes to fly under the radar, doesn't look for the limelight, and wants to do great work—and when he gets going, he can be a machine. His eye for mixing colors, especially in his pastel work, is beyond amazing. Layer upon layer of color goes into a piece. Weird greens, shocking oranges, intense purples— all stacked on top of each other—but the result has this intense depth and vibrancy. Frankly, his sketching abilities make me envious. I am lucky to call Mark my friend and business partner.

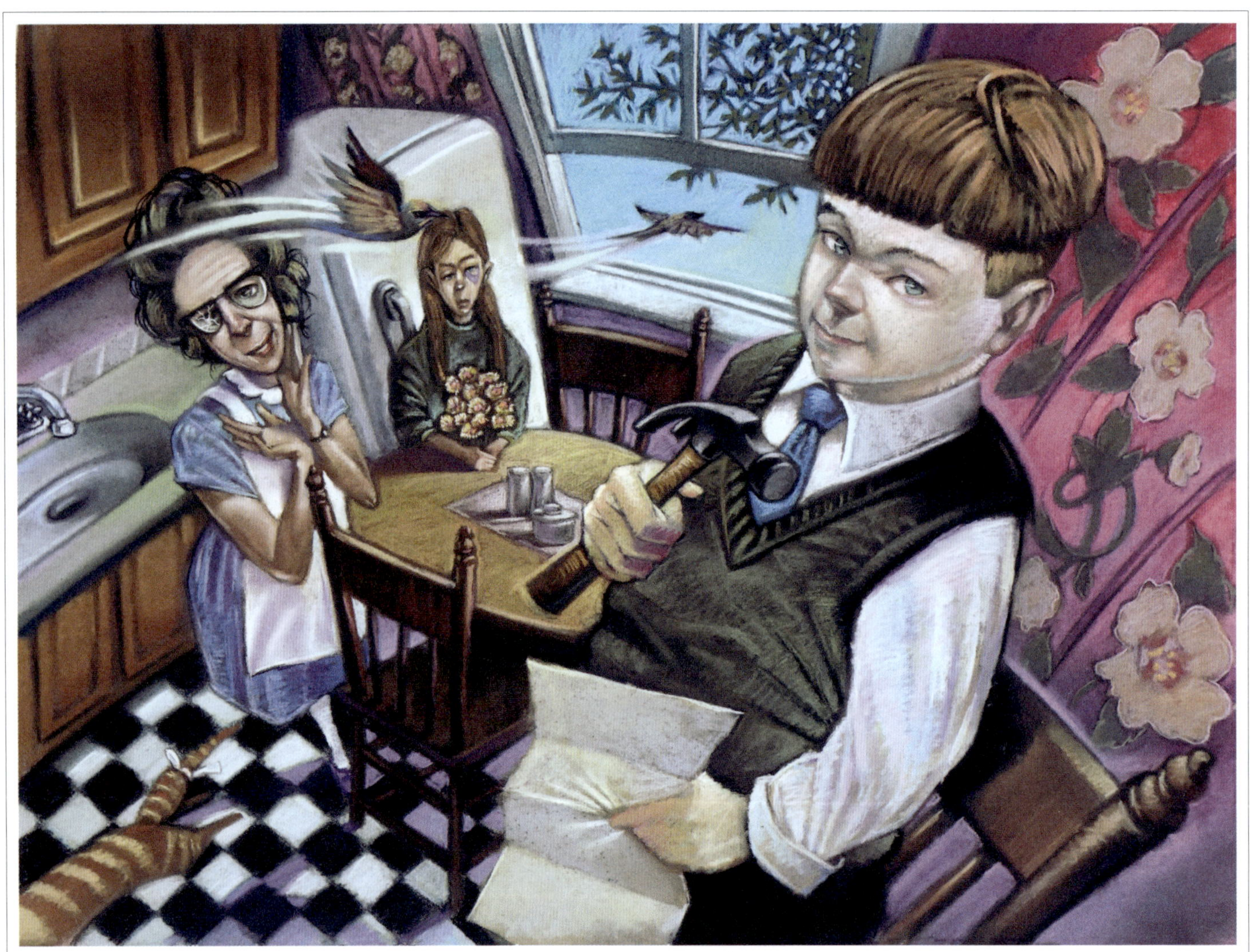

*Title: Momma's Favorite. AD: Brian Miller. Client: Moore Langden. Year: 1984.*

# DRAWING WILL ALWAYS STAY IN STYLE. IT IS FUNDAMENTAL TO VISUAL COMMUNICATION LIKE THE ALPHABET IS TO WRITING.

**Mark Braught,** *Illustrator, Mark Braught Studios*

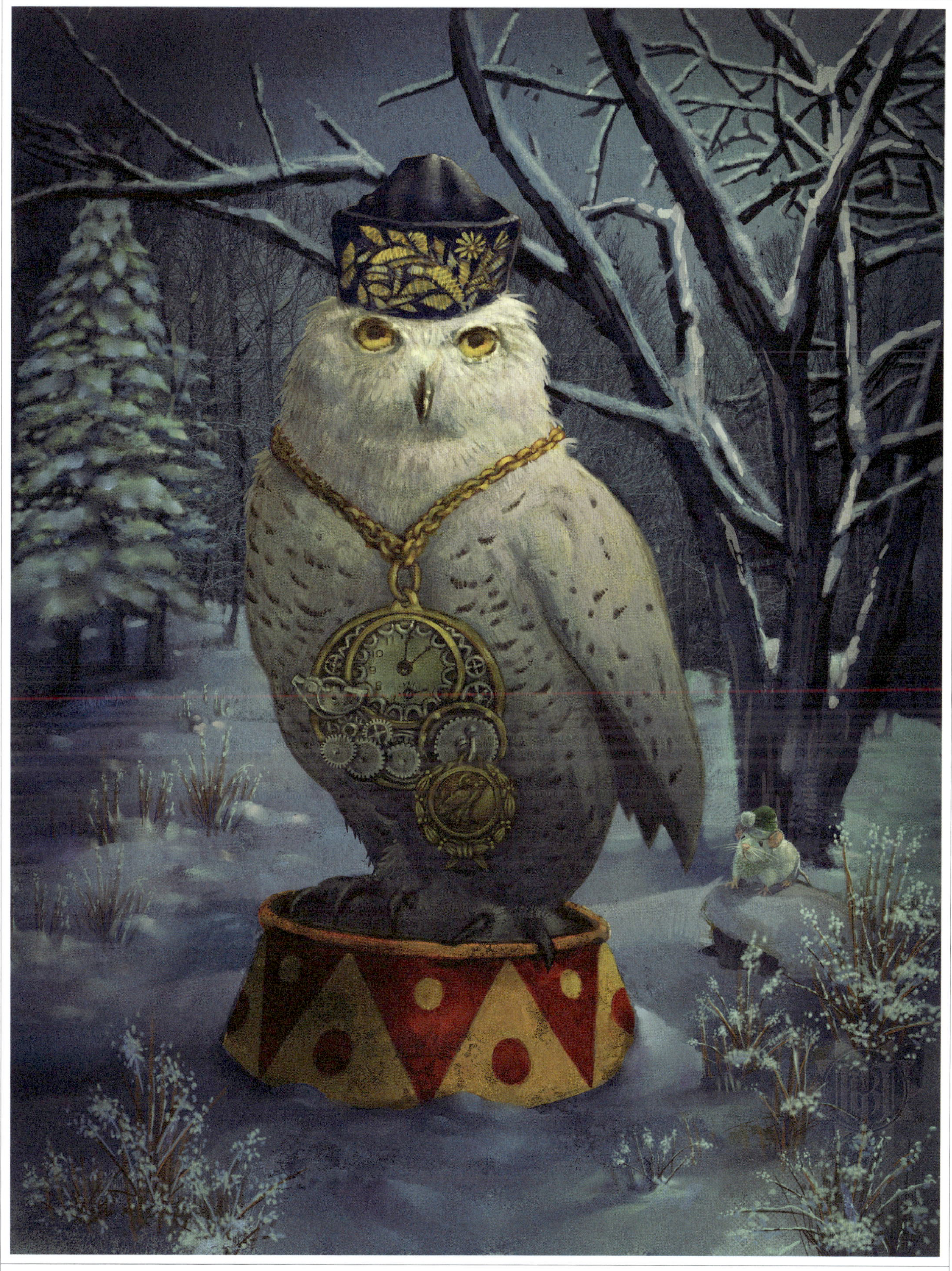

*Title: Another Year. AD: Roger Sawhill. Client: Up-Fun. Year: 2023.*

**What is your work philosophy?**
Does the solution address the problem within the parameters supplied to the best of my abilities?

**Who is or was your greatest mentor?**
John Laska, Hazel Gamec, and Rob Lawton.

**What is it about illustration that you are most passionate** about?
Effectively communicating a message to an audience.

**Who have some of your greatest past influences been?**
Herb Lubalin, *Mad* magazine, Mary Cassatt, N. C. Wyeth, Brad Holland, John Collier, Bernie Fuchs, Jack Unruh, and Norman Rockwell.

**Who among your contemporaries today do you most admire?**
Greg Manchess, C. F. Payne, Bill Mayer, Laura Freeman, and Tim Jessell.

**What would be your dream assignment?**
Something involving a series of images establishing a brand or a great children's book manuscript.

**Who have been some of your favorite colleagues or clients?**
Tom Gundred, Lloyd Brooks, Heather Hughes, Jennifer Bacheller, Mike Weed, Sleeping Bear Press, and Strange Duck Brewery.

**What are the top things you need from a client to do successful work for them?**
The parameters and goals of the project, as well as an environment of mutual respect conducive to collaboration.

**What do you consider your greatest professional achievement so far?**
To be able to continue to create solutions in this industry.

**What about your work gives you the greatest satisfaction?**
Creating successful, creative solutions.

**What part of your work do you find the most demanding?**
Striving for the standard my mentors embedded in me: "Good isn't good enough."

**What professional goals do you still have for yourself?**
Again, "Good isn't good enough."

**What advice would you give to students starting out today?**
Be curious, be passionate, be brave, and work hard.

**What interests do you have outside of work?**
Playing tennis and literary festivals.

**What do you value most in life?**
Family, friends, and time (all of these are finite and irreplaceable).

**What would you change if you had to do it all over again?**
Nothing. To change anything would risk where I'm at, and I'm pretty happy where that is.

**Where do you find inspiration?**
Just about anywhere. I love going down rabbit holes.

**How do you define success?**
Waking up excited and happy to face what the day has in store.

**Where do you see yourself in the future?**
I never saw my career developing as it has, and it became more than I could have dreamed, so I am more curious than most to see what the future holds.

**How do you balance your work with your personal life if there is a distinction between the two for you?**
In many ways, they coexist pretty seamlessly. They feed off each other most of the time.

**In what ways do you see your field changing over the years?**
The technical barrier between the industry and its consumers is, in a very broad general manner, continuing to disappear at break-neck speed. With our clients having access to resources to create solutions easily, it is a challenge for us to develop "a game" for better solutions and to earn our keep. It is an excellent opportunity to earn and/or maintain respect for what we do.

**You mainly do hand-drawn work, though you sometimes do digital illustrations. For you personally, why hand-drawn over digital, and is hand-drawn a dying art?**
Drawing will always stay in style. It is fundamental to visual communication like the alphabet is to writing. Does writing on a laptop make someone a better writer?

Digital is just another way to do it, not a way to replace it. I use a medium in response to the problem at hand and what is needed to get the image where it needs to be.

**You illustrate for publishing, editorial, and advertising. Is there a category you prefer to illustrate for, and are there similarities and differences between working on each one that might not be obvious?**
Each category offers unique challenges, but they all have a story that needs to be told visually. These challenges are very appealing.

**Some of your most recognizable works are your Harry Potter illustrations. How did you get to illustrate one of the biggest literary series of all time?**
LOL! That is a great question. You would have to ask Tom Gundred (the art director for the project). It was a great experience, and I am still very grateful for the opportunity. The short answer is that he called.

**Other than your illustration work, you also run UP-Ideas with Roger Sawhill. How was UP-Ideas founded, and how does that work differ from your illustrations?**
UP-Ideas evolved from both of us teaching at Creative Circus and collaborating on various freelance design projects we both had, including the identity of the school. We discovered that we have great chemistry when working together and felt that our combined experience would greatly expand our opportunities. I primarily function as a designer but occasionally illustrate if the project calls for it.

**You're a member of numerous organizations, such as the Society of Illustrators and the Illustrators Partnership of America. How have such memberships benefitted and shaped your work?**
Interacting in these organizations has been an incredible asset. So much was learned about our industry from some of the best it has to offer. Networking is also a great benefit. They helped me see the bar I wanted to meet and gave me information on how to meet it.

**Mark Braught Studios** www.markbraught.com

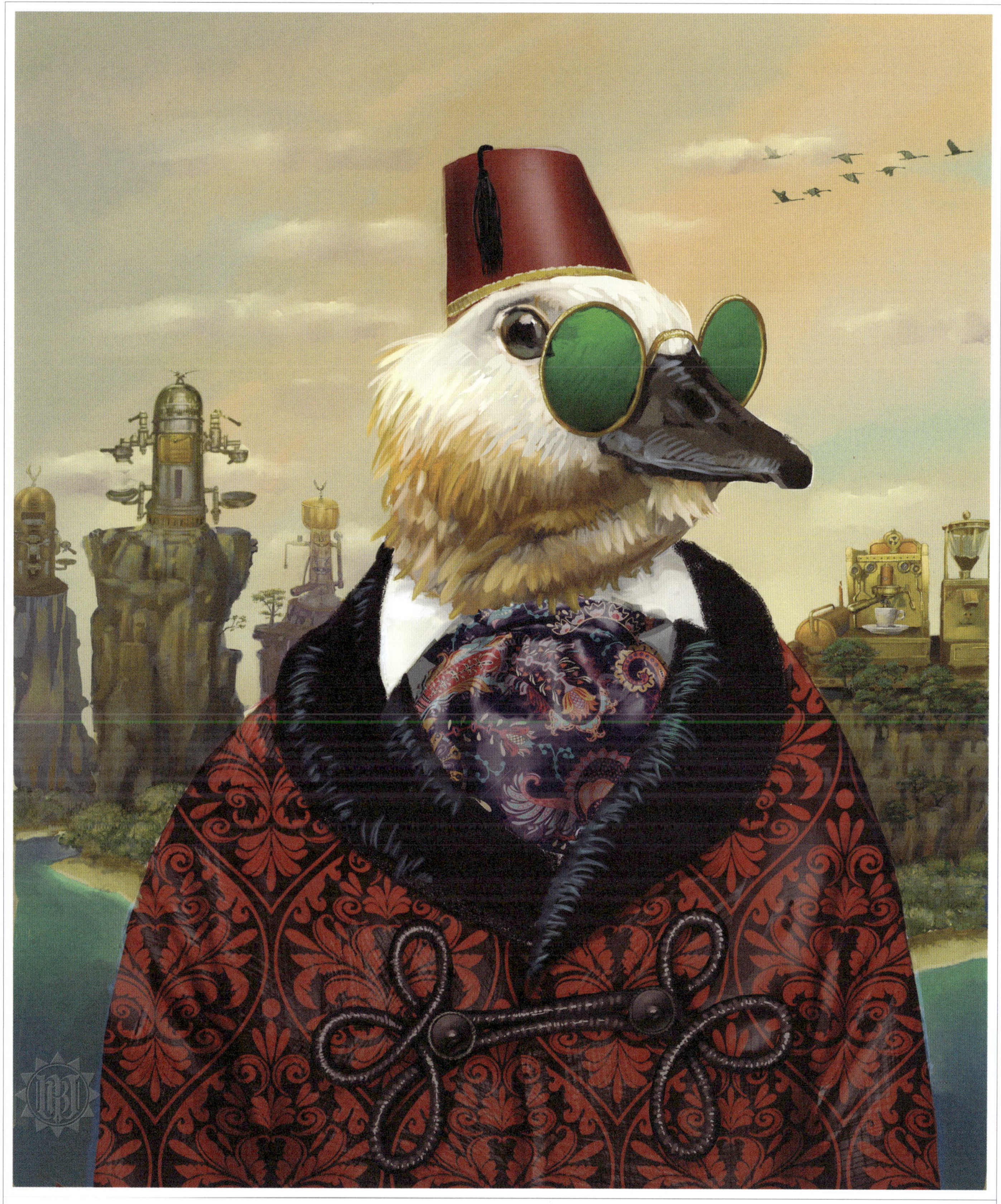

Title: *Capulus Anaticula. AD: Kristen Robertson. Client: Strange Duck Brewery. Year: 2021.*

# I USE A MEDIUM IN RESPONSE TO THE PROBLEM AT HAND AND WHAT IS NEEDED TO GET THE IMAGE WHERE IT NEEDS TO BE.

**Mark Braught,** *Illustrator, Mark Braught Studios*

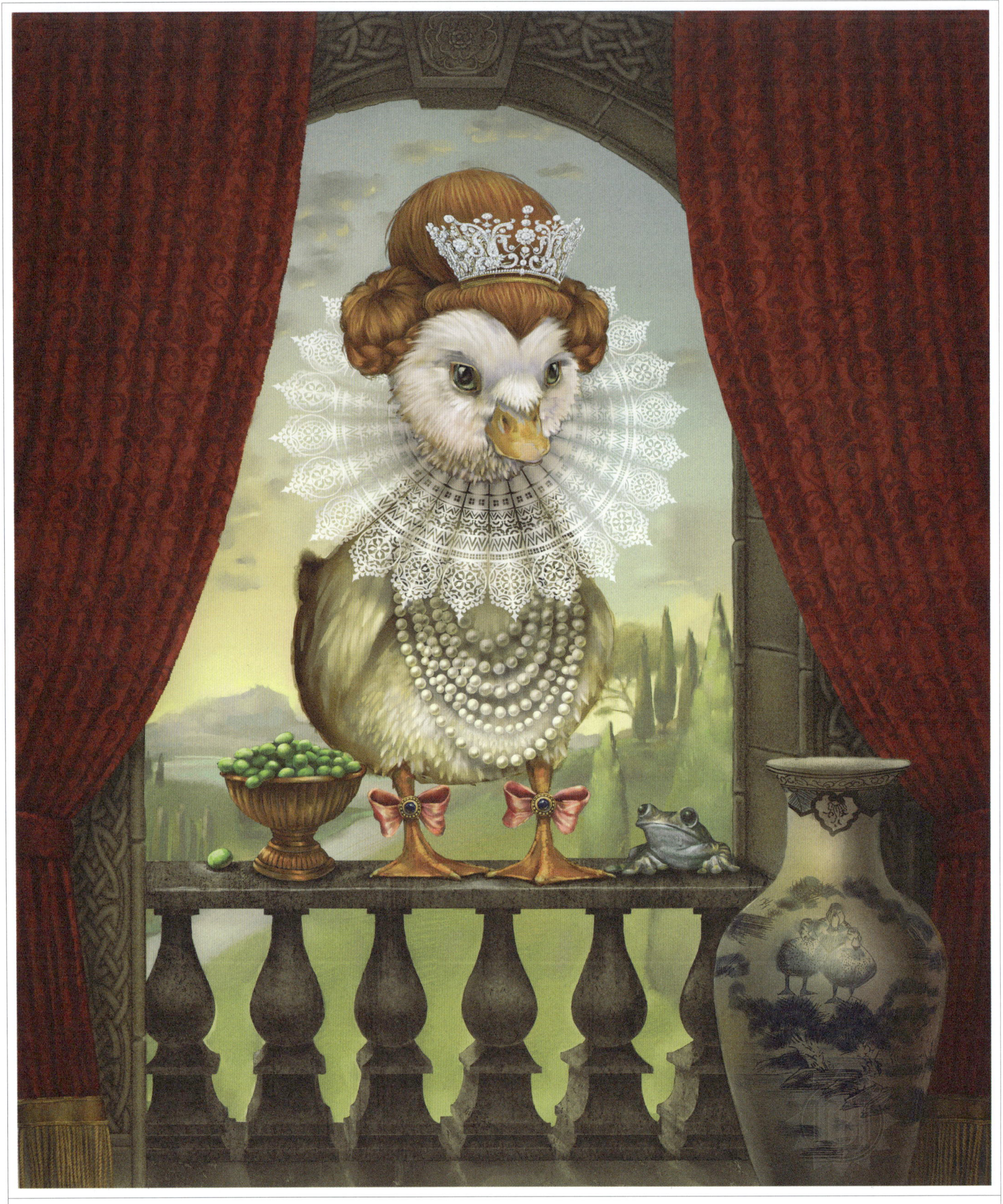

*Title: Lauda Regina. AD: Kristen Robertson. Client: Strange Duck Brewery. Year: 2022.*

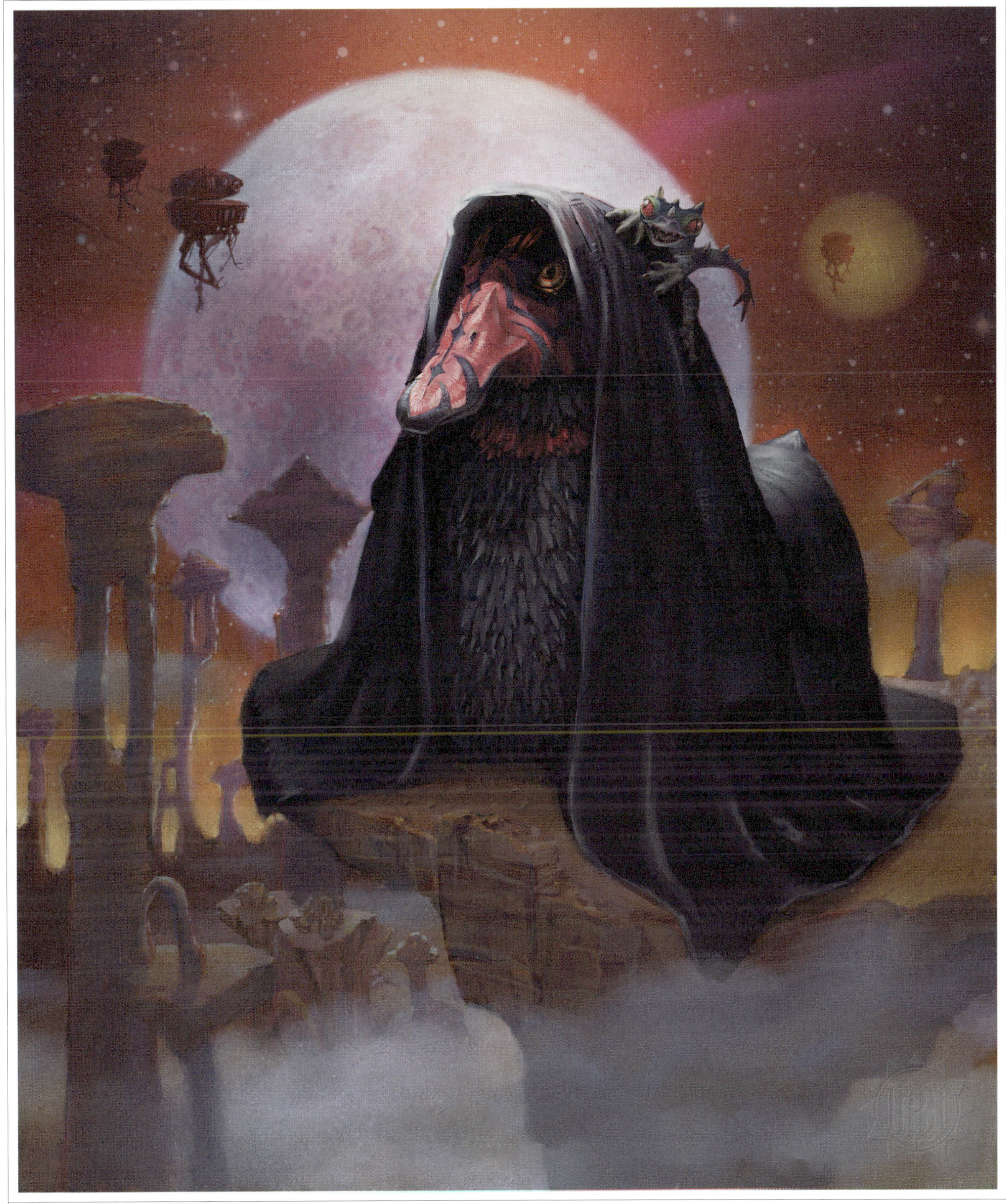

*Title: Fowl Apprentice. AD: Kristen Robertson. Client: Strange Duck Brewery. Year: 2021.*

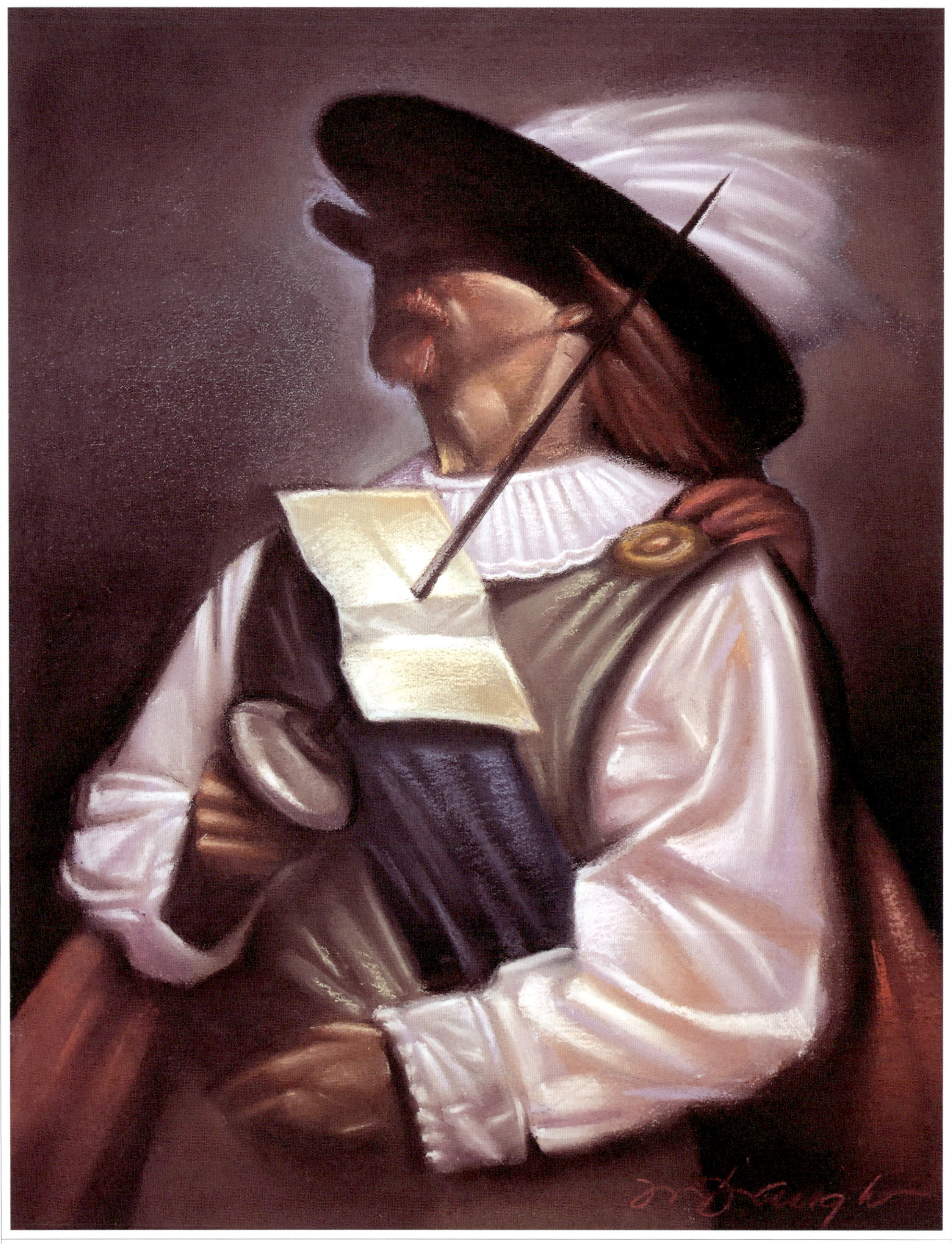

Title: Cyrano. AD: Chris Willett. Client: Scholastic Inc. Model: Tom Nynas. Year: 1995.

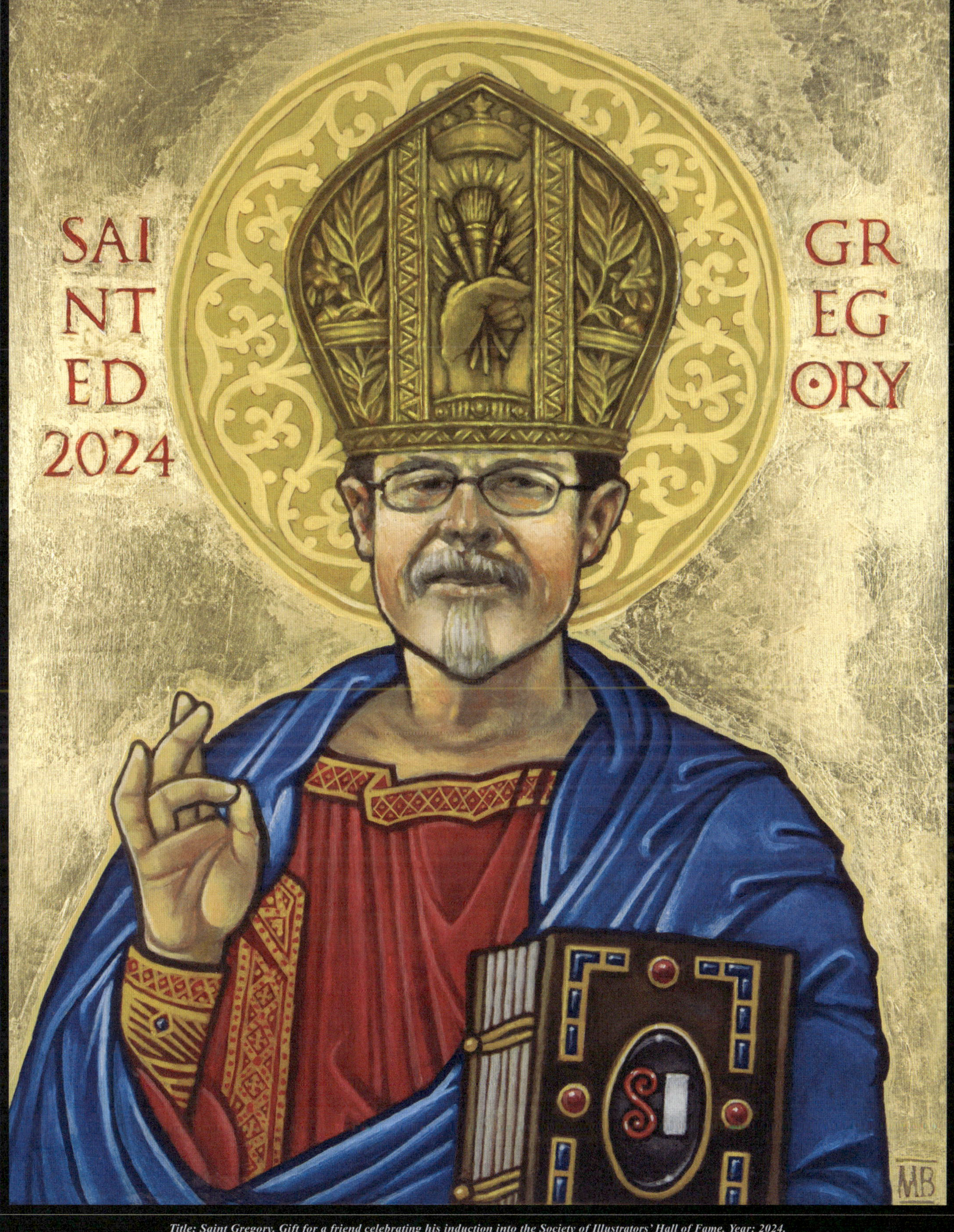

SAI
NT
ED
2024
GR
EG
ORY

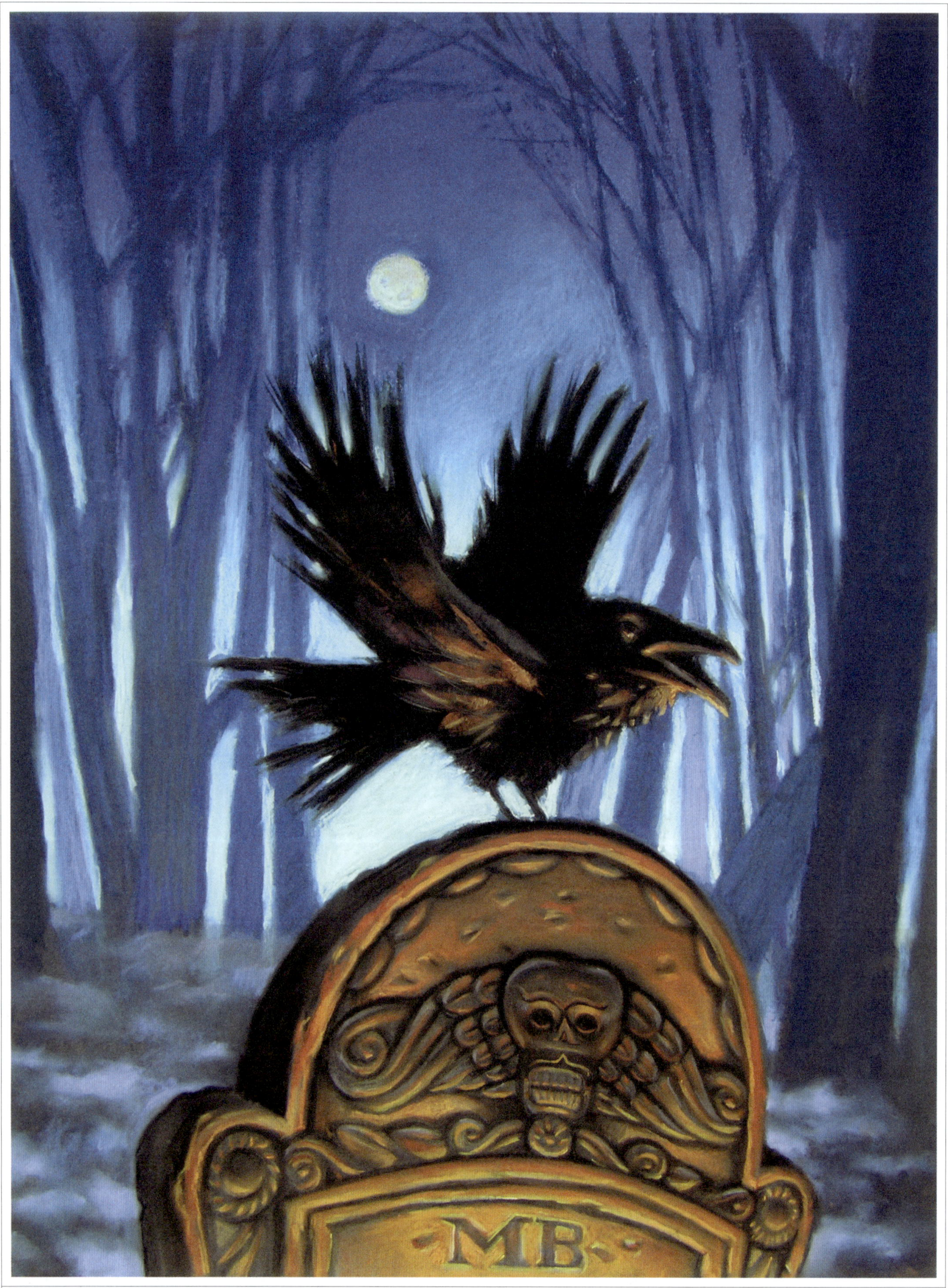

*Title: Campfire Storytelling Festival. AD: Tracy Walker. Client: Dawson County Library. Year: 2017.*

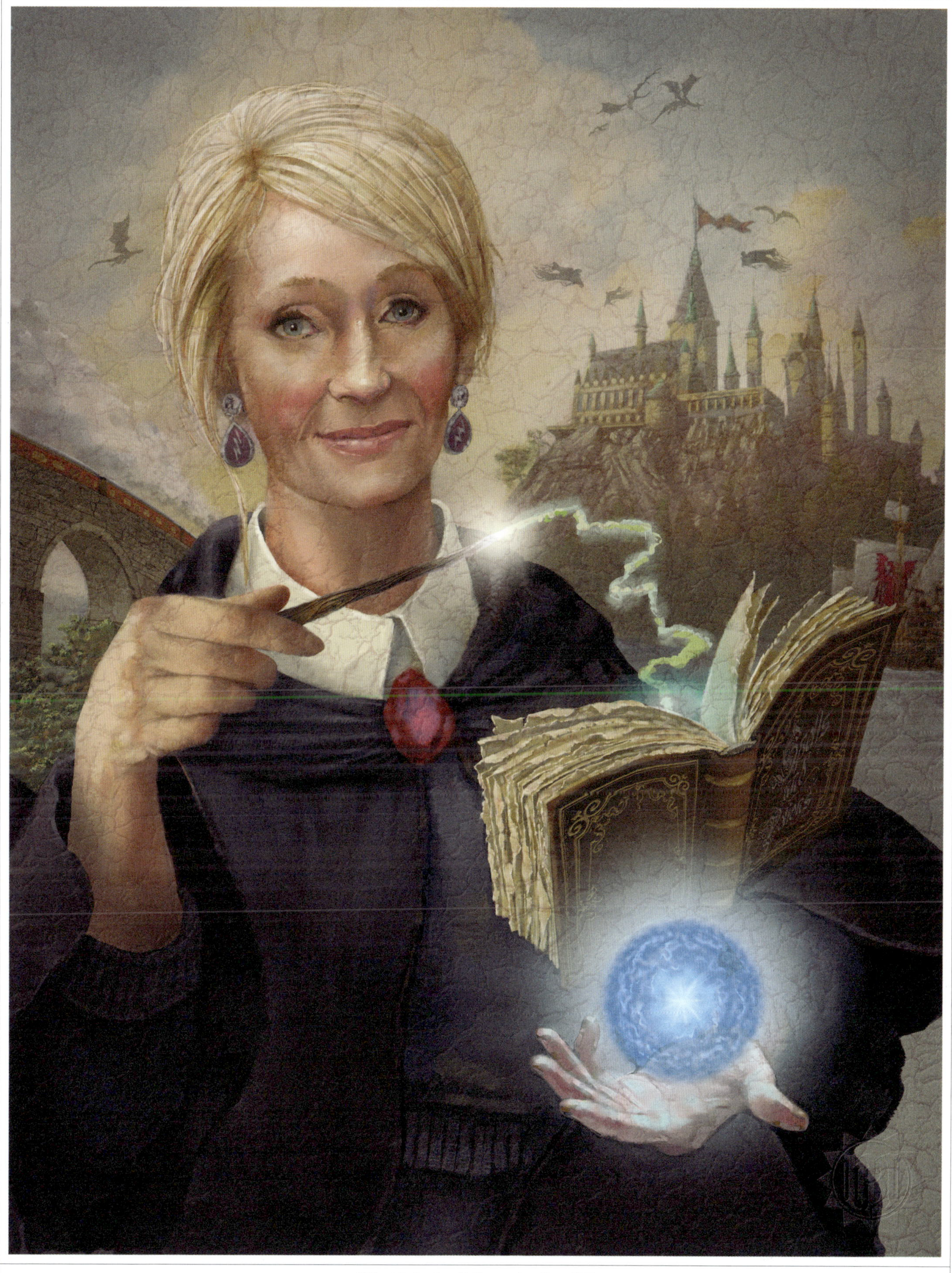

*Title: J.K. Rowling. Self-promotion. Year: 2022.*

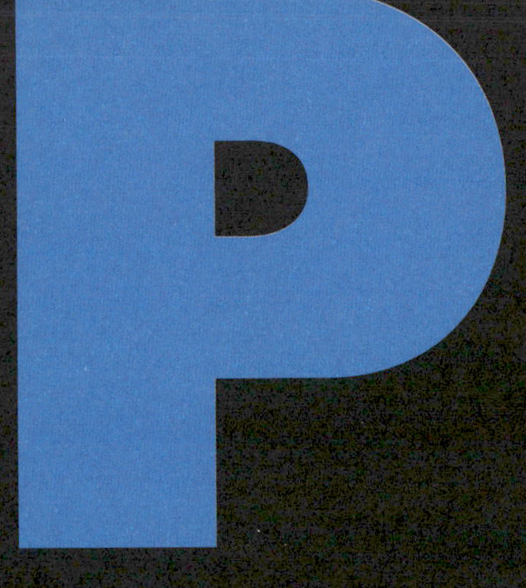



PRODUCT DESIGN

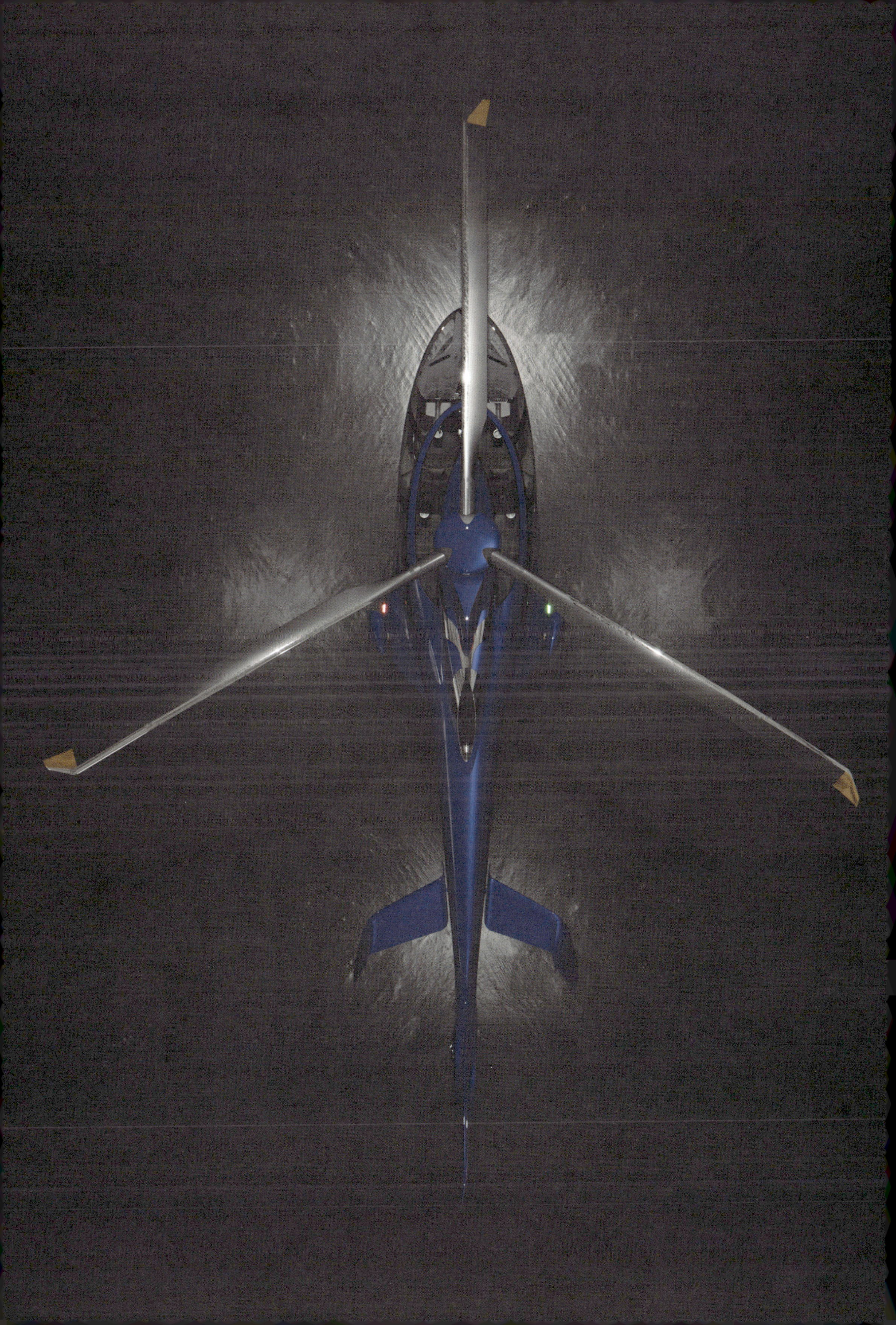

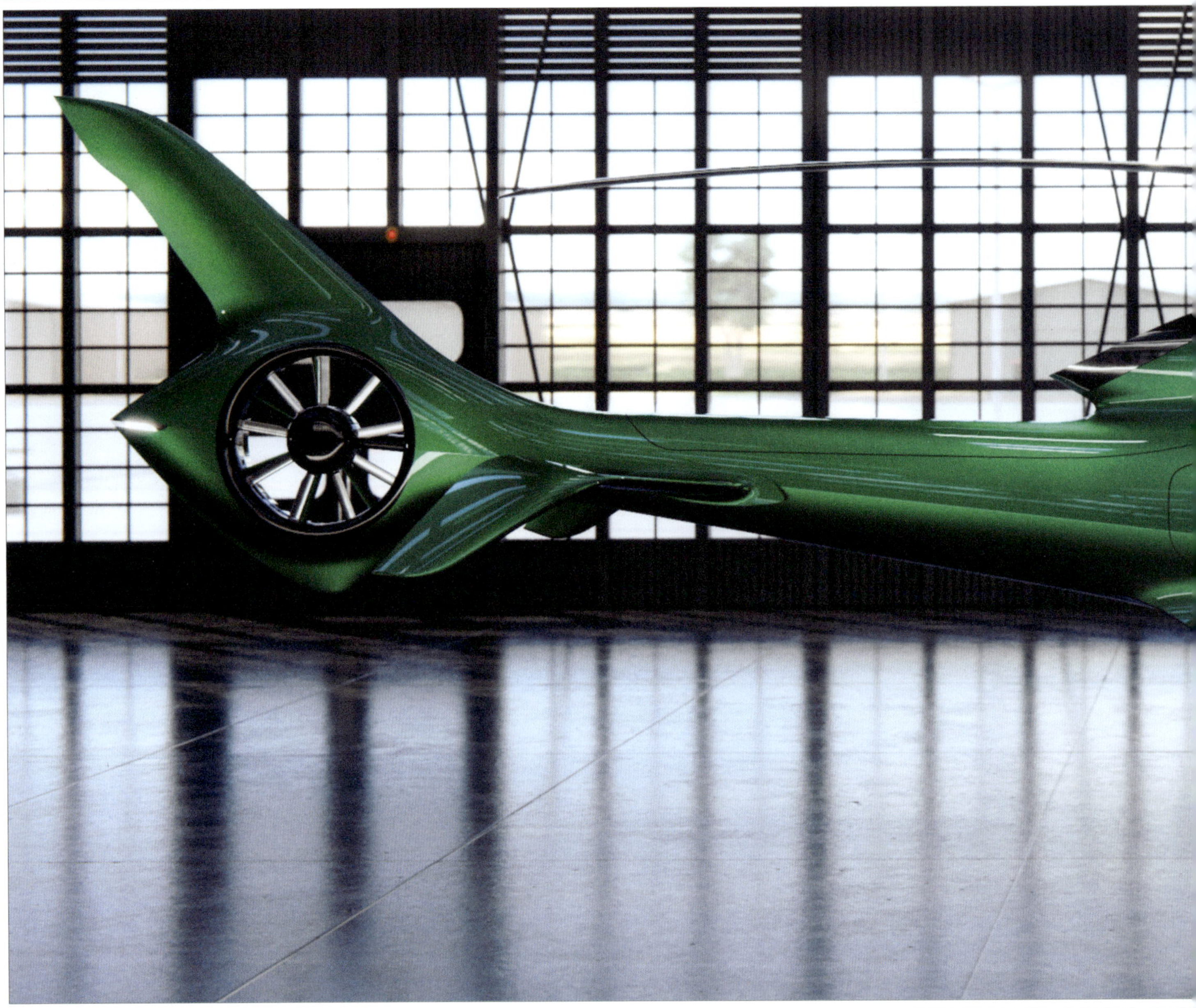

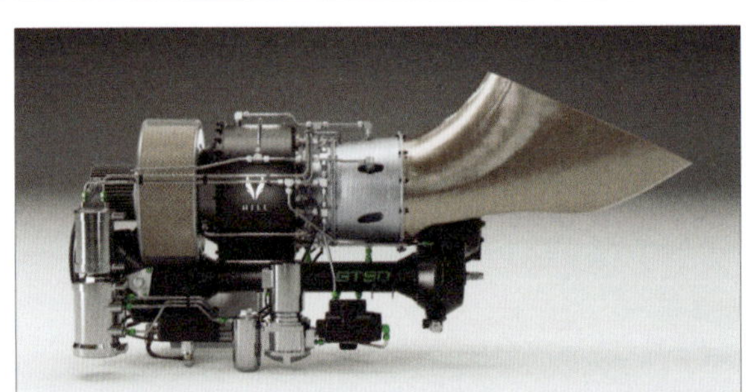

At first, I was stumped as to why the HX50 reminded me of my childhood in the United Kingdom. Then, after researching the organization a little further, it all clicked into place: Hill Helicopters is a UK company, and it proudly boasts that its products have an iconic British design. *Thunderbirds*, a beloved and often repeated British children's television show dating to the 1960s, must have been a particular inspiration. The Thunderbird crafts themselves seem to be almost woven into the fabric of the HX50, with their curvature and bold metallic finishes calling back to the show that inspired countless British engineers.

People unfamiliar with the *Thunderbirds* TV show must still admit that the HX50 is exactly the sort of product that harks back to a feeling of childhood wonder. Some elements that are unique to the helicopter, such as the glass skylights, certainly seem to be catered to those who have a childlike curiosity. Just imagine gazing up at the propellers through those roof windows and being hypnotized by their motion!

The luxurious interior is just as unique as the exterior. The five seats that fill the cabin are bursting with character. These ergonomic chairs separate at key points, implying that they have bodies and souls that could go on their own adventures. The headphones that sit on the headrests only reinforce this perception, suggesting that these seats are conversing with one another. The materials used to produce the interior are among the finest that could possibly be procured, including Nappa leather, Alcantara trim, and first-class brushed metal. An easy-to-miss outstanding design choice with these chairs is the fact that the rear three are elevated, ensuring that those sitting at the back enjoy superior views without being obstructed by the pilot seats. Hill offers ten different interior color schemes, all of which give the cabin a distinct feel. Perhaps the most authentic scheme is English Walnut, as its tone is taken from a genuine resource native to the British countryside.

One especially impressive claim regarding the HX50 is the fact that its controls have resulted in an aircraft that is remark-

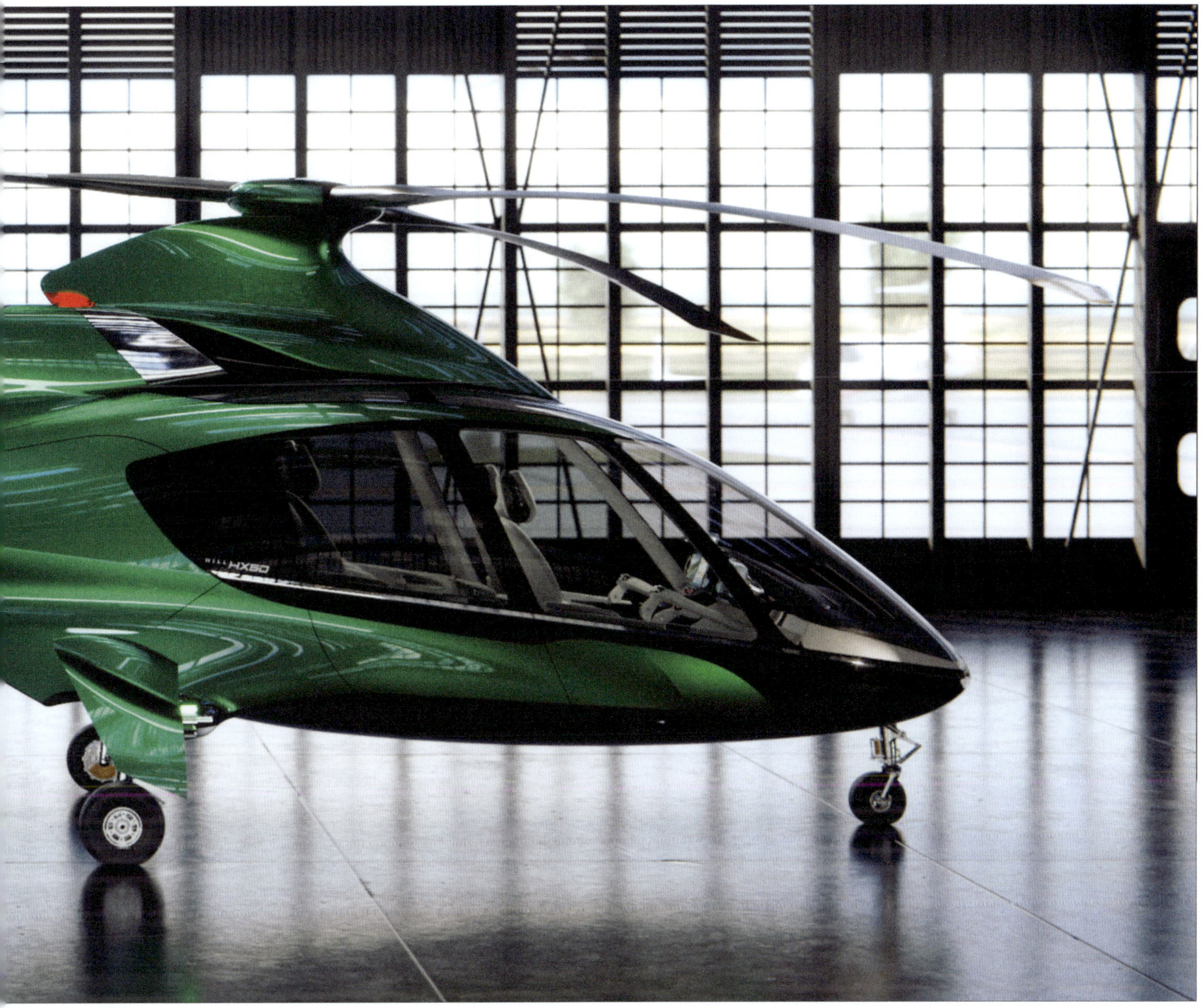

*HX50*

| **Horsepower:** 500 shp | **Payload:** 1.760 lbs (798 kg) | **Length including rotors:** 38.6 ft (11.8 m) | **Width:** 8.5 ft (2.6 m) |
| **Cruise speed:** 140 kn (161 mph) | **Max range:** 700 NM (1,296 km) | **Length excluding rotors:** 32.2 ft (9.8 m) | **Height:** 10.8 ft (3.29 m) |

ably easy to maneuver. Hill even claims that these "make flying the aircraft almost as simple as driving a modern car." The cyclic sticks positioned in front of the pilot seats certainly seem simple enough to get to grips with, even for a novice pilot. The three screens at the front of the cabin have been designed "to present the information elegantly and succinctly… This integrated and connected approach dramatically reduces pilot workload and effectively draws attention to changing conditions when neces-

sary." Anyone wondering how Britishness is integrated into this system will be comforted to learn that a key aspect of the flight controls was the idea of delivering information "in an emotionally sensitive manner so as to avoid panic or pilot over-reaction." Basically, the helicopter software employs a "keep calm and carry on" approach to essential flight information.

Few things make me proud to be British, but the HX50 certainly does!

# I WANTED AN AIRCRAFT THAT FUSED THE BEST OF PREMIUM AUTOMOBILE STYLING, REFINEMENT, AND BUILD QUALITY WITH THE CONVENIENCE AND EXCLUSIVITY OF POINT-TO-POINT PRIVATE AIR TRANSPORT. IT IS WITH THIS SIMPLE VISION IN MIND THAT I HAVE CREATED THE HX50.

**Jason Hill,** *Founder, Chairman, & Chief Engineer, Hill Helicopters*

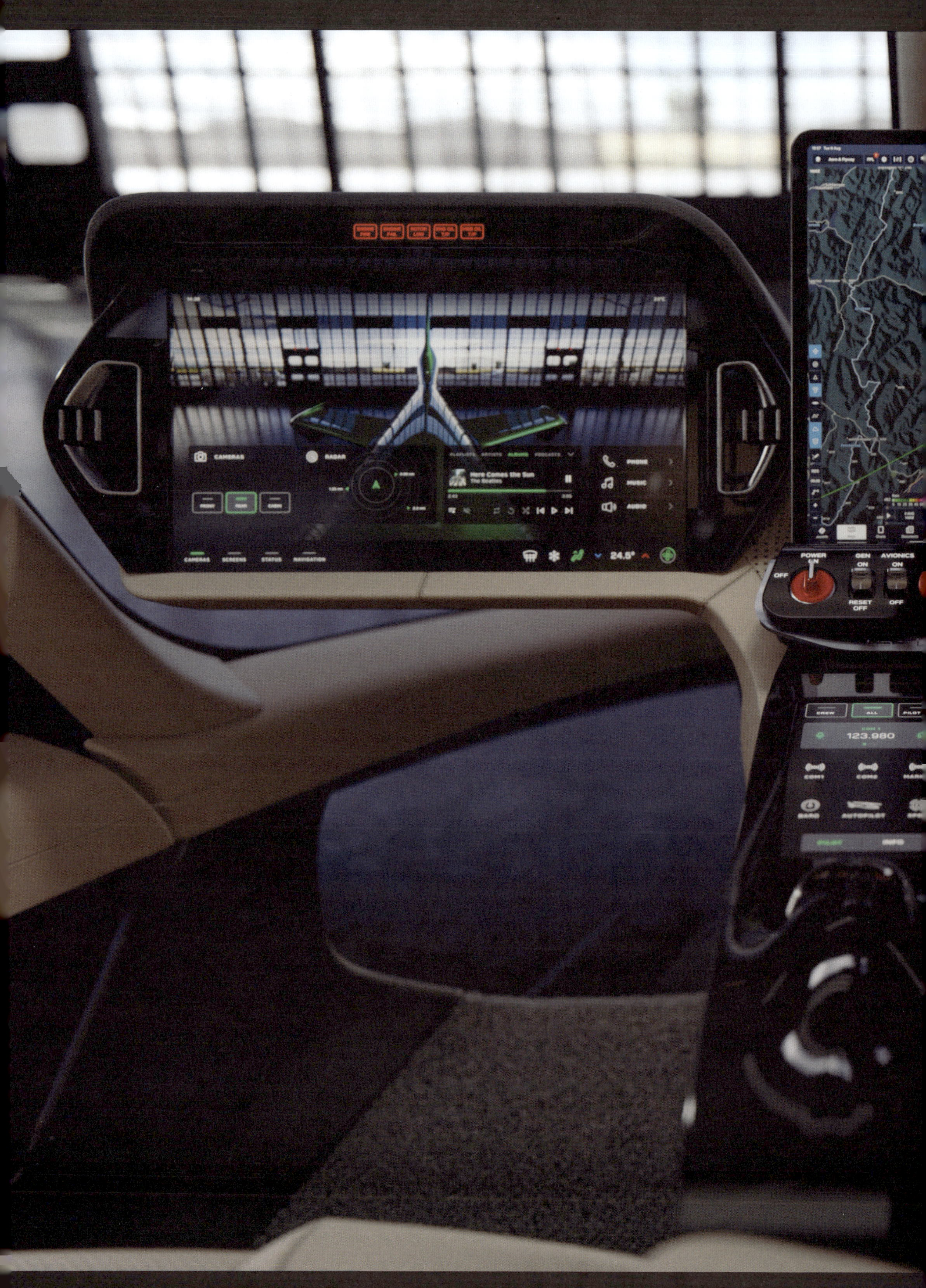

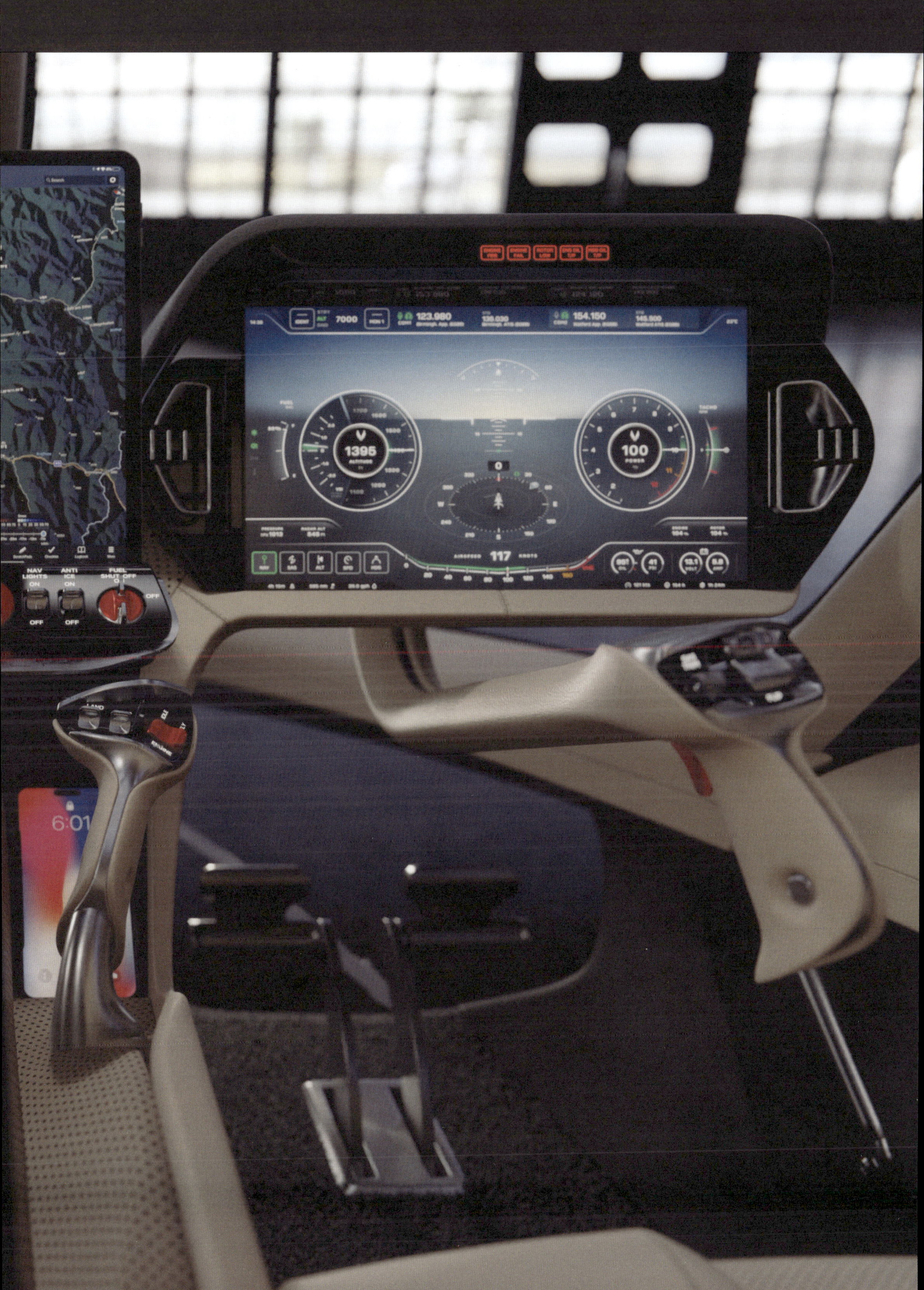

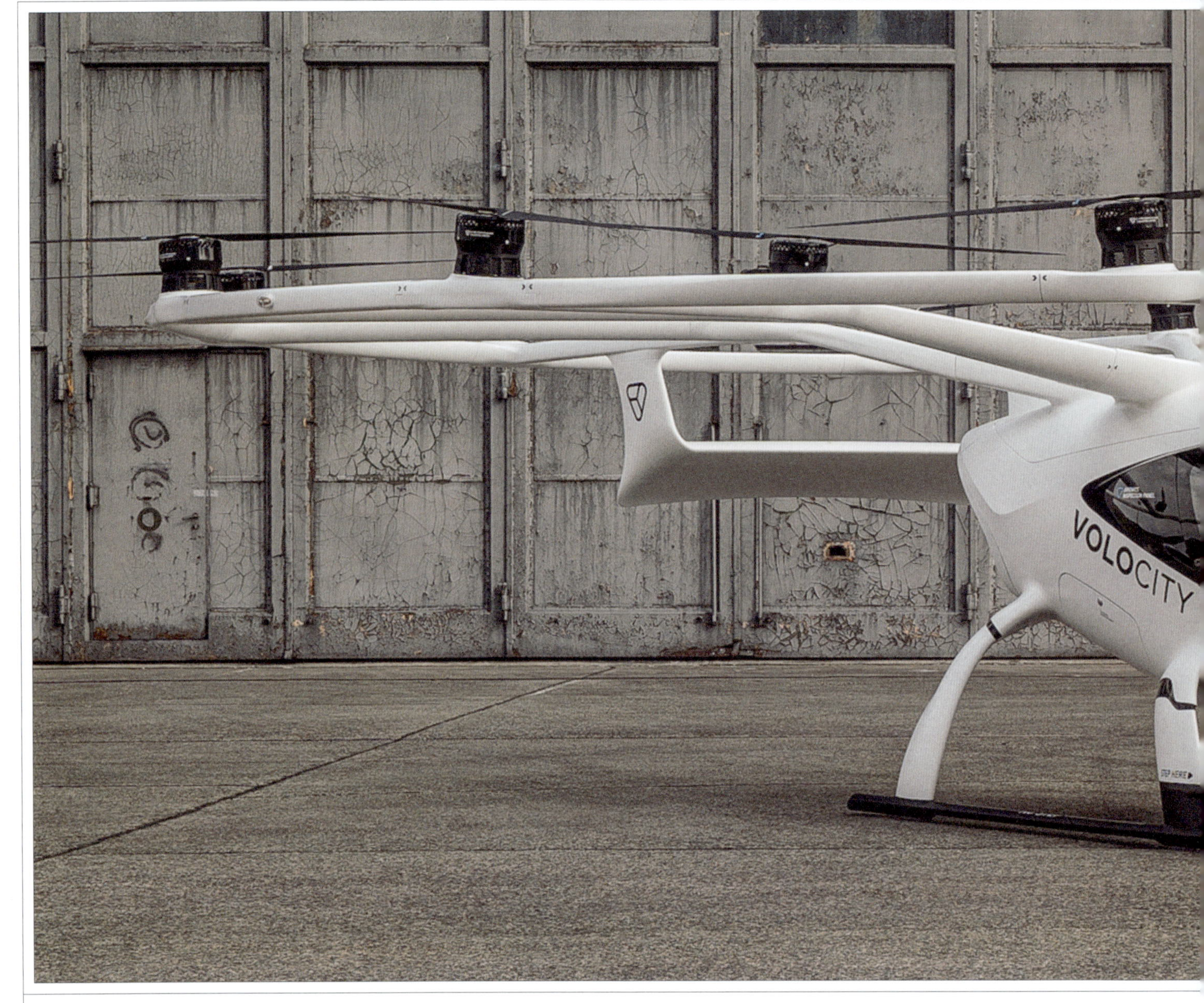


Volocopter has lofty ambitions, literally! The company states that its VoloCity vehicle will become the first internationally certified eVTOL aircraft and the first air taxi to serve Europe. If all proceeds as planned, there's a point in the not-too-distant future when air taxis will be as commonplace as drones are today, which currently number 1.6 million units in Europe alone.

While the introduction of VoloCity air taxis will take some time, Volocopter has already notched up some impressive achievements, the most recent being in August 2024, when a VoloCity successfully conducted a vertical take-off and landing flight test on the grounds of the Palace of Versailles. This once-royal residence is an apt location for the vehicle, given that the most immediately noticeable aspect of its design is the large circular crown above the cockpit, which houses 18 small propellers. In addition to being visually striking, this regal addition ensures that the VoloCity is four times quieter than a helicopter.

Below the crown is a cabin that appears to be a cross between a helicopter cockpit and a 1980s NASA space shuttle.

THE FIRST TIME YOU EXPERIENCE A VOLOCITY, YOU WON'T BELIEVE YOUR EARS! YES, FLYING REALLY CAN BE THIS QUIET. ALL 18 ROTORS OPERATE WITHIN A NARROW FREQUENCY RANGE, LARGELY CANCELING EACH OTHER OUT.

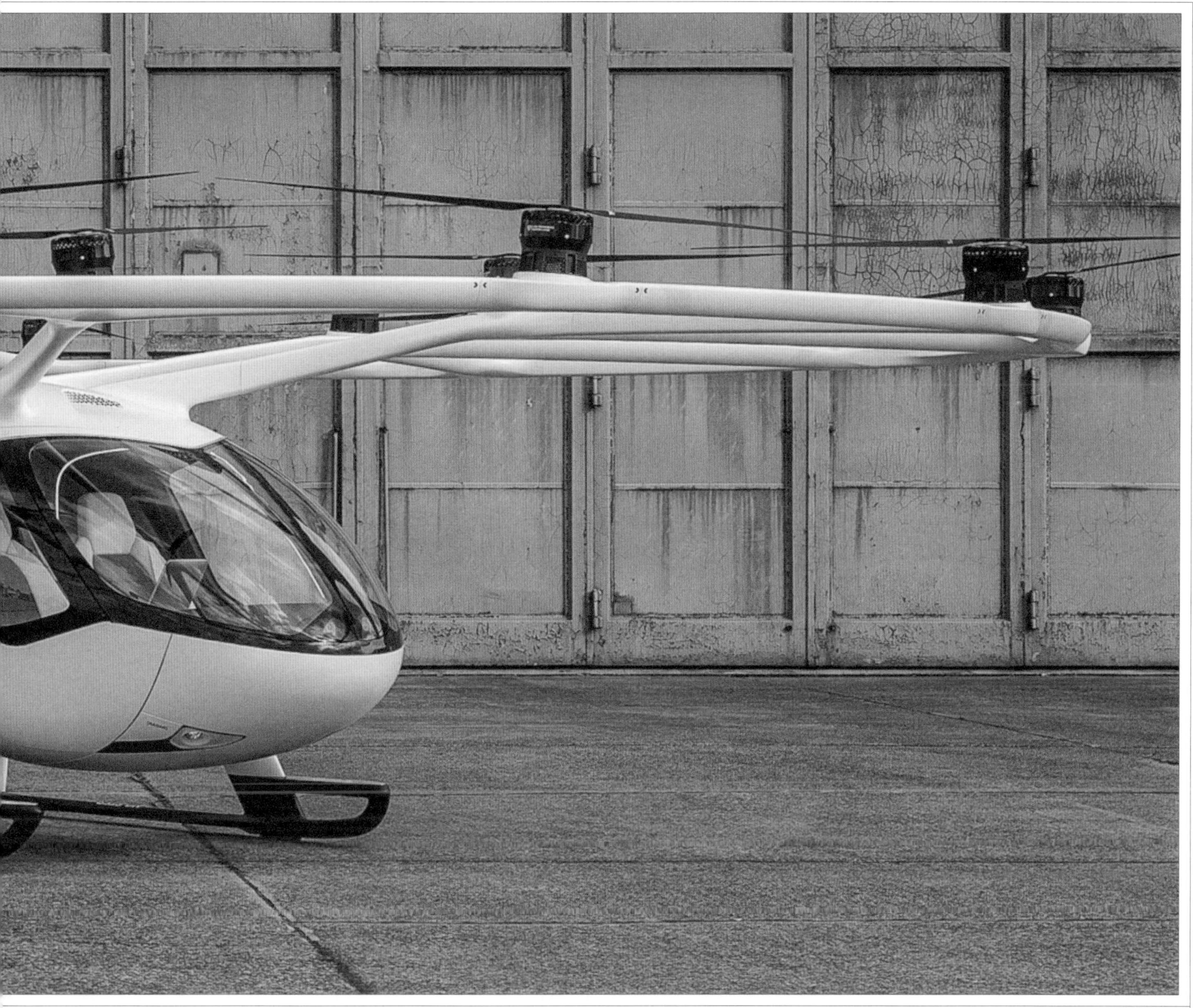

*Volocopter's VoloCity Air Taxi for commercial UAM services*

| **Max takeoff mass:** 2,205 lbs (1,000 kg) | **Max airspeed:** 54 kn (62 mph, 100 km/h) | **Diameter of rotor rim including rotor:** | **Power supply:** Battery electric, lithium-ion |
|---|---|---|---|
| **Range:** 12 mi (20 km) | **Height:** 8.9 ft (2.7 m) | 37.1 ft (11.3 m) | |

The snug compartment is as minimalistic as can be. Regardless, no one who rides a VoloCity will notice the details of the interior, thanks to the expansive windows offering panoramic views of whichever metropolis they are commuting through. The initial VoloCity will offer two seats and take passengers on journeys of up to 12 miles. Initially, one of the seats will be reserved for a pilot. Eventually, autonomous systems will ensure that two passengers can ride simultaneously. A version that will accommodate more passengers is already in the long-term pipeline. This vehicle, which will be known as the VoloRegion, aims to accommodate four passengers, transporting them over longer distances at speeds of up to 155 miles per hour.

In addition to the robust physical design of the VoloCity, Volocopter has gone all out in creating superior software. The company proudly boasts that its "state-of-the-art assistance systems and upwards of 100 microprocessors mean our VoloCity air taxis ensure exceptional stability and control." It has also developed VoloIQ, a cloud-based platform that will manage vehicle safety, including monitoring weather conditions.

Anyone who is still doubting whether or not air taxis will become a viable option in the near future should ask themselves why some of the wealthiest, most influential companies in the world, such as BlackRock, Microsoft, Toyota, and Intel, have partnered and invested in Volocopter. With backing like this, the organization stands a strong chance of achieving its world-changing goals! In addition to Paris, the VoloCity has already flown in cities as diverse as Dubai, Helsinki, and Singapore. As a New Yorker, all I can say is that I'm looking forward to the day when they're painted yellow and hovering all over Manhattan. And yes, the VoloCity has already performed a test flight in New York City, suggesting that the Big Apple will be one of the first locations to benefit from Volocopter's services. Fingers crossed that this becomes a reality sooner rather than later!

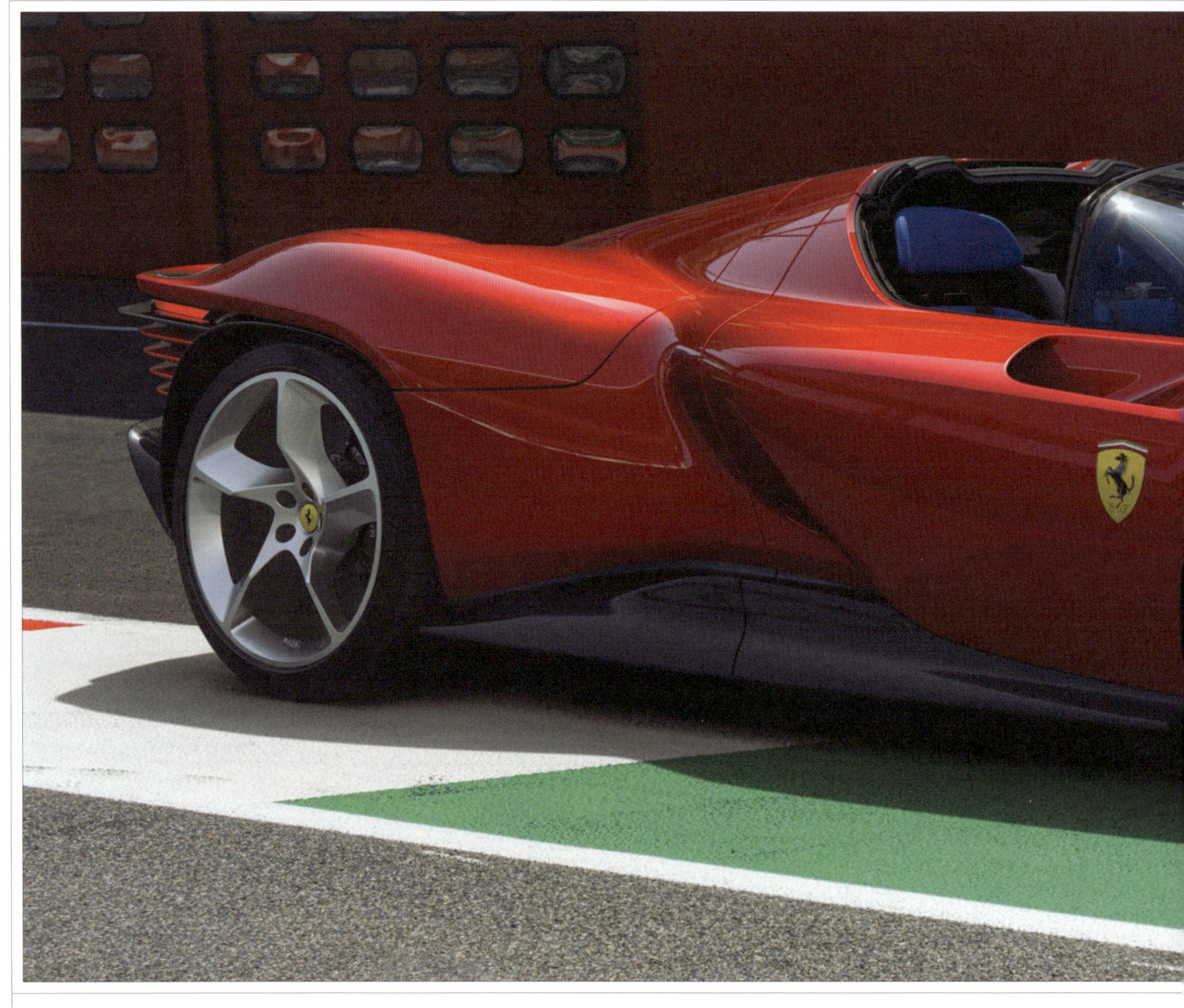

There's a risk that comes with designing any product aimed at evoking a company's golden era. It could indicate that the organization has nothing new to offer. However, anyone with even a slight knowledge of Ferrari knows this legendary automobile manufacturer is the opposite of risk-averse. The Daytona SP3 is a masterclass in showing how to highlight heritage while also soaring into the future.

1967 is remembered as a defining year in ways impossible to summarize in a single article. Over the course of February 4th, 5th, and 6th of that year alone, two landmark events took place within 100 miles of each other. In Florida, a lunar orbiter, which would take critical photographs of the Apollo Moon Landing locations, launched from Cape Canaveral, and just 60 miles to the north, the 24 Hours of Daytona racing event resulted in Ferrari vehicles clinching first, second, and third place. This feat alone would be impressive enough, yet even more astounding is the fact that two of the three finalists maintained their lead for 20 hours of the race's runtime. The Daytona SP3 takes direct inspiration from the three cars that pulled off this victory.

As a vehicle intended to evoke Ferrari's 1967 track dominance, the Daytona SP3 needed to be nothing less than stunning.

# ALTHOUGH INSPIRED BY THE RACING CARS OF THE 1960S, THE FERRARI DAYTONA SP3 IS CLOTHED IN ORIGINAL, MODERN FORMS. Ferrari

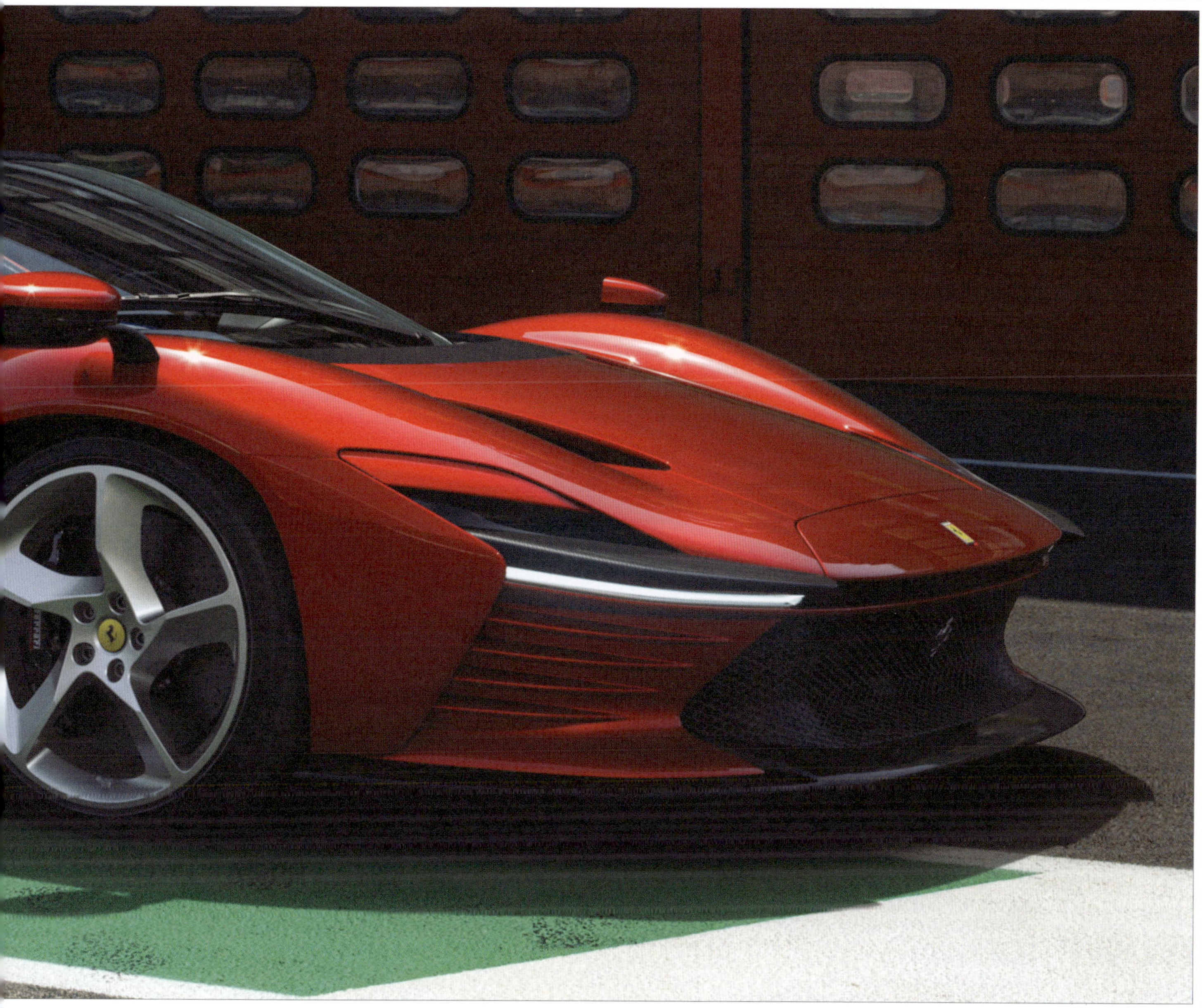

_Daytona SP3_

| | | | |
|---|---|---|---|
| **Top speed:** 211 mph (34 km/h) | in 2.85 seconds | **Max torque:** 697 Nm at 7,250 rpm | **Length:** 184.4 in (4.7 m) | **Height:** 45 in (1.1 m) |
| **Acceleration:** 0-62 mph (100 km/h) | **Engine:** V12 - 65° | **DIMENSIONS:** | **Width:** 80.7 in (2.1 m) | **Fuel tank:** 22.7 gal (86 L) |

It's impossible to deny that the finished product looks like anything other than how a Ferrari should, with its beak-like hood extending smoothly in harmony with an aerodynamic windshield and prominent cobra-neck-like backbone rear engine cover, providing that stand-out "Wow!" factor only one automobile organization on the planet can deliver with such panache.

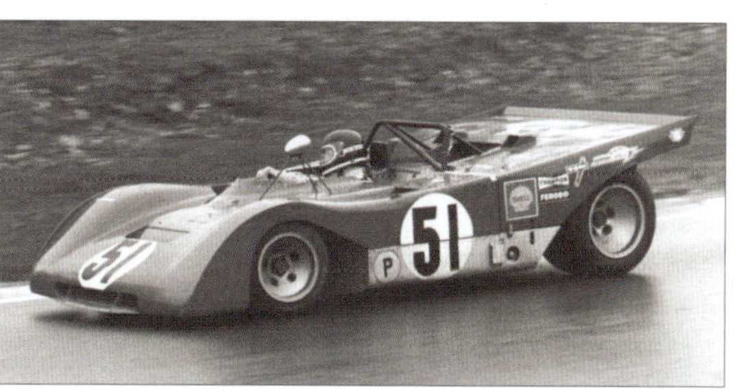

Naturally, the Daytona SP3 echoes a number of key design elements from all three of the winning 1967 vehicles. A photograph of the cars aligned at the finishing line of the race all feature slightly different iterations of that iconic cobra-neck backbone, for example. Yet the subtle modernizations that have gone into the Daytona SP3, such as its curtailed headlamps and metallic paint finish, ensure that it is a product of the 21st century. Possibly the most notable change to the exterior of the Daytona SP3 is the addition of two nostril-like hood scoop air vents, which deboss where the circular bump wings on either side of the vehicle meet the hood. This feature differs from the Daytona race vehicles that inspired the modern automobile, which all feature a large singular hood scoop. It's easy to see why this change was made. These inset nostril slits enhance the impression that the Daytona SP3 is somehow reptilian, suggesting that it may strike out with fury at any second.

Ferrari describes the exterior view of the vehicle's cabin as akin to "a dome set into a sensual sculpture with sinuous wings emerging boldly on either side." From the inside, this sensuality manifests itself in an entirely different manner. The vibrant blue seats, which are built into the chassis to enhance performance, stand in stark contrast to the red exterior, encouraging the driver to be fearless when taking their place behind the wheel. The bulky five-point harness seat belts would look silly in most cars, even the majority of sports cars. However, the clear influence of track vehicles makes this addition feel like a natural choice and works with every other feature to incite adrenaline in even the most steadfast person.

Once again, Ferrari has been unashamedly bold, and the result is yet another car that pushes the limits of sports car design.

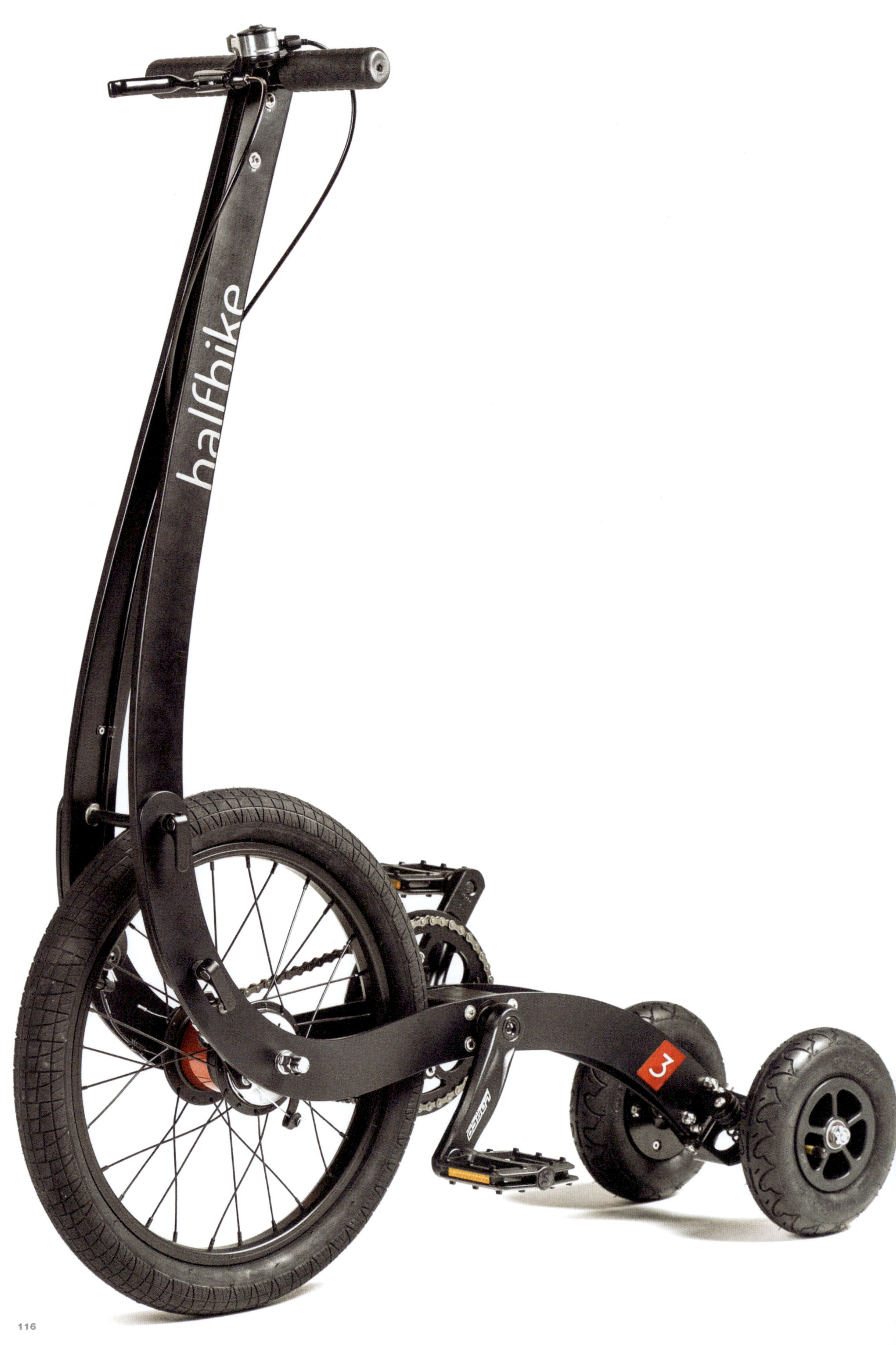
halfbike
3

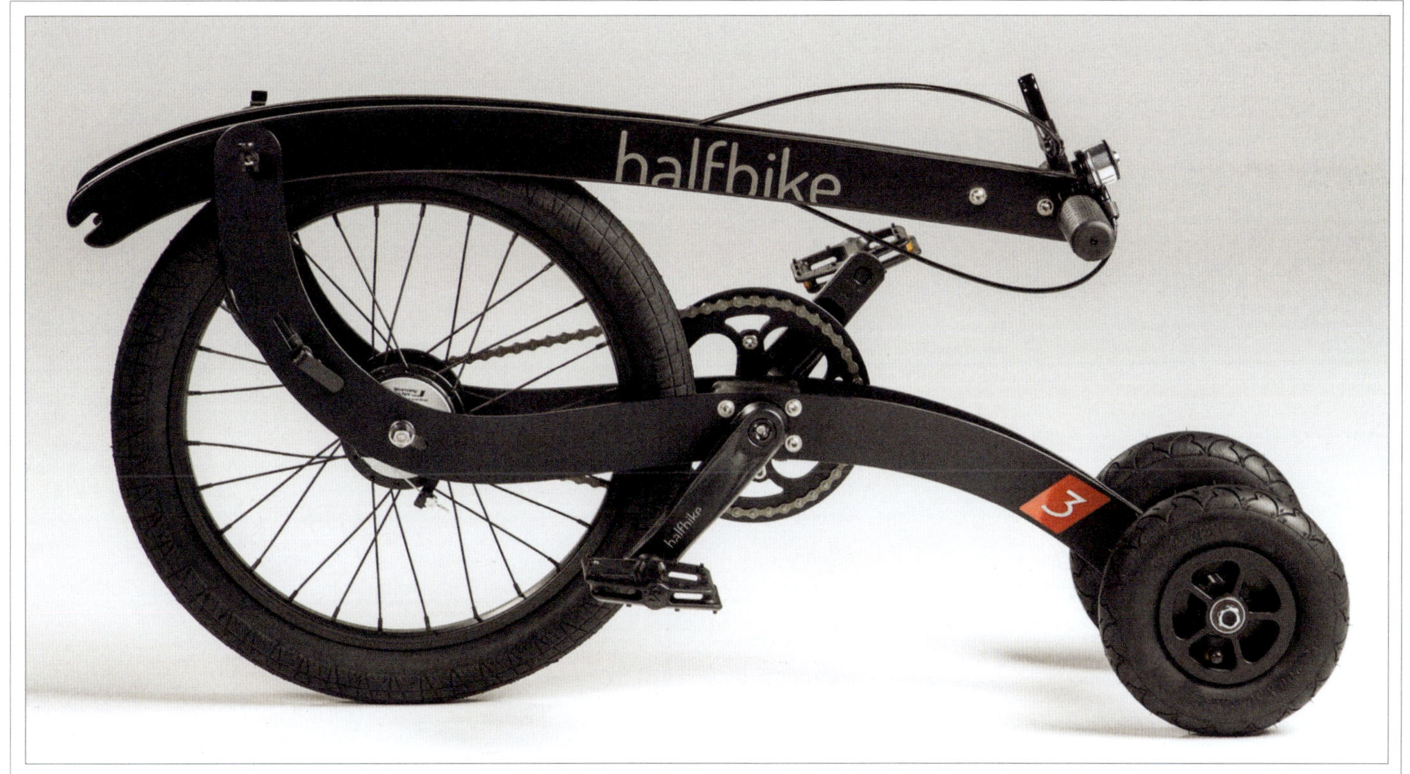

*Halfbike*

| **Material:** Aerospace-grade aluminum | **Weight:** 21 lbs (9.5 kg) | **Width:** 38 in (95 cm) |
| **Gears:** 4 | **Length:** 43 in (109 cm) | **Height:** 15.5 in (39 cm) |

The prospect of blending cycling, running, and skiing into a single product sounds extremely complex. Many would imagine a Swiss Army knife-like contraption with a wide array of complex components. The team behind the Halfbike went in the opposite direction, offering something so simple in appearance and execution that it's hard to believe no one else had previously envisioned it.

Despite the simple construction of the Halfbike's design, it does bear one significant similarity with the Swiss Army knife in that it utilizes a folding mechanism, allowing the product to be stored and carried with greater ease than standard bikes. Using the folding mechanism requires little effort, as does carrying the product, thanks to the use of aerospace-grade aluminum, resulting in a weight of just 21 pounds. This is essentially in line with typical adult bicycles sans the bulk.

The curving blades that form the body of the Halfbike reveal another simple yet impactful design difference the product utilizes. Two slender yet sturdy-looking pieces of metal resembling hockey sticks bend smoothly from the tip of the handlebars, joining with two more blades at the front wheel to form the folding mechanism. These slim strips certainly convey a more aerodynamic experience than the tubular poles most similar products employ!

In addition to structural curves, the product's learning curve is one interesting indicator of just how distinct the Halfbike is, especially when compared with the everyday bike. Halfbike describes riding the product as requiring a technique "unlike anything you've tried before." It goes on to elaborate: "In that sense, knowing how to ride a bicycle, for example, would be of little help." Instead, the Halfbike requires around 20 minutes to get to grips with the basics, with the finer details developing along the same timeframe as any well-designed item of personal transportation/exercise equipment. Perhaps these facts indicate why the Halfbike's creation took place almost 200 years after the seated bike while highlighting the spark of genius that eventually brought it into the world. Designers of pedal vehicles generally take it as a given that the product should have a seat, resulting in the same general body positioning as a bike. By taking a risk in eliminating this expected feature, the Halfbike's inventor, Martin Angelov, has opened up a whole new facet of personal transportation.

The Halfbike makes the Segway, with its motors, batteries, and AI mobility enhancements, feel hopelessly over-engineered. Even without electronic gadgetry, the Halfbike feels more modern and innovative than anything a company with numerous technology awards is currently introducing to the market. On the other end of the personal transport device spectrum, it's perfectly acceptable to start wondering if the typical seated bike design was a major step in the wrong direction, and its popularity has suppressed the development of interesting products like the Halfbike until now!

The true test of outstanding design is how a product makes the user feel. From this perspective, the Halfbike is undoubtedly leagues ahead of the competition. Without resorting to gaudy embellishments, it gives the rider a sensation of finesse just by pumping pedals and turning the body in an intuitive motion, providing an experience that feels almost like flight.

# 55% OF OUR TEAM ARE ARCHITECTS, WE HAVE ONE MAD-GENIUS PHYSICIST ONBOARD, OVER TWO-THIRDS ARE KEEN ROCK CLIMBERS, AND OUR SKI-TO-SNOWBOARD RATIO IS ABOUT 6:1.

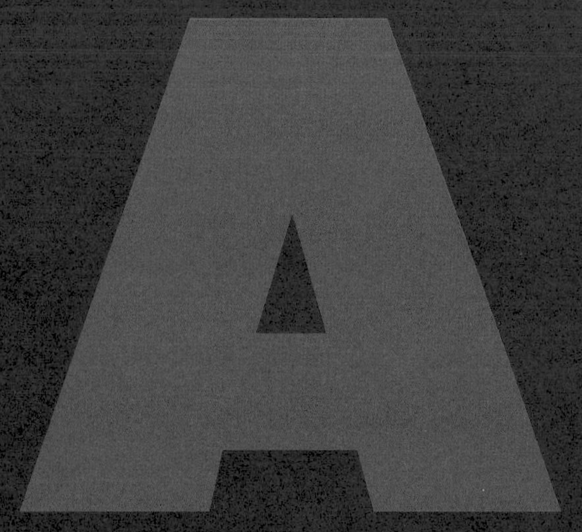


**ARCHITECTURE & EXHIBITS**

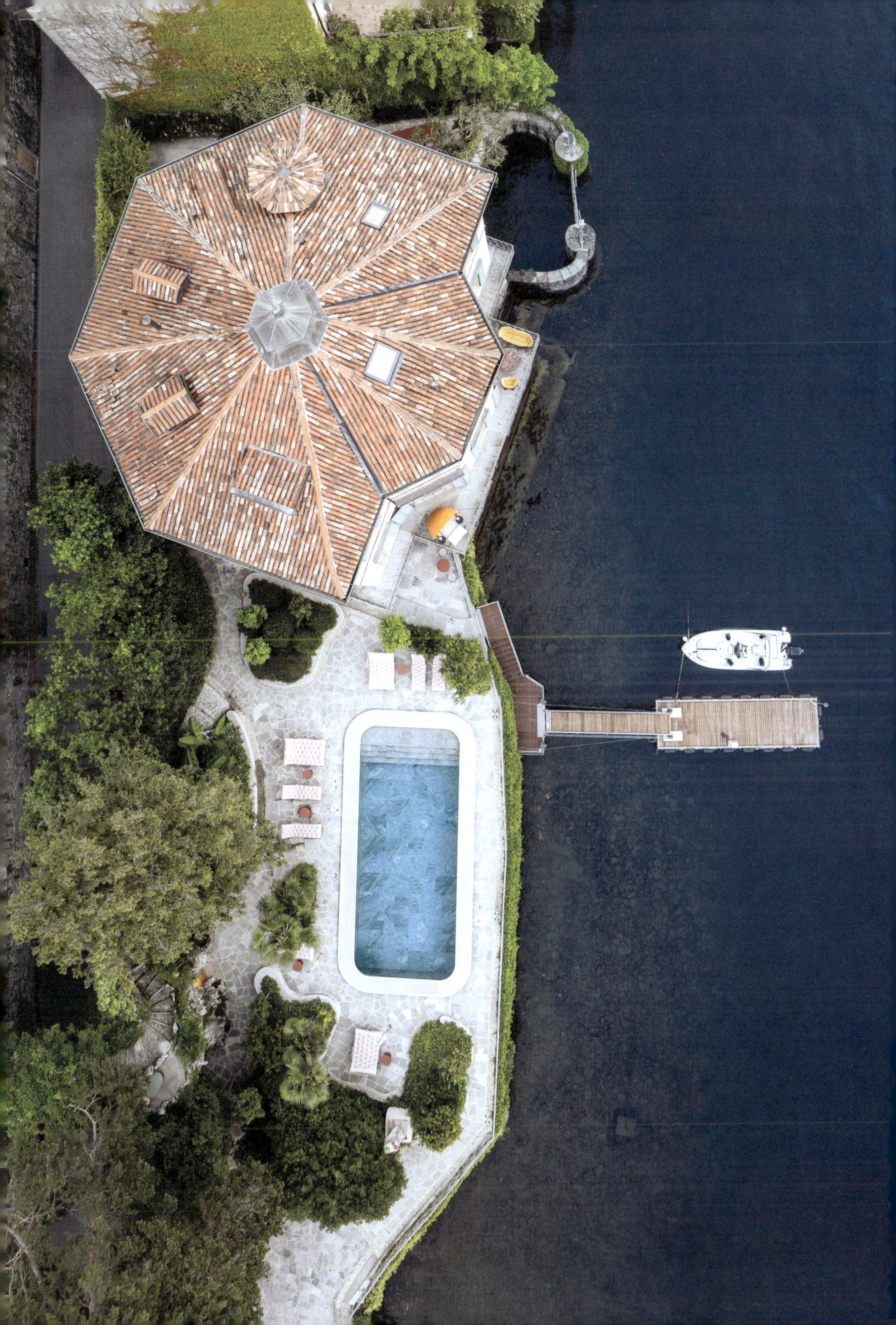

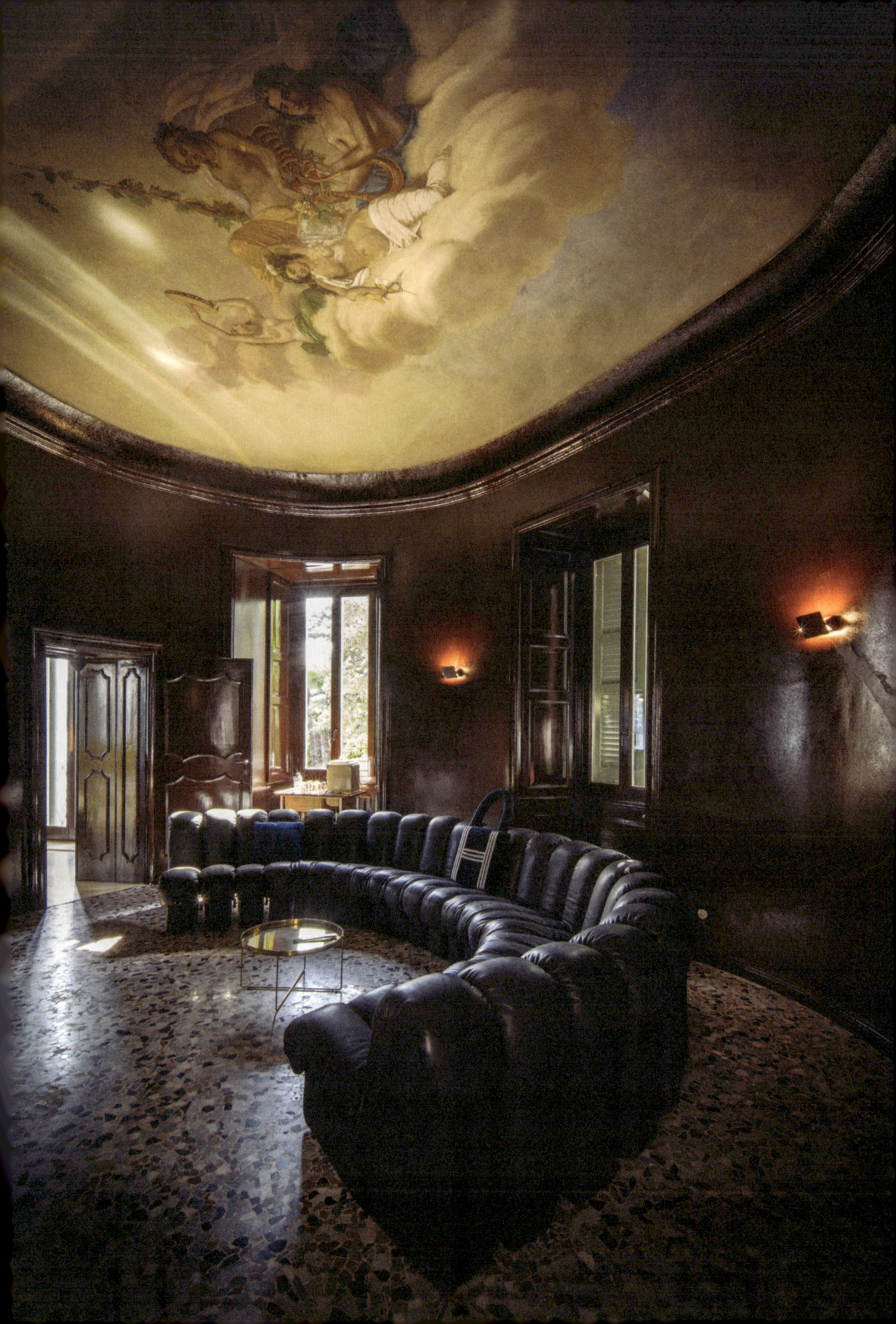

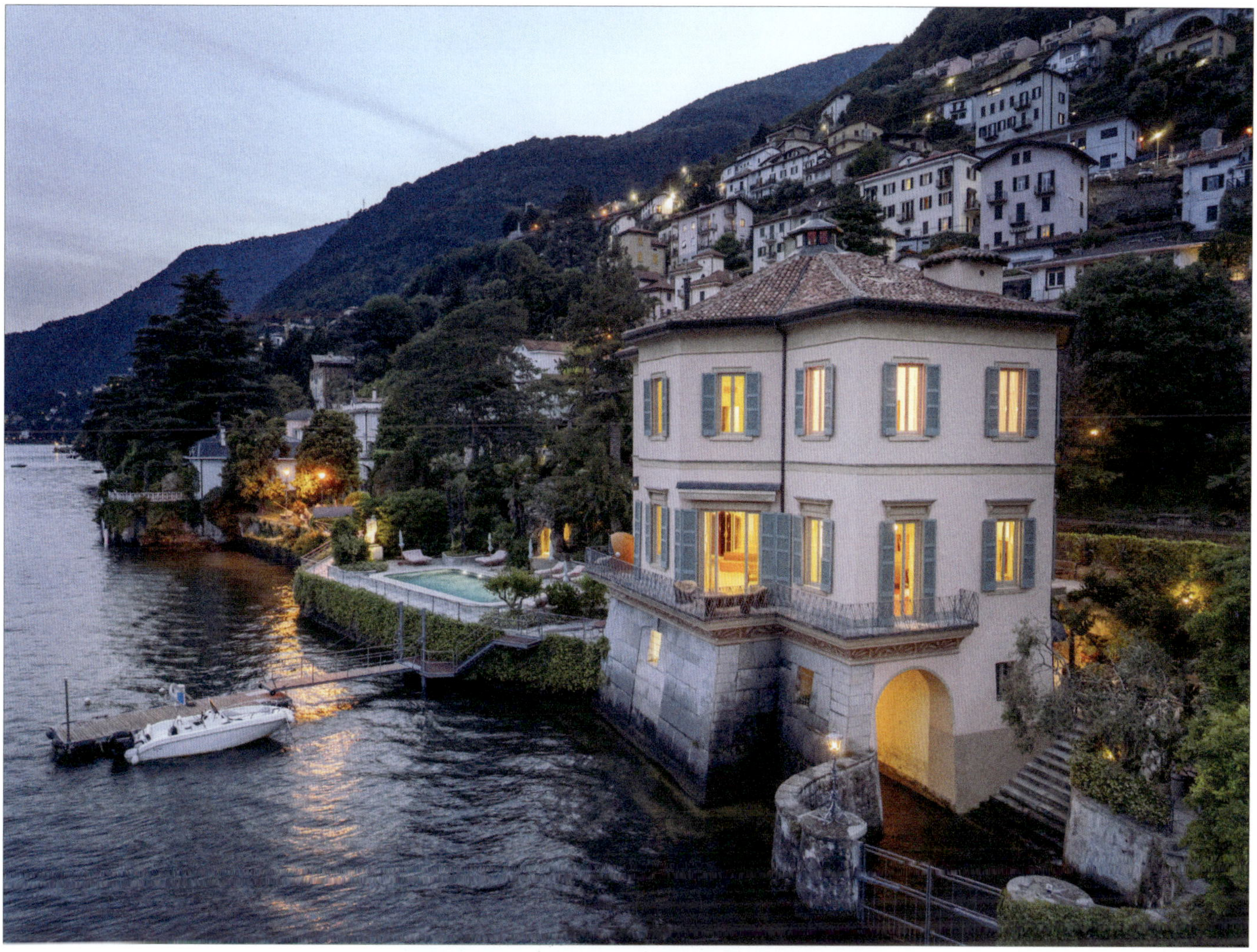

Photo: Dave Franck

The preservation efforts that went into the House on Lake Como restoration are almost as remarkable as the original structure. This 18th-century building went without a major renovation in the 19th and 20th centuries. In the 21st century, an update was finally commissioned. J. Mayer H., the architecture firm awarded the project, respected the building in ways that require detailed analysis to truly appreciate. For instance, instead of covering

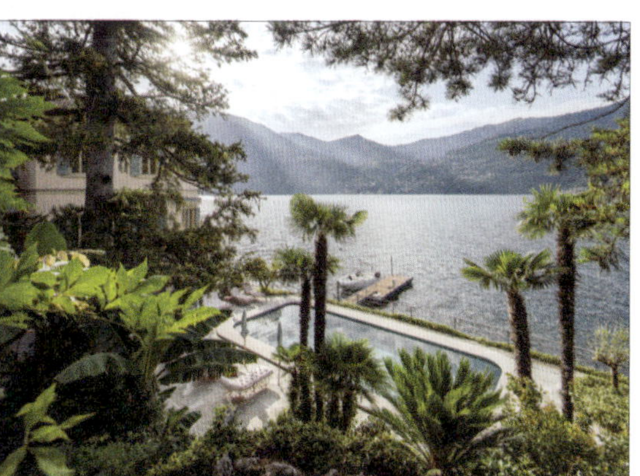

up signs of the house's age, such as cracks in the walls, the renovators chose to not only keep them visible but also decorate these surfaces with a glossy finish, making these wrinkles more distinguished.

Naturally, some new materials had to be added to the House on Lake Como. Yet, in many instances, these new additions blend into the character of the structure. One example is the marble found in the bathroom, which comprises the flooring and the square sink. Identifying these features as recent additions is somewhat easy, but they are also perfectly in keeping with the materials that would have originally been used on

houses of this era. Also, bear in mind that, eventually, time and usage will weather this material, making it harder to discern as a new addition.

The exterior had much the same treatment as the interior. The facade's original overall color was retained, while the window frames were adjusted, with new awnings and shutters added. The turquoise green used for these shutters only reinforces the building's historic integration with the surroundings, being between the shades of the lake and the surrounding wildlife. The green stone tiling added to the floor of the adjoining pool also matches these awnings, giving the overall exterior a subtle cohesion.

In an area such as Lake Como, which is dotted with numerous luxury villas, it takes something truly special to stand out. Anyone who has worked on the House on Lake Como over the last 300 years has undoubtedly contributed to the creation of an amazing structure. Part of what makes the House on Lake Como so appealing is the fact that it's essentially a celebration of the past by taking those who are lucky enough to experience it into history.

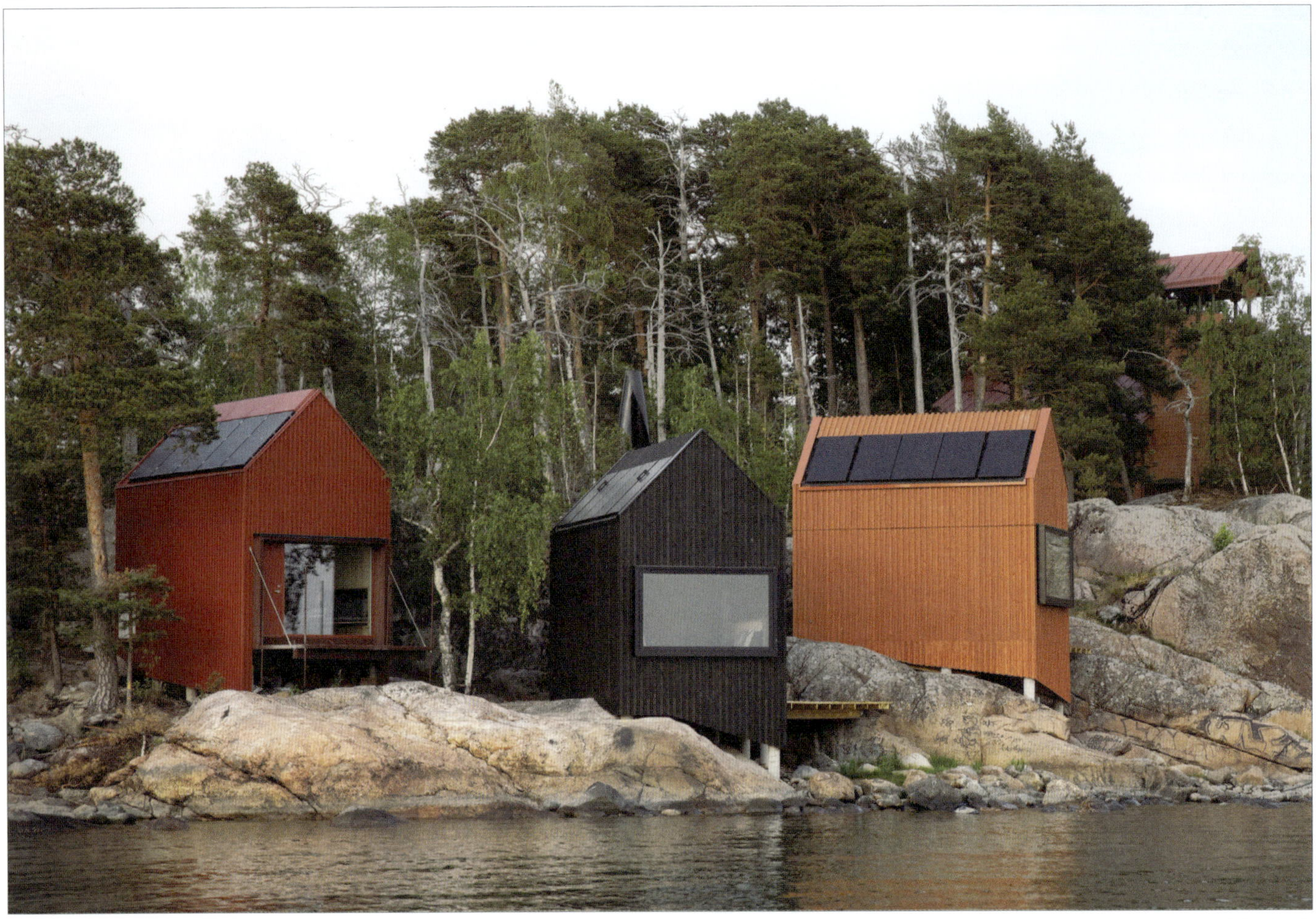

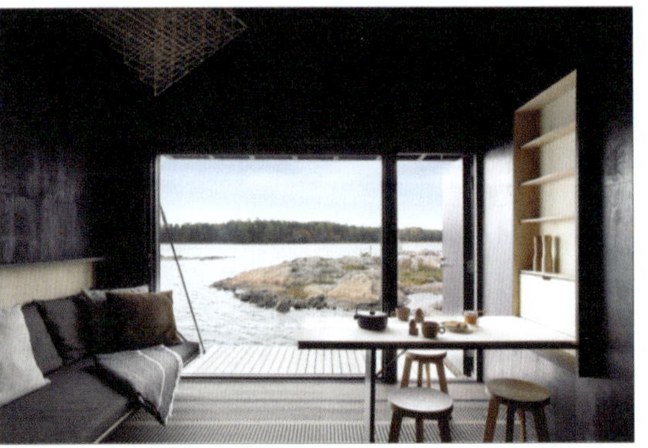

*Joonas Linkola and Chikako Harada. www.majamaja.com*

A humble arrangement of prefabricated structures in an isolated environment may just be the future of housing. Located on a remote edge of the Helsinki archipelago, the Majamaja Off Grid Village lives up to its name by being able to function entirely independently and without harming the environment. Thanks to a "patented autonomous sanitary-kitchen module, coupled with an energy storage system and a wastewater treatment system," it's possible to live here away from society, with no roads, ground sanitation, or any connection to wider civilization indefinitely.

The prefab cabins used to create this little reclusive utopia ran the risk of tarnishing their stretch of land. After all, if it appeared as if a group of dumpsters was lining the water's edge, then that would stain the village's cause. Luckily, thanks to the unique earthy tones used for each prefab, they feel at home among the trees. Their jagged alignments also ensure that the entire village flows alongside the rocks that stretch across the surrounding coast, reinforcing the idea that these cabins belong. Their pointy roofs also hint that these structures are a new species of beach hut that has evolved to this environment, adding a certain fairytale-like charm to the overall concept.

Inside these cabins, the minimalistic design is exactly the stuff of Scandinavian aesthetics. Interestingly, the carpeting and fold-down nature of the amenities also give the impression of traditional Japanese interiors. Ensuring that hygge/zen is maintained at all times are huge windows, which all provide dramatic views of the surroundings, and with waves breaking just feet away on the hard shore.

Off-the-grid living currently suffers from a certain "crackpot" conception in wider society. Could the Majamaja project make this sort of living more normalized? Anyone who can look at pictures of this community and not be swayed by the idea, even a little, must surely be lying!

# THE LONG-TERM GOAL IS TO MAKE THIS INNOVATIVE APPROACH THE TREND FOR ALL FUTURE HOUSING SOLUTIONS. AFTER TWO YEARS OF TESTING, THE FIRST MAJAMAJA MINI-VILLAGE IS NOW OPERATIONAL IN HELSINKI.

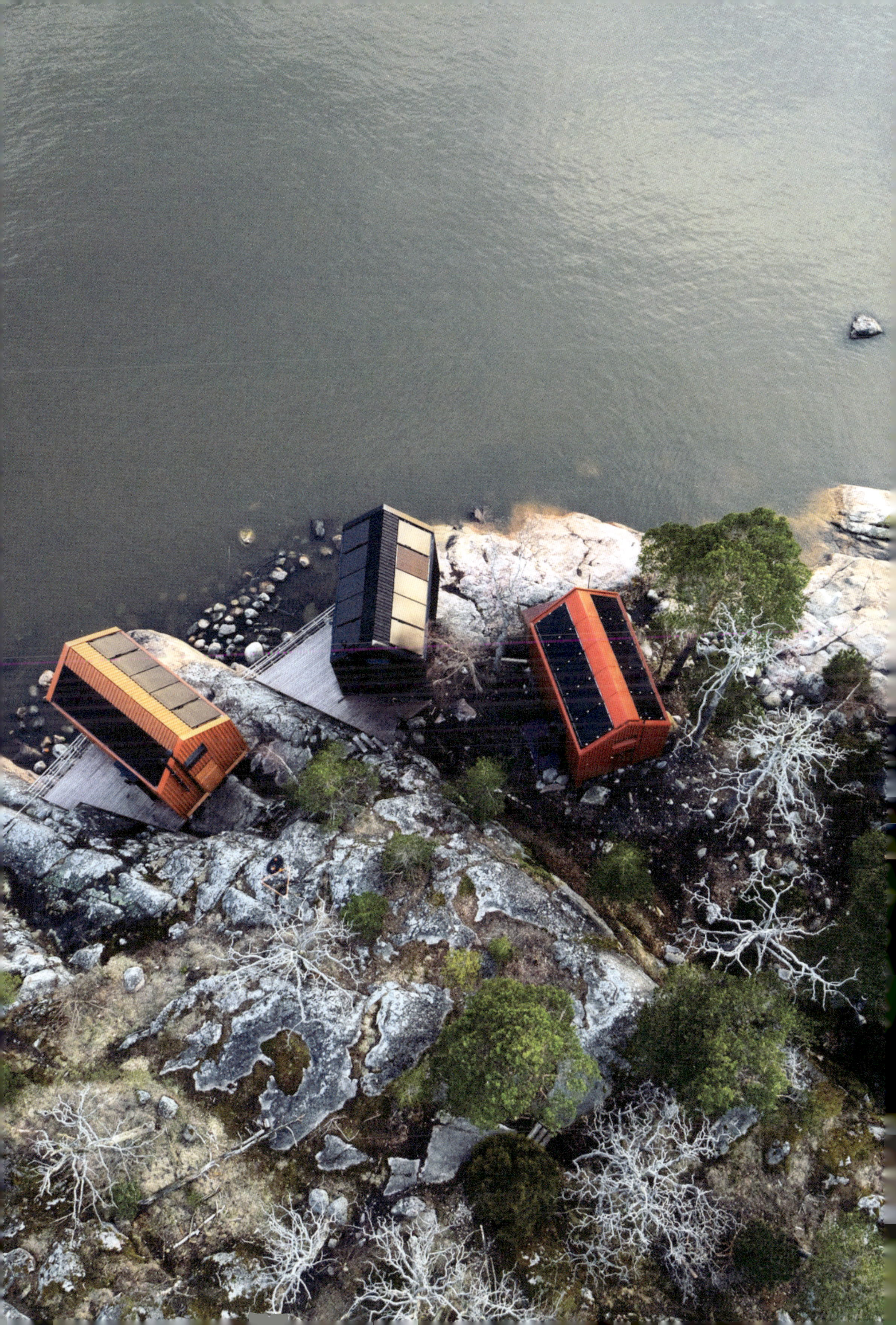

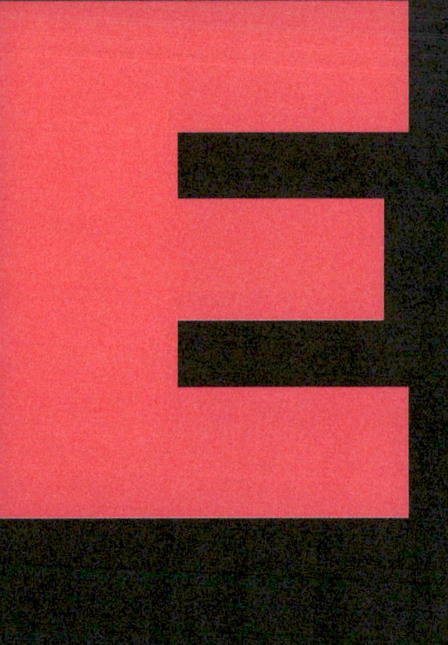

# E

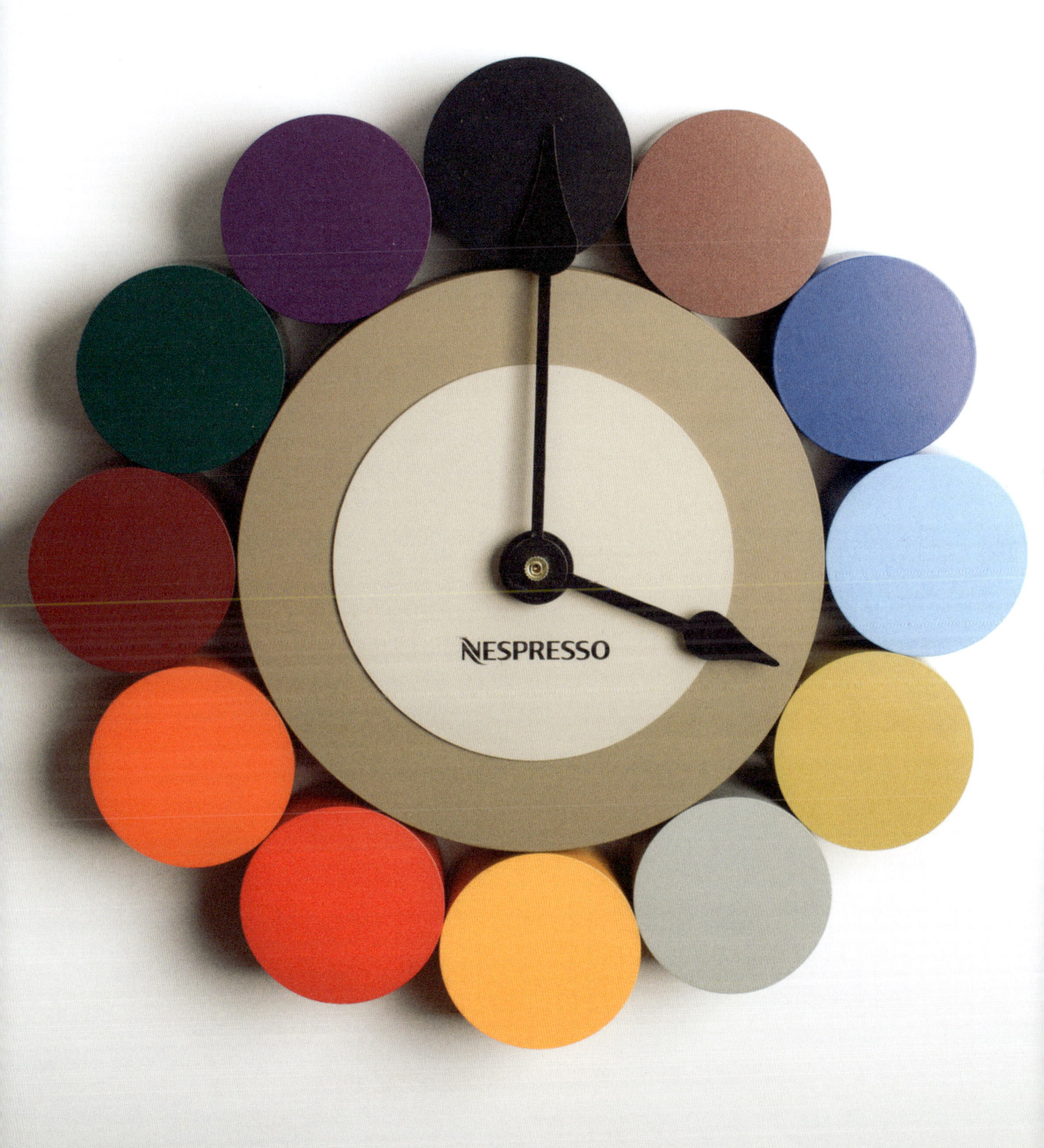

NESPRESSO

THE GIFT THAT ENABLES TOM TO GET THE VERY
BEST OUT OF HIS STUDENTS STARTS WITH
HIS INFINITE PATIENCE AND ENDS WITH HIS ABILITY
TO INSPIRE THEM WITH HIS VAST KNOWLEDGE
OF BRANDING AND CREATIVE TEACHING.

**Mary Scott,** *Director Emerita, School of Graphic Design, Academy of Art University*

THERE ARE A FEW "LEGENDS" WITHIN THE CIRCLE
OF INSTRUCTORS HERE AT THE ACADEMY,
AND TOM IS AMONG THEM. HE IS CONSISTENTLY
ONE THAT STUDENTS RECALL AS THE INSTRUCTOR
WHO HAD THE GREATEST IMPACT ON THEM.

**Hunter Wimmer,** *Professor & Associate Director, School of Graphic Design, Academy of Art University*

WHEN I THINK OF A TRUE MASTER OF BRANDING,
THOMAS IMMEDIATELY COMES TO MIND.
HE'S A LEGENDARY DESIGNER AND INSTRUCTOR
WITH THE UNCANNY ABILITY TO BALANCE
RIGOROUS STRATEGY WITH BOUNDLESS CREATIVITY.

**Fred Carriedo,** *Former Student & Staff Product Designer, TikTok Shop*

TOM MCNULTY BRINGS A LIGHT HEART AND
A KEEN EYE TO THE CLASSROOM DAILY, IGNITING
A PASSION FOR DESIGN IN HIS STUDENTS.

**Mary Rauzi,** *Former Student & Founder, Embr Creative*

*Backhouse, New Talent Annual 2017. Professor: Thomas McNulty. Platinum-winning student: Yuya Yoshida*

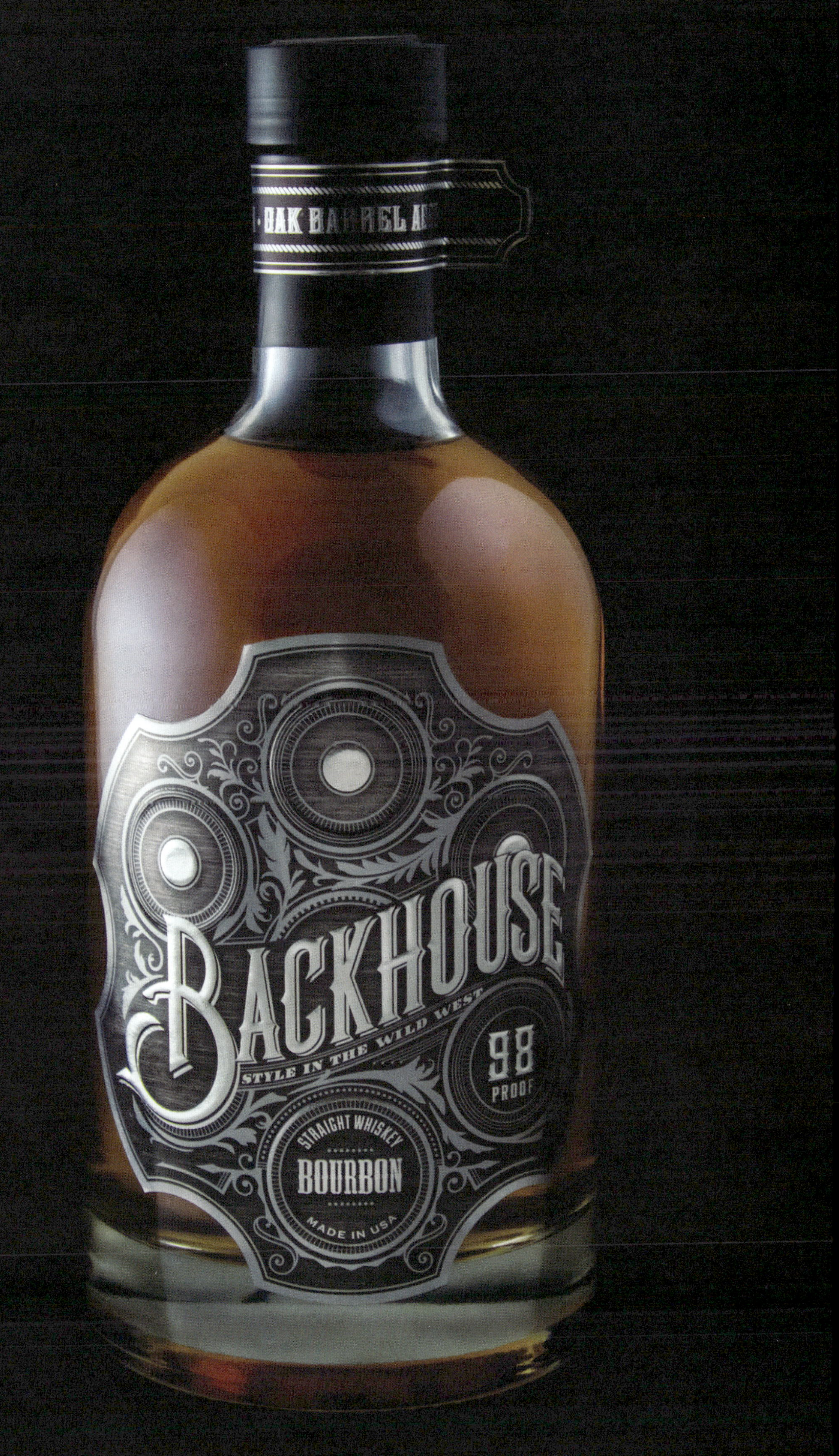

OAK BARREL AG
BACKHOUSE
STYLE IN THE WILD WEST
98 PROOF
STRAIGHT WHISKEY
BOURBON
MADE IN USA

As the executive director of the School of Graphic Design at the Academy of Art University, I am truly honored to have Thomas McNulty as a cornerstone of our faculty. Over the years, he has taught numerous branding and packaging courses, sharing his vast design expertise and genuine passion for mentoring students. His dedication to teaching has helped many of his students launch extraordinary careers, working for renowned brands like Starbucks, Amazon, and TikTok. Tom's ability to inspire creativity and guide students toward success has enriched our program and helped maintain its reputation as one of the most respected in the field. His unwavering commitment to our school and students makes him an exceptional educator and a cherished member of our faculty.

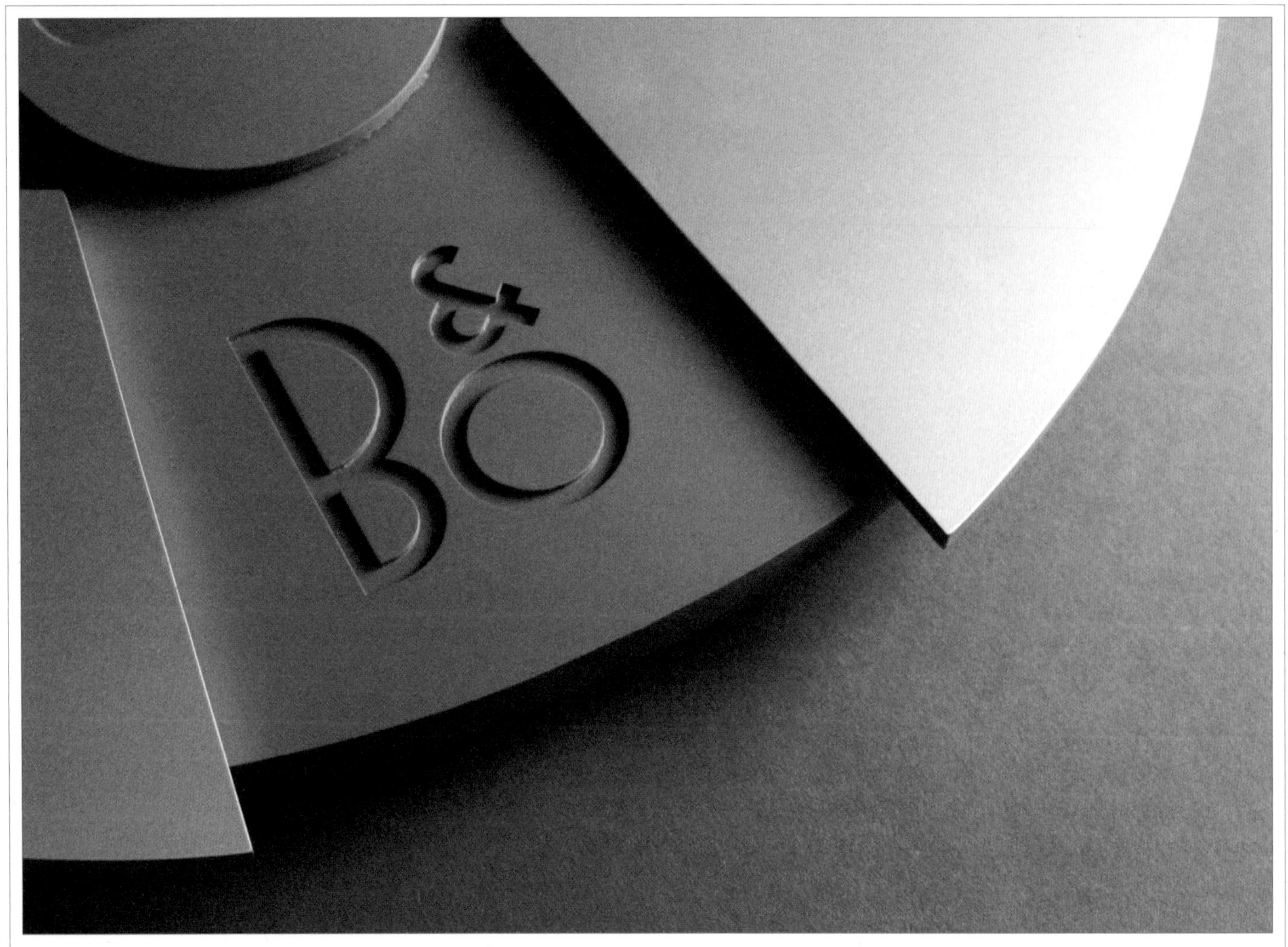

*Pluto by Bang & Olufsen, New Talent Annual 2012. Professor: Thomas McNulty. Gold-winning student: Karen Liong*

# TOM'S POSITIVE IMPACT ON STUDENTS WITH HIS REAL-LIFE DESIGN ASSIGNMENTS CREATES SIGNIFICANT LEARNING MOMENTS IN GRAPHIC DESIGN EDUCATION.

**Troy Alders,** *Professor, School of Graphic Design, Academy of Art University*

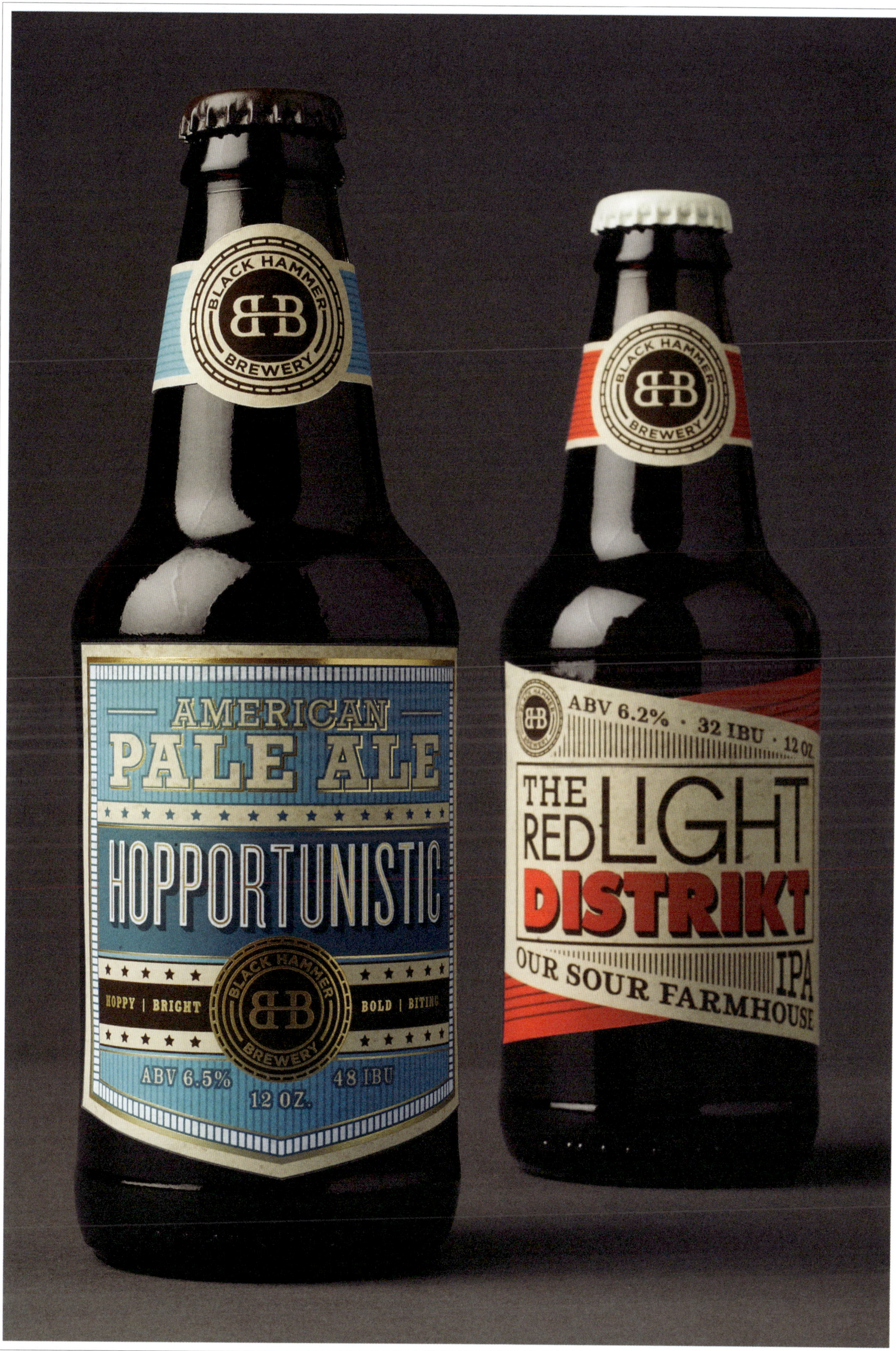

BLACK HAMMER
BREWERY
AMERICAN
PALE ALE
HOPPORTUNISTIC
BLACK HAMMER
BREWERY
HOPPY | BRIGHT
BOLD | BITING
ABV 6.5%
12 OZ.
48 IBU

BLACK HAMMER
BREWERY
ABV 6.2% · 32 IBU · 12 OZ.
THE
RED LIGHT
DISTRIKT
OUR SOUR FARMHOUSE
IPA

*What is your process for selecting students for your classes? Are there specific qualifications they have to meet?*
The Academy of Art University requires a no-portfolio policy to apply. That said, some students attending the university may have some art or design training, while others do not. In either case, this makes the job especially interesting as an educator when trying to help students define their path to becoming successful graphic designers.

*Is there anything that would make you turn down a prospective student?*
No. My role as an educator is to help students sharpen the skills necessary for them to enter the job market with an outstanding portfolio. I remind students that agencies look for designers who think strategically, are problem-solvers, and understand the design process when they graduate.

*Have you ever dismissed a student from your class? If so, for what reason?*
No. As an educator, I never had to dismiss a student from any classes. Maybe luck? I believe if you set the expectations and standards required in class at the start of each semester, you can stop a situation from happening. Keep it simple: Mutual respect, a willingness to learn, and professionalism go a long way in the class.

*What might be a typical first assignment?*
This depends on the nature, subject, and course. I prefer to give assignments based on process and problem-solving methods. For example:
- Provide a clear lesson plan that clarifies the course expectations and course learning outcomes (CLO).
- Require students to conduct in-depth and comprehensive research.
- Require students to create a written design strategy plan.
- Require students to explore and create visual mood boards.
- Require students to create ideation sketches.
- Require students to execute a final project.

*Do you ever have students work on assignments for real clients?*
Yes. I believe allowing students to work and interact with a real client provides excellent learning outcomes and experience while in school. Students learn that teamwork, collaboration, and communication with their peers are invaluable skills when preparing for the job market.

*Do you ever ask them to include something they're passionate about in their work for your class?*
Periodically, I get a student who is passionate about drawing or illustration and wants to incorporate this skill into their final assignment. In this case, I encourage the idea of adding illustration work to their graphic design work. Sometimes, it proves successful; other times, it might be best to collaborate with a student illustrator for better outcomes. If an assignment requires photography, the same may apply. Working with a student photographer might also be the best option moving forward.

What has come into the conversation more and more these days is AI imaging. Instructors are now encouraged to get students to explore the visual opportunities available to help broaden their use of photography or illustration skills. The university now offers courses that support the use of AI imaging capability.

*Do you work with students individually or in groups?*
I work in both scenarios for different reasons… When conducting a class critique, I tend to work in groups where I have students present the work and then receive input and comments from their peers. I like to select individuals to comment on the work and create discussion topics. Conducting individual assessments will depend on the class size and nature of the assignment.

*How do you develop and raise your students' visual awareness?*
I start by encouraging students to get out and explore their surroundings, especially the city of San Francisco. The city offers a rich culture of design, music, museums, libraries, architecture, and nature to raise awareness. Another exercise I conduct in class that helps raise students' visual awareness occurs in my packaging courses. Each week, I ask students to bring an effective and/or ineffective package design to discuss with the class. This exercise raises awareness of 3D thinking and creates a dialogue around package and structural design.

*How do you develop and raise your students' verbal standards?*
One challenging area for most students is speaking in front of a classroom and presenting their work or design strategies. Cue cards and rehearsing are great ways to help prepare important points they want to communicate to the class when presenting. I also point out that communicating an idea (verbally) is just as important as the work itself.

*What percentage of a typical class goes on to create award-winning work?*
I can't be exact on the percentage. I can tell you that students from the Academy of Art University's School of Graphic Design program win more award competitions year after year in design. Speaking from the advanced-level courses I teach in packaging or branding at the university, our graduates continue to produce award-winning agency work.

*What kind of advice do you give your class at the end of the semester?*
Believe in yourself and be passionate, and success will follow.

*Can you name a few of your past students who have gained success? If so, what are they doing now?*
Most of our graduates go on to become successful graphic designers once they enter the job market. One student, Fred Carriedo, has gained great success in the industry. Fred's success includes lead design for Starbucks, Amazon, Wayfair, and Walmart. His design work extends across so many successful brands in the marketplace.

*What attracted you to teaching at your current school?*
What attracted me most about teaching at the Academy of Art University was the reputation, leadership, and mentorship of Mary Scott, the director emerita of the School of Graphic Design. When I joined the department 22 years ago, I knew that joining forces as the associate director and educator would be a great adventure for teaching so many students. Thank you, Mary Scott!

**Thomas McNulty, Academy of Art University**
www.academyart.edu/art-degree/graphic-design/faculty

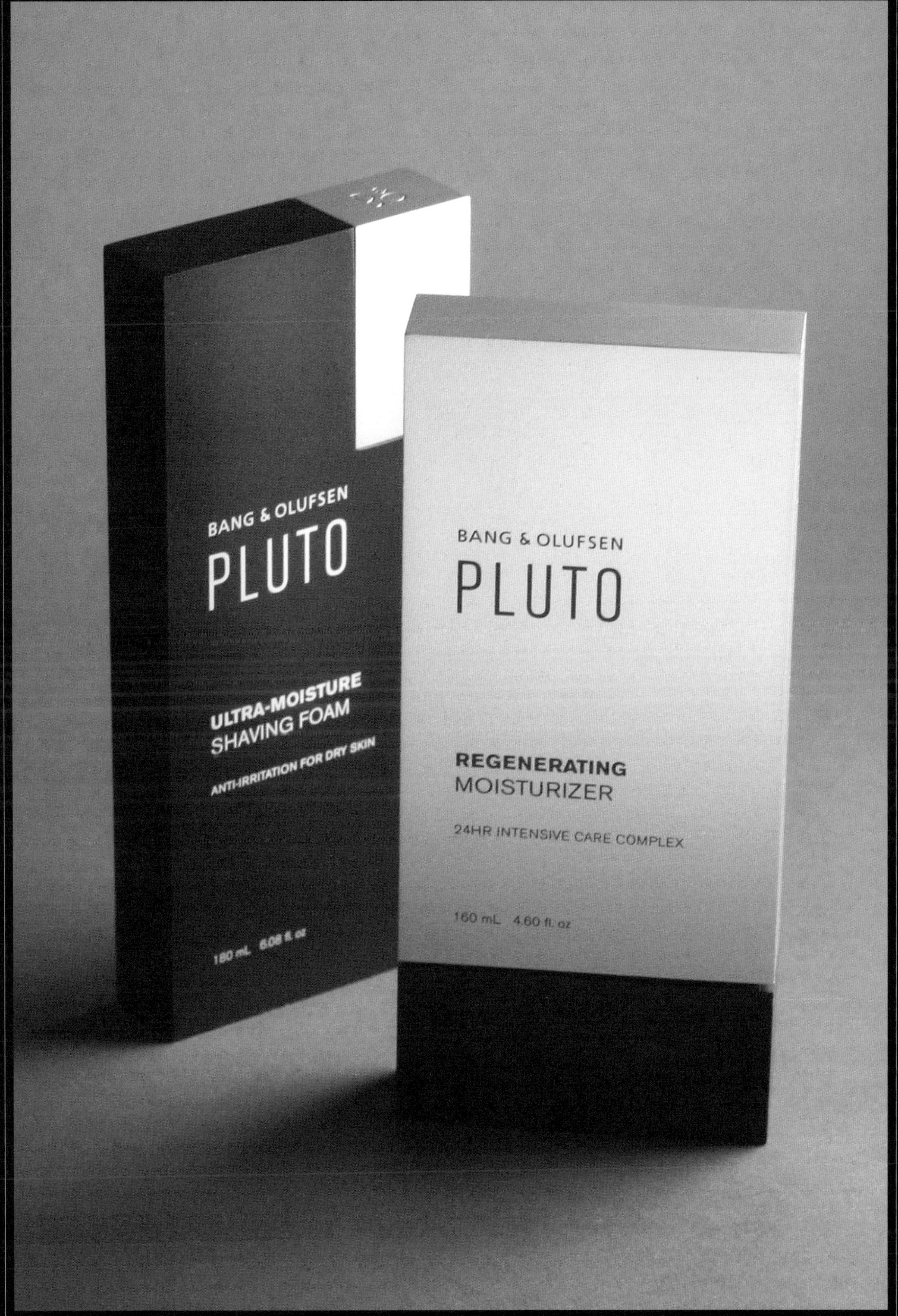

*Pluto by Bang & Olufsen, New Talent Annual 2012. Professor: Thomas McNulty. Gold-winning student: Karen Liong*

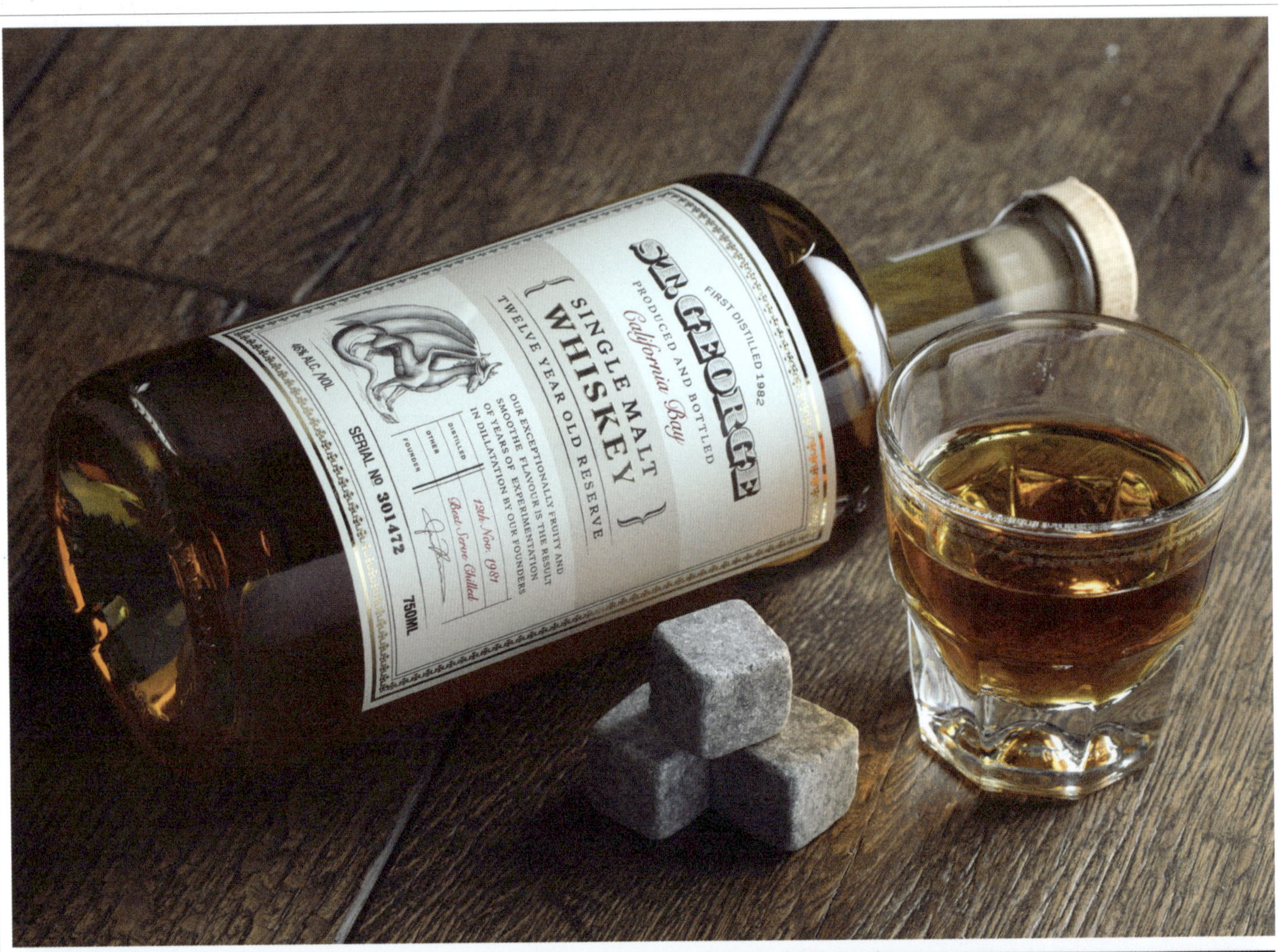

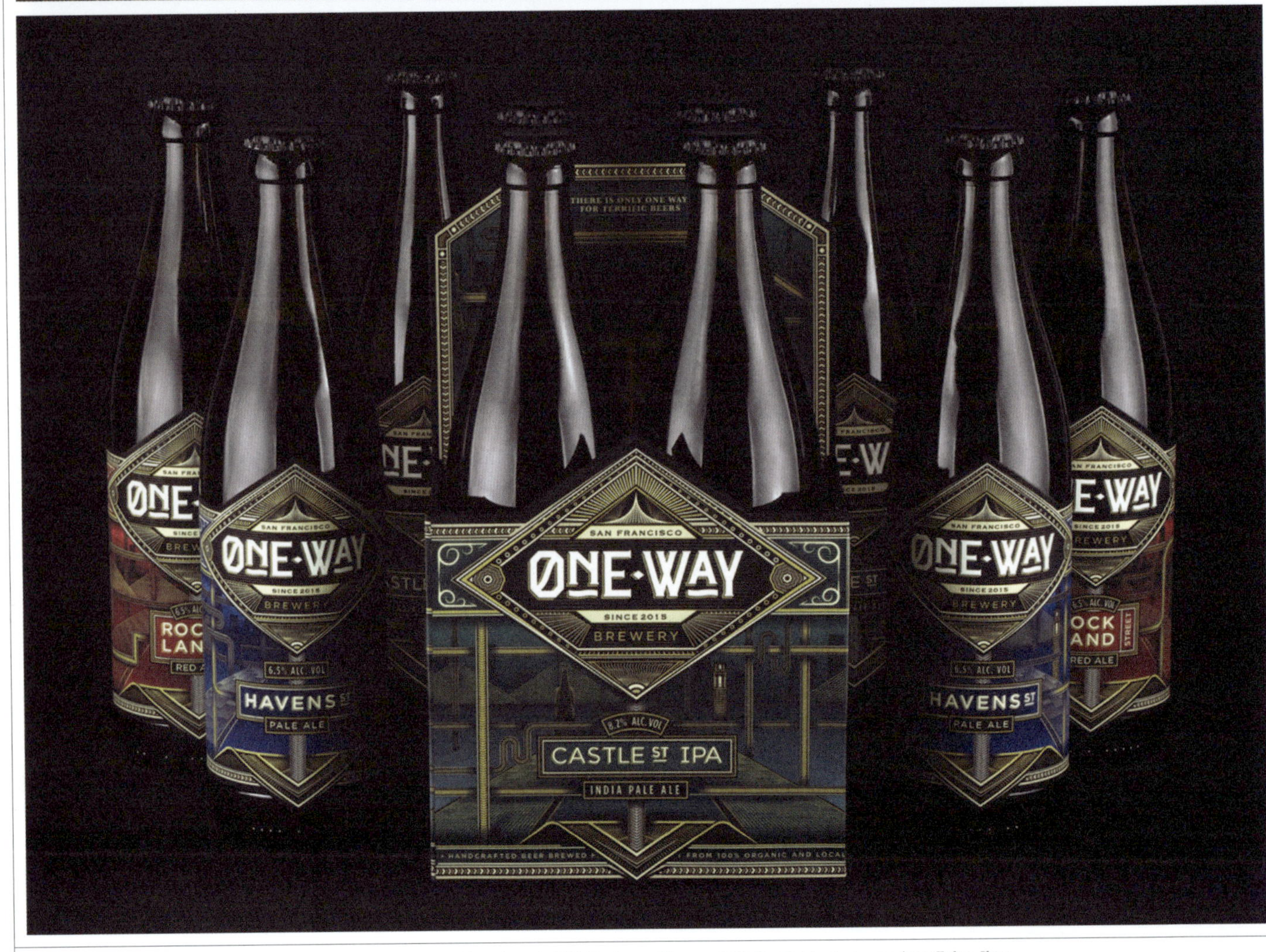

*St. George Whiskey, New Talent Annual 2018. Professor: Thomas McNulty. Gold-winning student: Zahra Ilyas*
*One Way Beer, New Talent Annual 2017. Professor: Thomas McNulty. Gold-winning student: Jacob Bang*

**Alireza Jajarmi,** *Former Student & Lead Brand Designer, Humane*

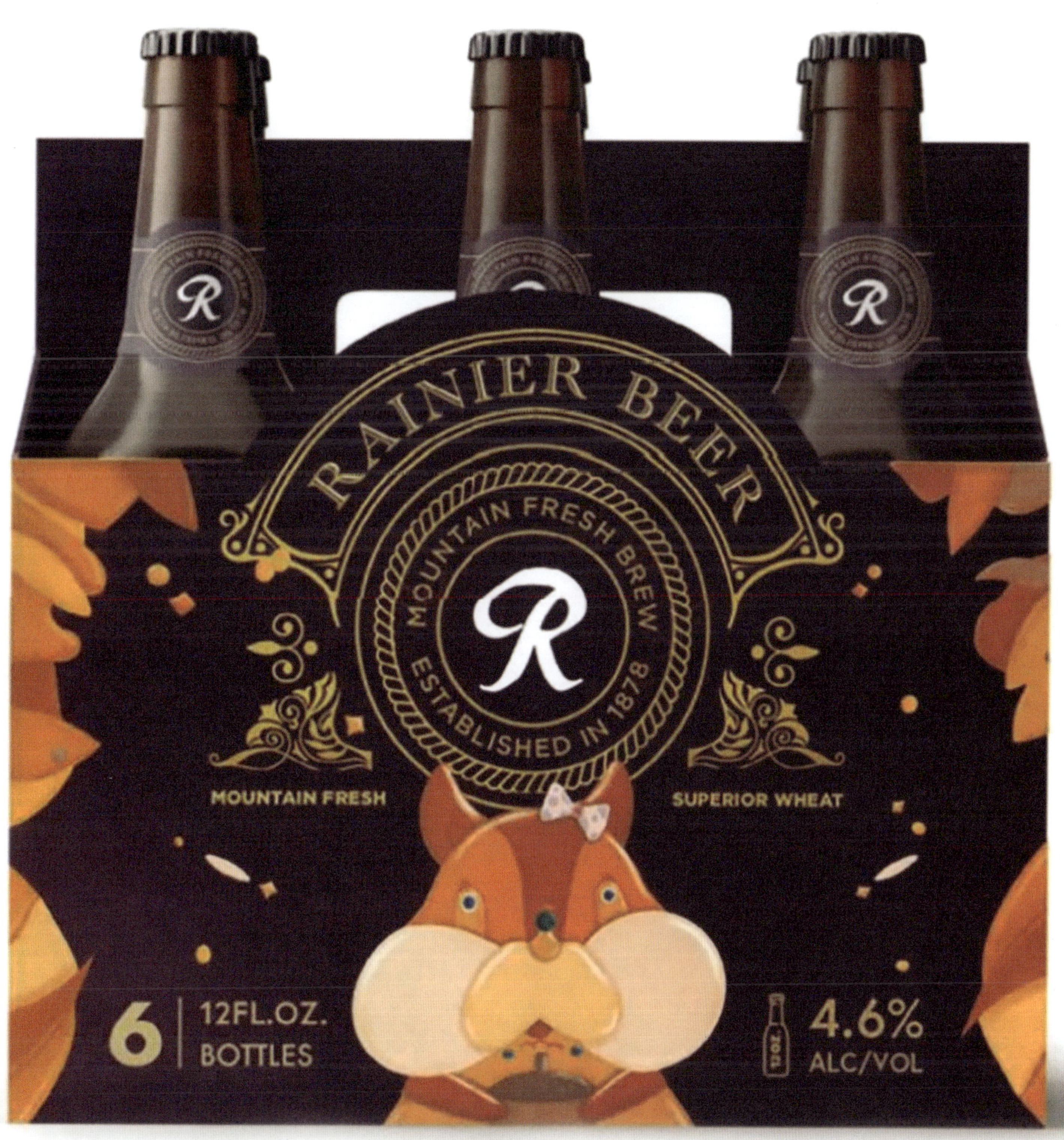


*Rainier Beer, New Talent Annual 2025. Professor: Thomas McNulty. Gold-winning student: Sissi Chen*

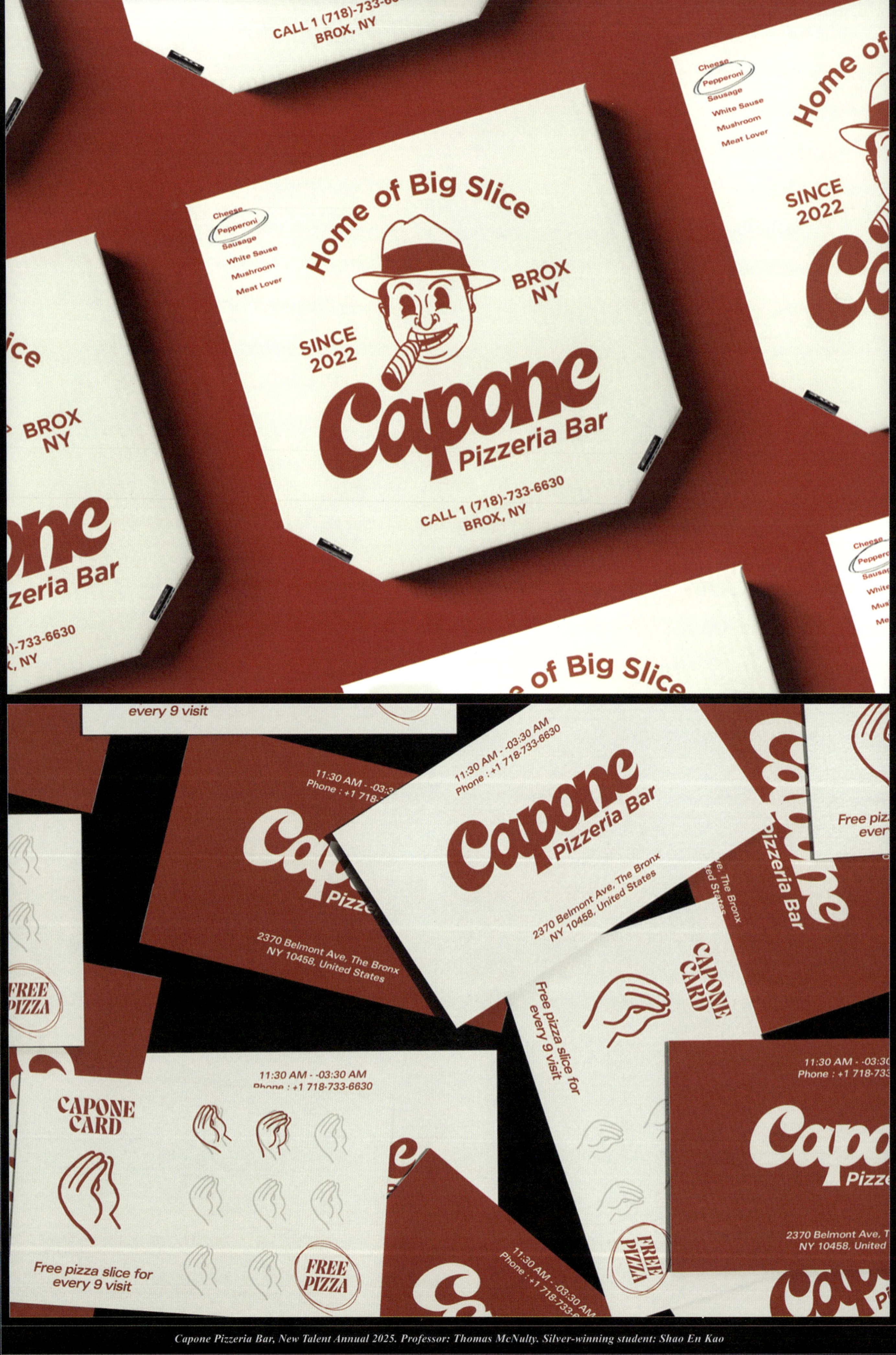


*Capone Pizzeria Bar, New Talent Annual 2025. Professor: Thomas McNulty. Silver-winning student: Shao En Kao*

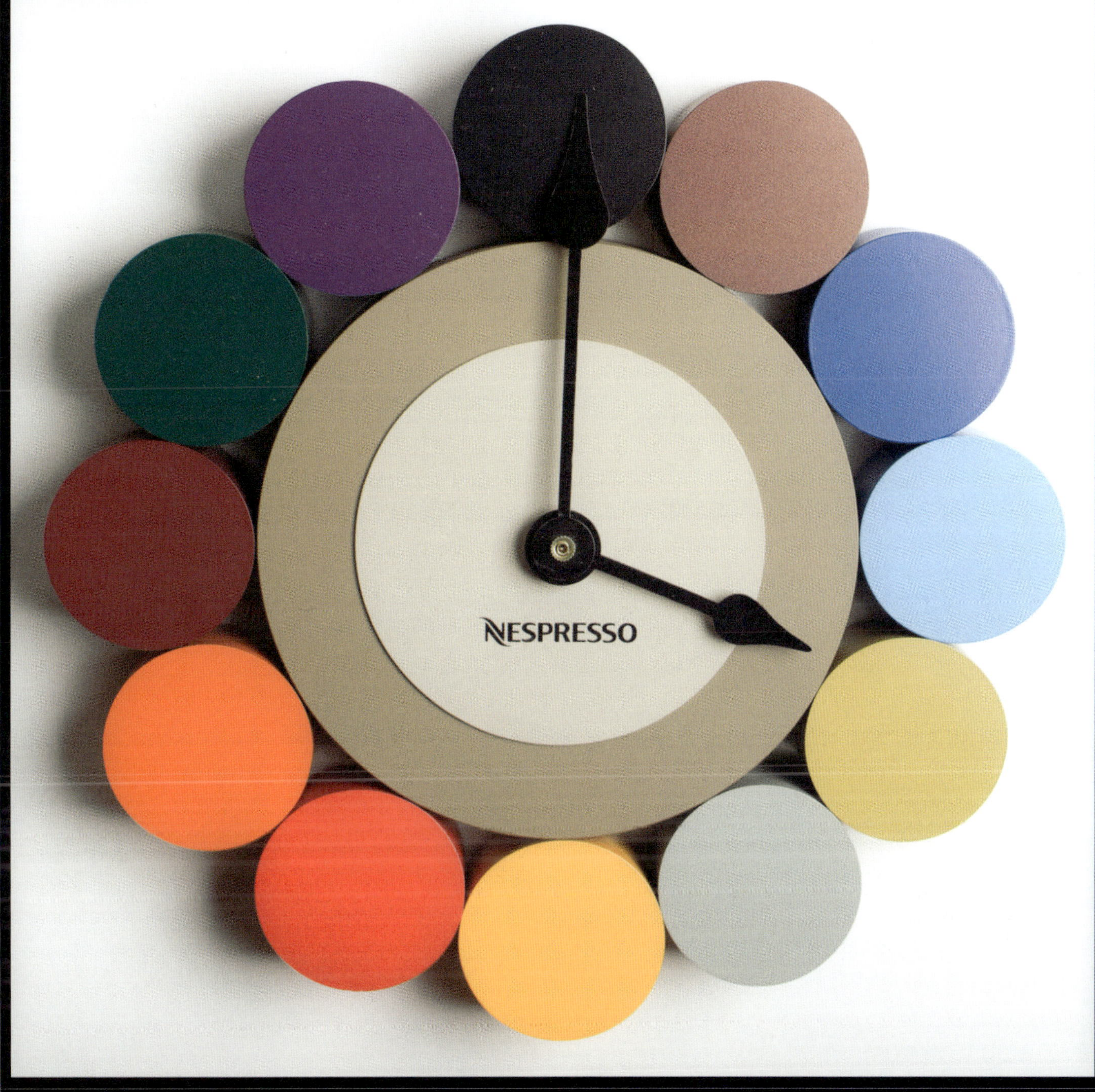

*Nespresso Clock, New Talent Annual 2017. Professor: Thomas McNulty. Gold-winning student: Moonyonng Ro*

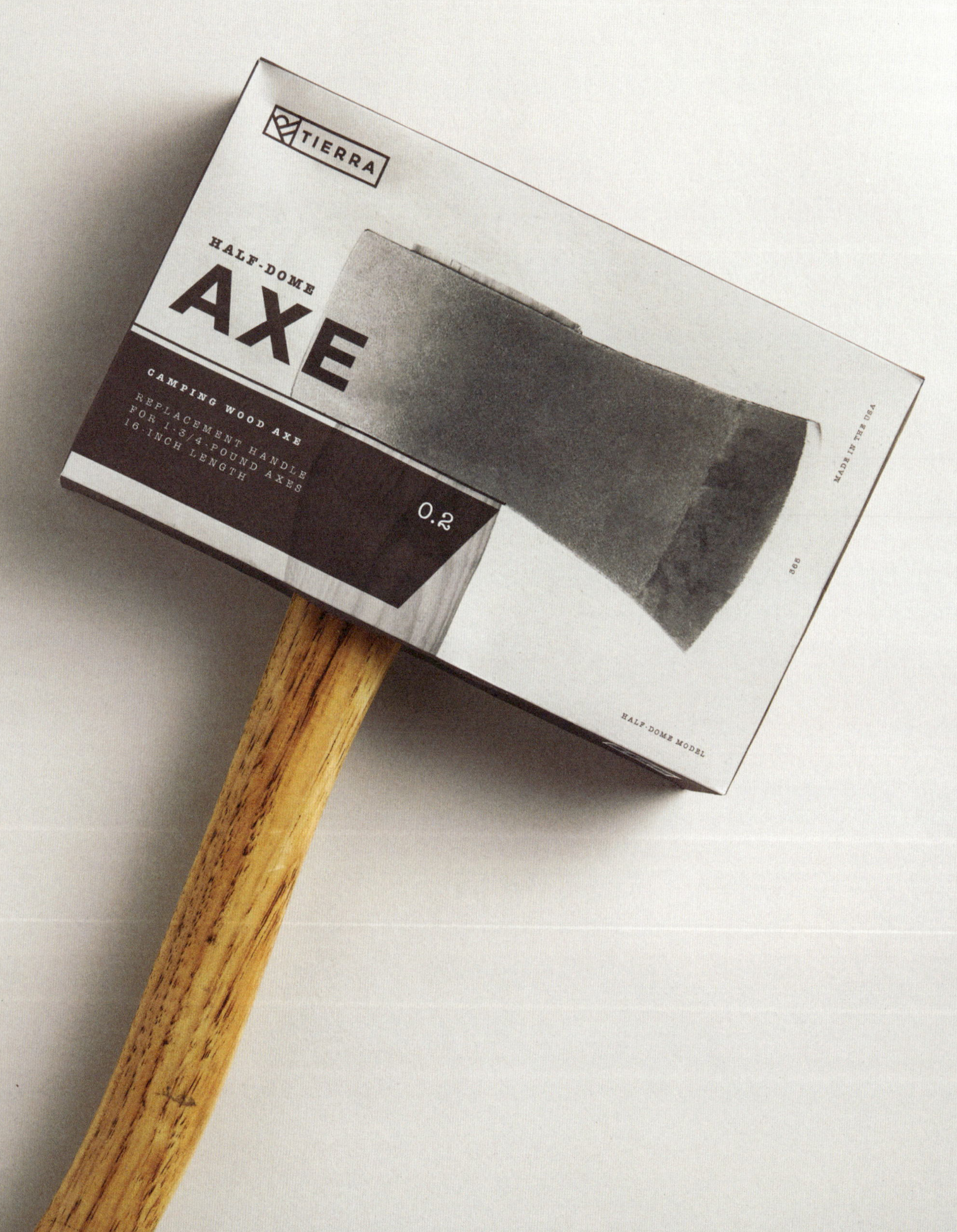

TIERRA
HALF-DOME
AXE
CAMPING WOOD AXE
REPLACEMENT HANDLE
FOR 1-3/4-POUND AXES
16-INCH LENGTH
0.2
MADE IN THE USA
365
HALF-DOME MODEL

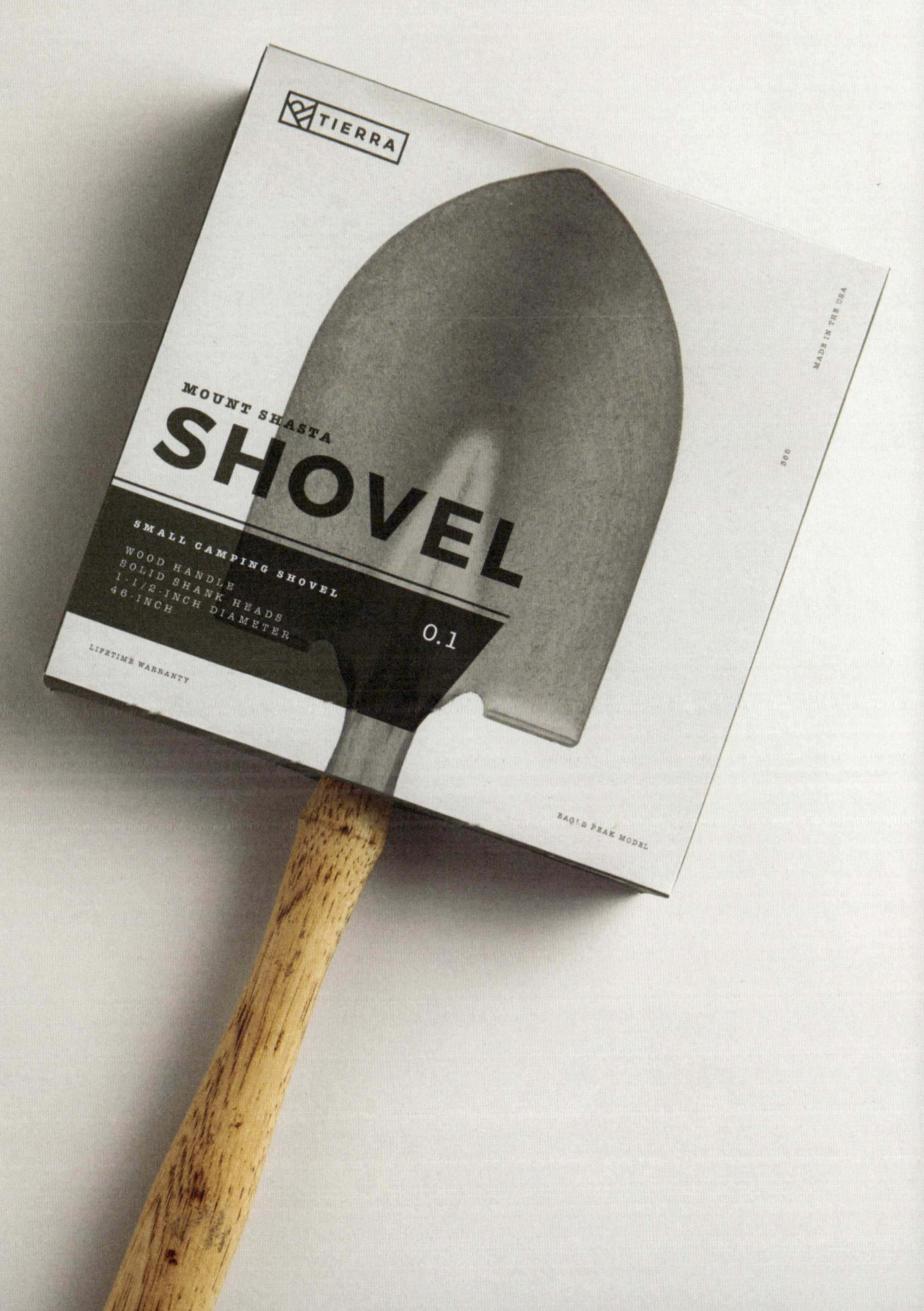

TIERRA
MADE IN THE USA
MOUNT SHASTA
SHOVEL
SMALL CAMPING SHOVEL
WOOD HANDLE HEADS
SOLID SHANK HEADS
1-1/2-INCH DIAMETER
46-INCH
0.1
LIFETIME WARRANTY
EAGLE PEAK MODEL

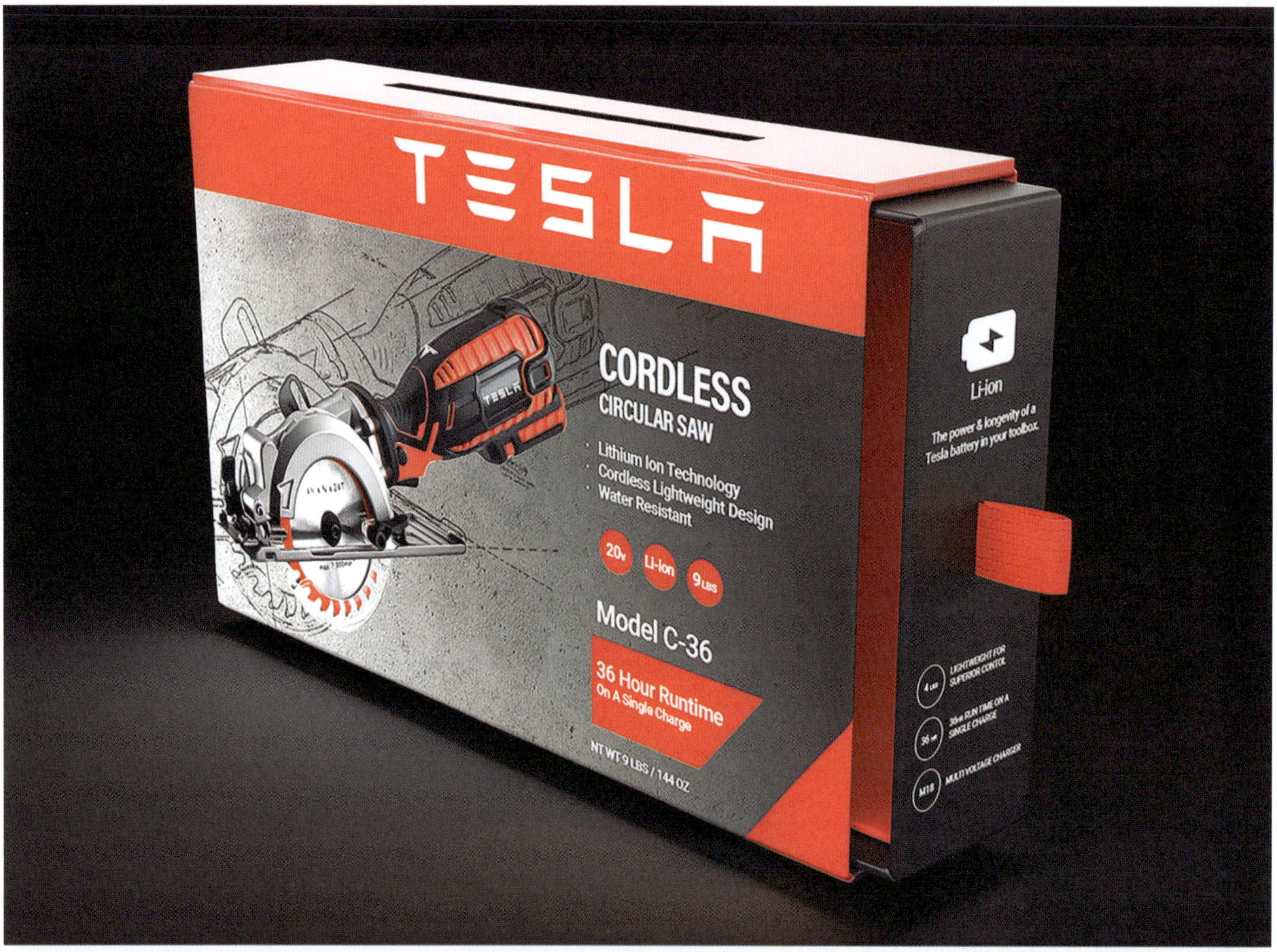

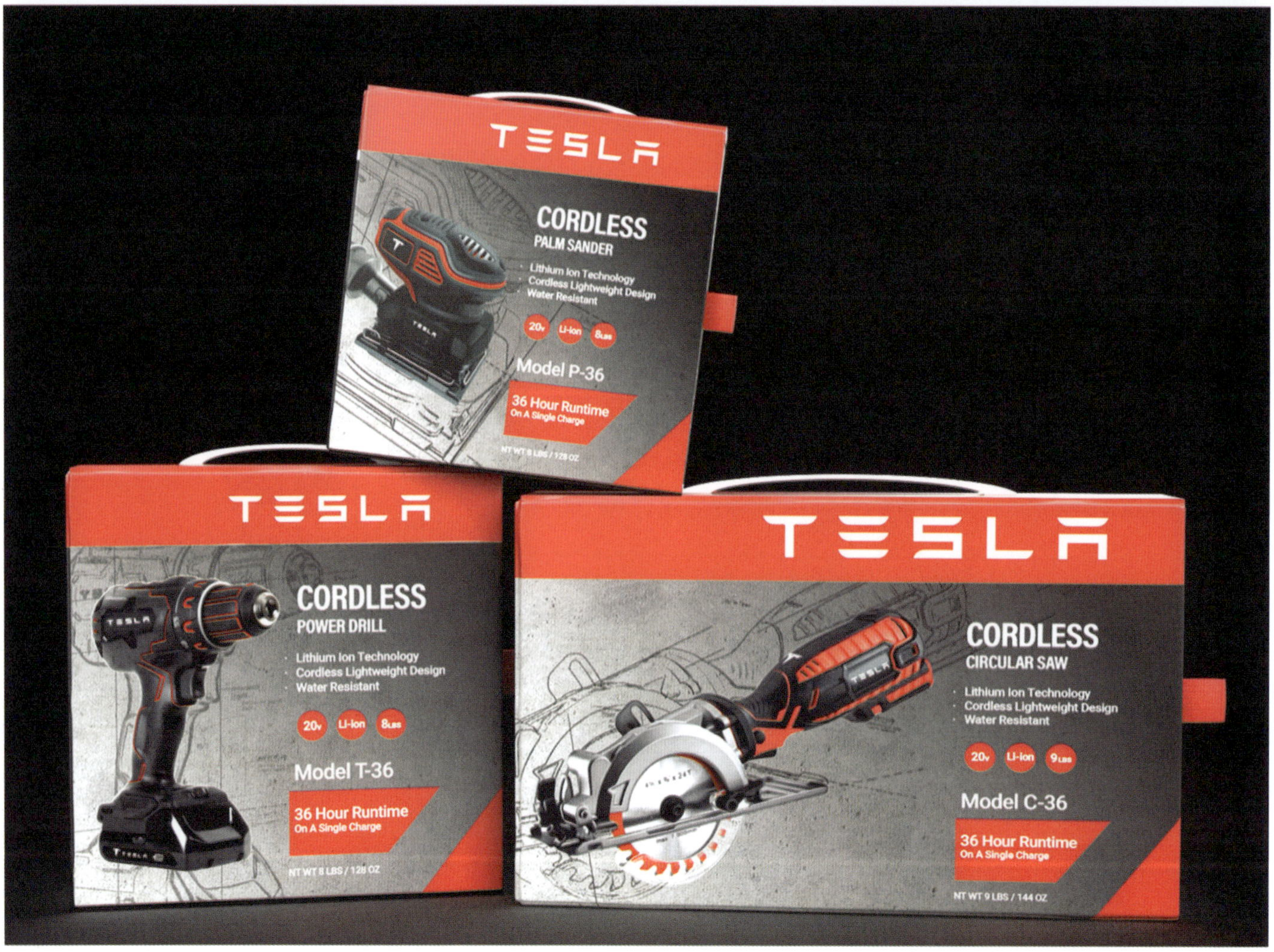

*Tesla Power Tools, New Talent Annual 2025. Professor: Thomas McNulty. Silver-winning student: Cristina (Cris) Meconi*

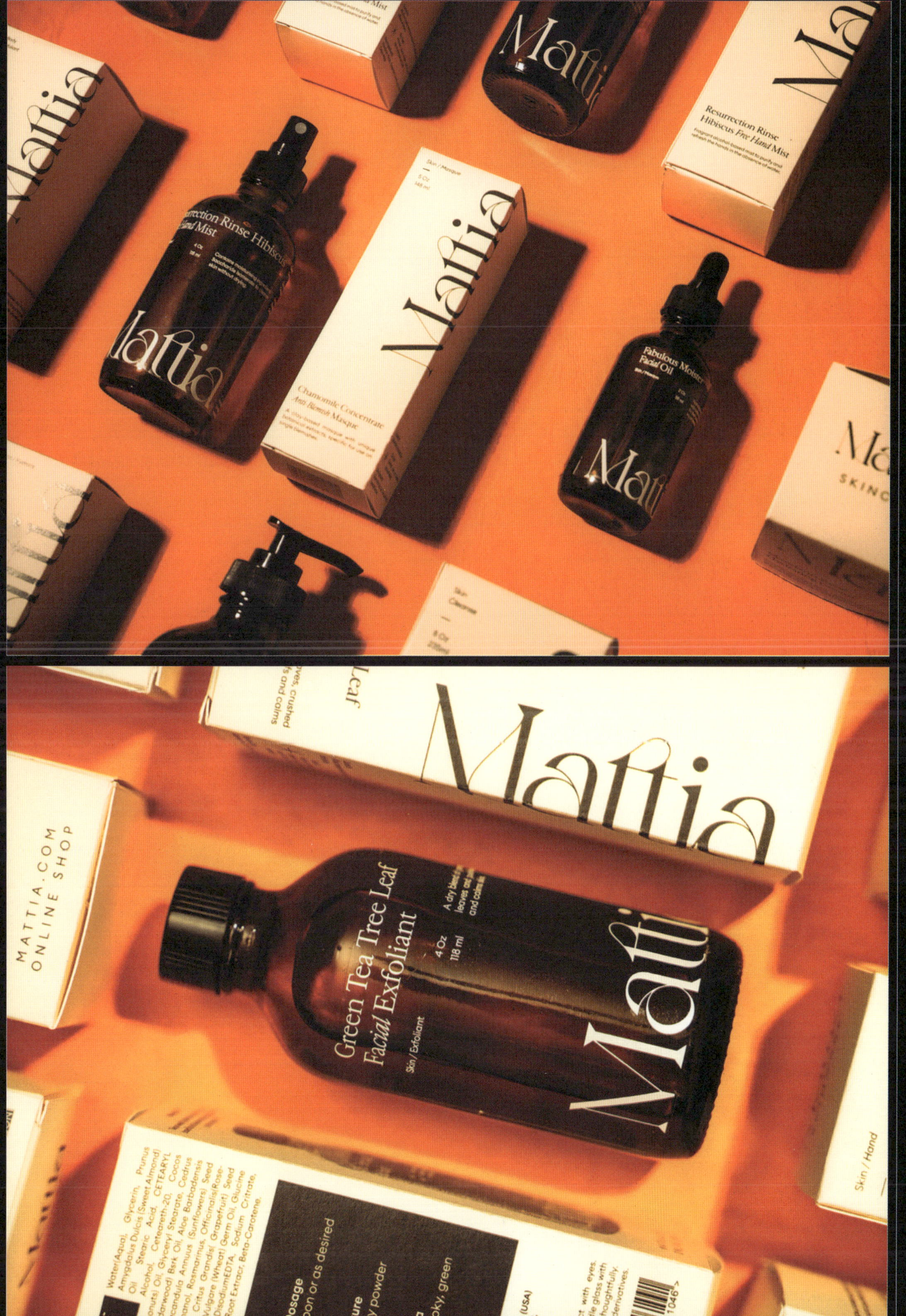


*Mattia Skin Care, New Talent Annual 2025. Professor: Thomas McNulty. Gold-winning student: Shao En Kao*

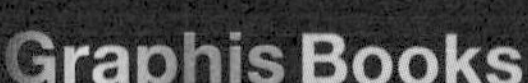

Graphis Books

POSTER

DESIGN

ADVERTISING

PHOTOGRAPHY

NUDES

TYPOGRAPHY

PROTEST POSTERS

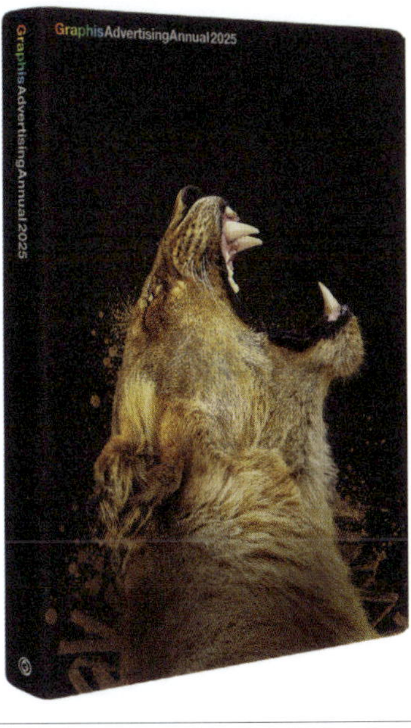

# Advertising Annual 2025

*2025*
*Hardcover: 192 pages*
*200-plus color illustrations*
*Trim: 8.5 x 11.75"*
*ISBN: 978-1-954632-35-6*
*US $75*

**Awards:** Graphis presents 12 Platinum, 78 Gold, and 68 Silver Awards, along with 19 Honorable Mentions, to many international advertising firms who explored what advertising can do with innovative, creative works.
**Winning Entrants:** ARSONAL, Barlow.Agency, Canyon, Chang Liu, Darkhorse Design, Eight Sleep, Lewis Communications, Ogilvy Brazil, PETROL Advertising, PPK, and Vanderbyl Design.
**Judges:** Scott Bucher, Steve Chavez, Quinnton Harris, Mike Kriefski, Dan Magdich, and Courtney Richardson.
**Content:** This hardcover book displays full-page images of Platinum-winning work from talented advertising firms. Gold and Silver-winning work is also presented, and Honorable Mentions are listed in the physical copy. All work is presented equally on our website. Award-winning work from the judges, an In Memorium list of advertisers who have passed away in the past year, and a section of Platinum-winning works from 2015 are also included.

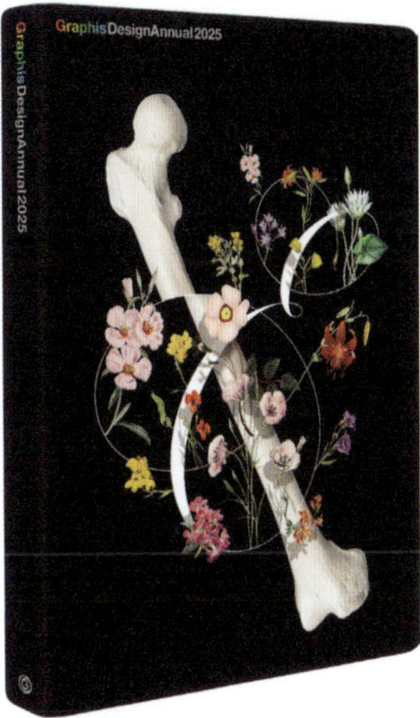

# Design Annual 2025

*2025*
*Hardcover: 272 pages*
*200-plus color illustrations*
*Trim: 8.5 x 11.75"*
*ISBN: 978-1-954632-34-9*
*US $75*

**Awards:** Graphis presents 12 Platinum, 163 Gold, and 401 Silver Awards, along with 118 Honorable Mentions, to many international designers who explored what design can do with innovative, creative works.
**Winning Entrants:** 33 and Branding, Dankook University, EJ Communication Studio, National Kaohsiung University of Science and Technology (NKUST), Sol Benito, Stranger & Stranger, Studio Del-Rey, Studio Hinrichs, and The Balbusso Twins.
**Judges:** Eduardo Aires, Toshiaki & Hisa Ide, Jennifer Morla, Brendán Murphy, and Richard Poulin.
**Content:** This hardcover book displays full-page images of Platinum-winning work from talented designers. Gold and Silver-winning work is also presented, and Honorable Mentions are listed in the physical copy. All work is presented equally on our website. Award-winning work from the judges, an In Memorium list of designers who have passed away in the past year, and a section of Platinum-winning works from 2015 are also included.

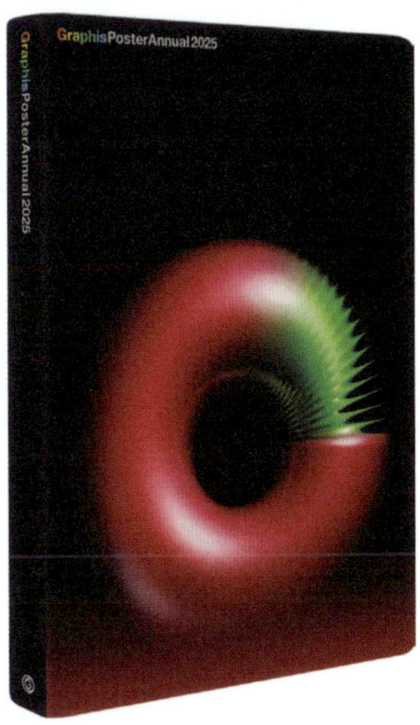

# Poster Annual 2025

*2024*
*Hardcover: 256 pages*
*200-plus color illustrations*
*Trim: 8.5 x 11.75"*
*ISBN: 978-1-954632-33-2*
*US $75*

**Awards:** Graphis presents 12 Platinum, 100 Gold, and 328 Silver Awards, along with 90 Honorable Mentions, to many international poster designers who challenged what poster design can be with innovative, creative works.
**Winning Entrants:** Atelier Bundi AG, CollierGraphica, Dankook University, dGwaltneyArt, Freaner Creative, Gallery BI, João Machado Design, Katarzyna Zapart, Melchior Imboden, Skolos-Wedell, The Union Design Company, and THERE IS STUDIO.
**Judges:** Liz English, Paul Garbett, Brad Hochberg, Sven Lindhorst-Emme, DaeKi Shim, and HyoJun Shim.
**Content:** This hardcover book displays full-page images of Platinum-winning work from talented poster designers. Gold and Silver-winning work is also presented, and Honorable Mentions are listed in the physical copy. All work is presented equally on our website. Award-winning work from the judges and a section of Platinum-winning works from 2015 are also included.

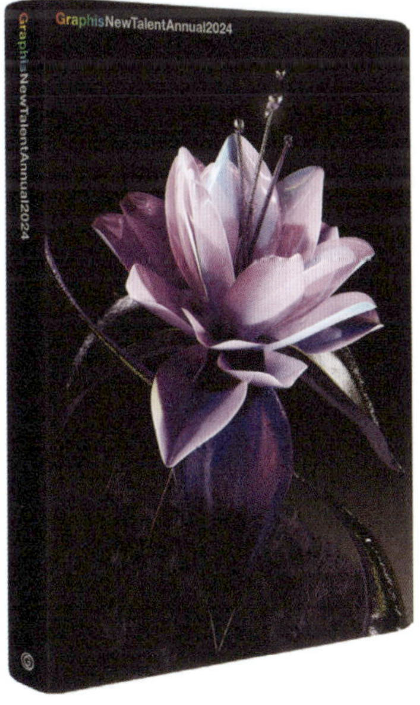

# New Talent Annual 2024

*2024*
*Hardcover: 256 pages*
*200-plus color illustrations*
*Trim: 8.5 x 11.75"*
*ISBN: 978-1-954632-29-5*
*US $75*

**Awards:** Graphis presents 13 Platinum, 132 Gold, and 587 Silver awards, along with 858 Honorable Mentions.
**Winning Entrants:** Design: Peter Bergman, Justin Colt, Rob Clayton, Natasha Jen, Simon Johnston, Billy Magbua, William Meek, Richard Mehl, Nathan Savage, Stephen Serrato, HyoJun Shim, Ming Tai, and David Tillinghast.
**Judges:** David Bernstein, Scott Bucher, Hoon-Dong Chung, Patti Judd, Jim Ma, Kah Poon, Frank P. Wartenberg, Lisa Winstanley, and others listed in the book.
**Contents:** This book contains award-winning entries in Advertising, Design, Photography, and Film/Video. There are full-page images of Platinum-winning work from talented teachers and students. Gold and Silver-winning work is also presented, and Honorable Mentions are listed. We also present A Decade of New Talent, featuring Platinum-winning works from 2014.

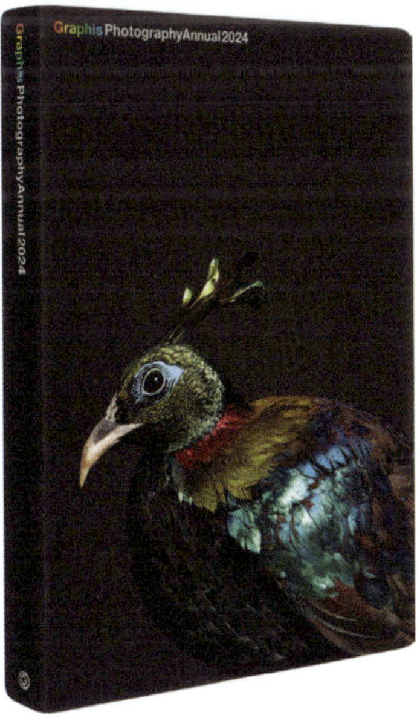

# Photography Annual 2024

*2024*
*Hardcover: 256 pages*
*200-plus color illustrations*
*Trim: 8.5 x 11.75"*
*ISBN: 978-1-954632-28-8*
*US $75*

**Awards:** Graphis presents 12 Platinum, 102 Gold, and 216 Silver awards, along with 54 Honorable Mentions.
**Winning Entrants:** Craig Cutler, Lindsey Drennan, Jonathan Knowles, James Minchin, Artem Nazarov, Peter Samuels, Howard Schatz, John Surace, and Paco Macías Velasco.
**Judges:** Per Breiehagen, Nick Hall, Takahiro Igarashi, RJ Muna, and Hadley Stambaugh.
**Content:** This book is full of exceptional work by our masterful judges, our Platinum, Gold, and Silver award winners, and our Honorable Mentions. It also includes a retrospective on our Platinum 2014 Photography winners, a list of international photography museums and galleries, and an In Memoriam list of photographers who have passed away this past year. The digital copy has an extra 52 pages of additional content for you to peruse.

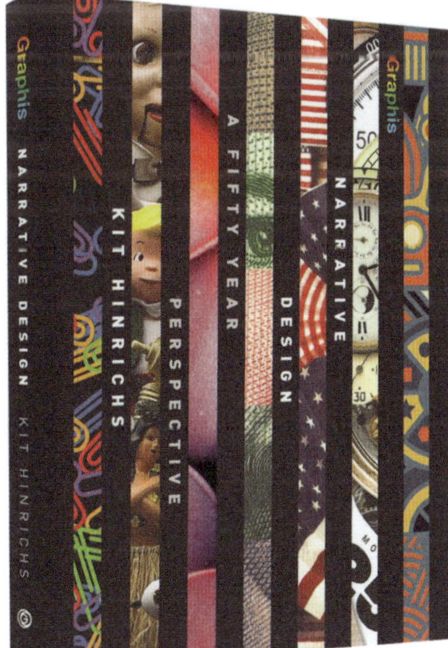

# Narrative Design: Kit Hinrichs

*2023*
*Hardcover: 248 pages*
*200-plus color illustrations*
*Trim: 9 x 12"*
*ISBN: 978-1-954632-03-5*
*US $65*

**Narrative Design: A Fifty-Year Perspective** is a collection of over 50 years of work from the obsessive graphic designer Kit Hinrichs. To the legendary AIGA medalist, author, teacher, and collector, design is the business of telling a story. It's not just about communicating a product or a corporate ethos—it's about contributing to the collective culture of storytelling. Presented in the book are not individual case studies but rather categories of work and graphic approaches to assignments that have wowed clients and dazzled viewers. The work is arranged to communicate Hinrichs' creative thinking, which always leads to a unique and effective solution to any design conundrum.

**Books are available at graphis.com/publications**

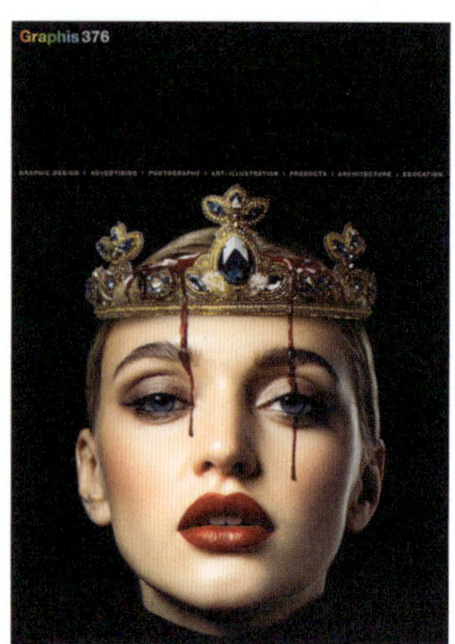



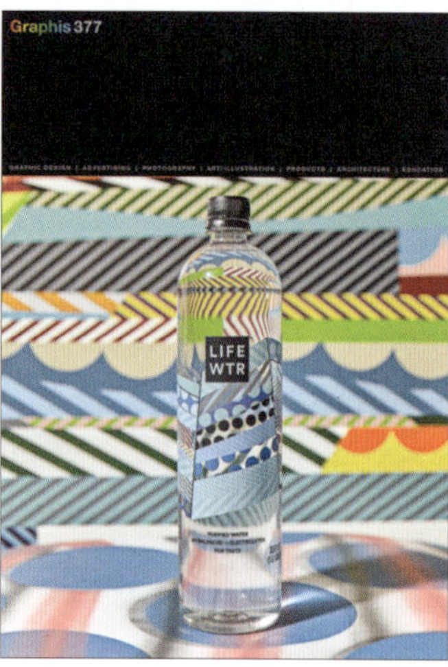



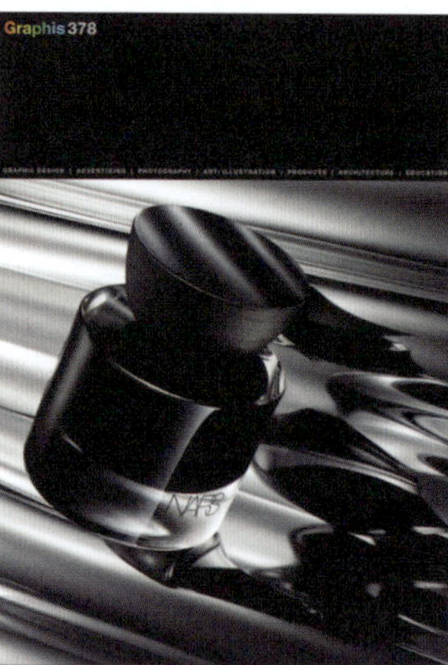



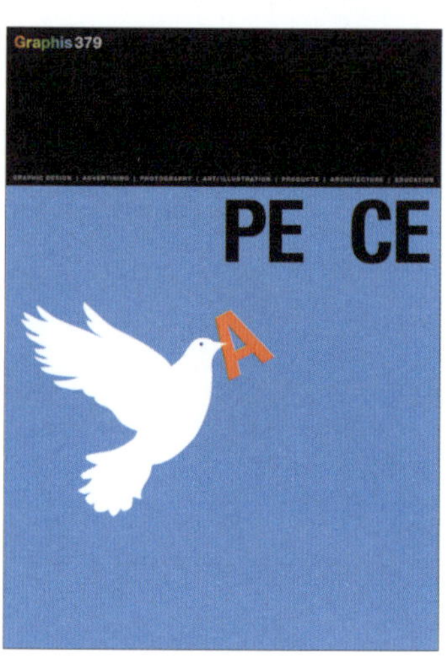



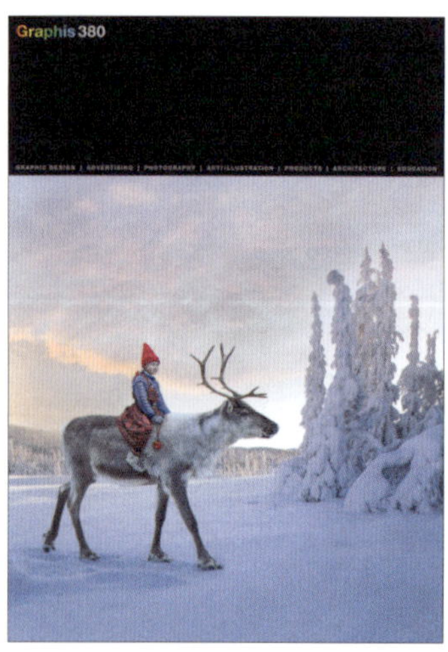



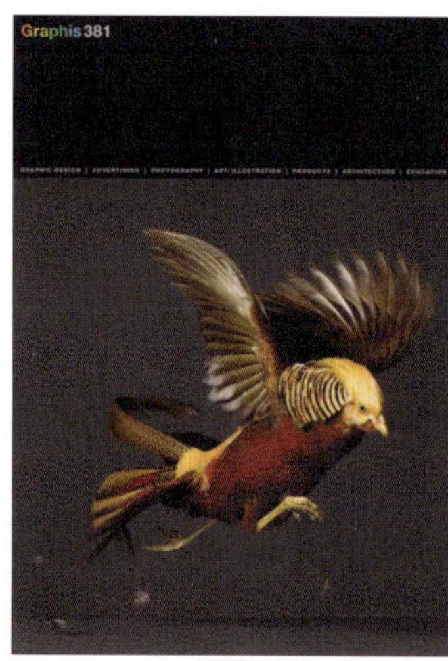



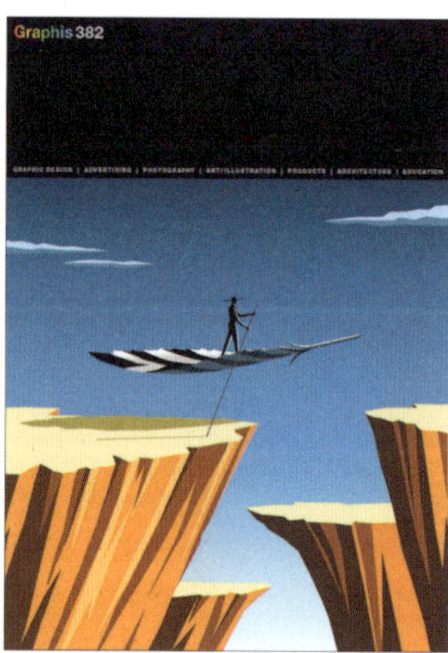
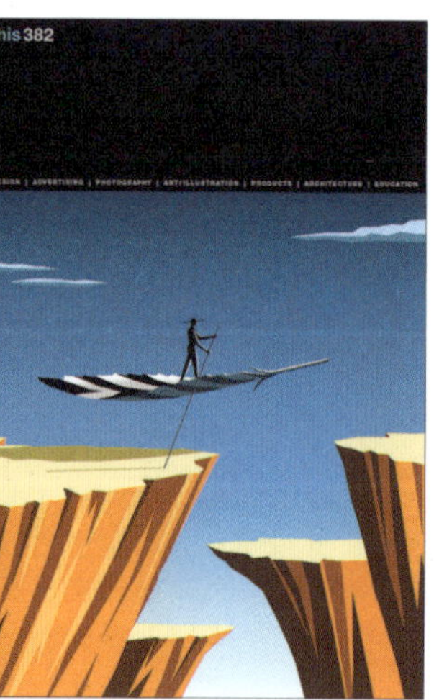



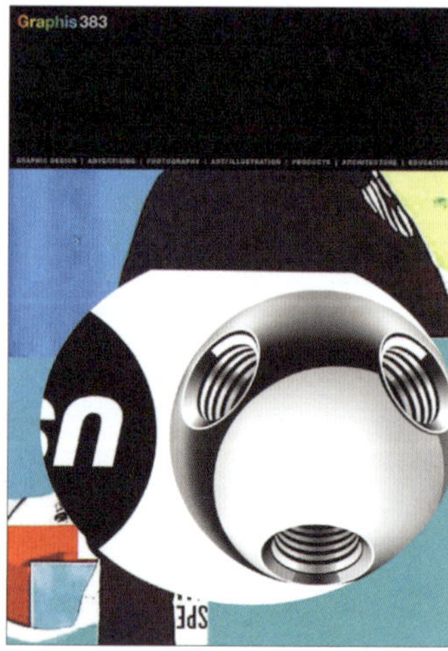

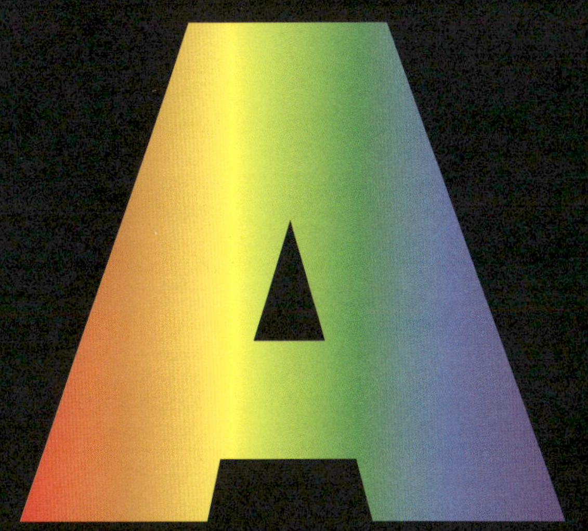

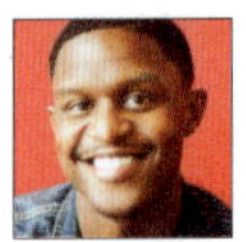

### Quinnton Harris

Retrospect co-founder and chief executive officer, Quinnton J. Harris is a creative leader and entrepreneur living in Brooklyn, New York. His new venture focuses on building products and digital experiences that are radical, culturally nuanced, and more accessible for untapped or overlooked market opportunities. Previously, he served as Publicis Sapient Group's creative director within experience design as well as co-leader of global computational design, which focused on evolving the organization's design systems practice. He played a critical role in accelerating CXO John Maeda's vision for fostering a more inclusive, multi-dimensional, and cohesive experience design capability. He also served as head of experience for San Francisco. In early 2020, he completed a short tenure as John Maeda's chief of staff, finding much success in pushing critical CXO initiatives, implementing systems for global collaboration, and enhancing internal communication strategies. Quinnton also led the #hellajuneteenth movement and got over 600 companies committed to observing Juneteenth as a paid holiday for its employees. Prior to joining Publicis Sapient, he served as inaugural creative director at Blavity, Inc., and before that led design at Walker & Company Brands, a start-up consumer products and tech company notably acquired by Procter & Gamble. He is an MIT alum, graduating with a SB in mechanical engineering and dual minors in architecture and visual arts.

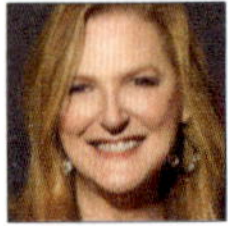

### Patti Judd

An award-winning creative director, accomplished marketing and film executive, and co-founder of the San Diego International Film Festival, Patti Judd joined Graphis as chief visionary officer. A key initiative was forming the Graphis Industry Advisory Board to promote greater industry insights and connections globally. Patti blends business savvy gained from 20+ years at her agency with the entertainment biz acumen garnered from working in music and film. Her studio, Judd Brand Media, champions her passion for creating innovative work, receiving over 100 awards in design, advertising, and marketing. Her work includes notable global brands such as WME, Disney, Mattel, the Montreux Jazz Festival, Century 21, Aramark, Service America, and Hilton, alongside numerous emerging brands, recording artists, and filmmakers. Her influence goes from helping launch a major live music venue, where she was a key player in its growth, to one of the top live jazz venues in the world to co-founding the San Diego International Film Festival. She holds two executive producer credits for a children's TV series on Nickelodeon and a feature film in association with the BBC, which premiered at Sundance (acquired by Universal Pictures). Currently, she is in development as executive producer on an exciting new animated children's series. Patti's nonprofit work includes being a foster youth board member and a past president of an arts and culture board benefiting Balboa Park, the largest urban cultural park in the US. Recently, she was awarded as an Altruist Honoree by *Modern Luxury* magazine.

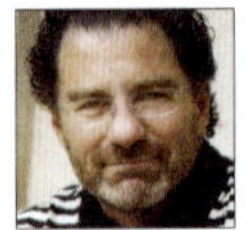

### Michael Pantuso

As a multidisciplined graphic designer and artist, Michael Pantuso thrives at the intersection of creative thinking, artistic expression, and strategically inspired ideas. Throughout his career, Michael has managed his own design practice, partnered with the branding agency IDEAS360°, and held positions inside TBWA Worldhealth (formerly CAHG) and Discover Financial. Located in the Chicago area, Michael is focused on creating design and art for clients, collectors, and organizations that make a social impact—these include charities, not-for-profits, NGOs, educational and arts bodies, social enterprises, and for-profit businesses who want to do more good. Michael's practice creates all the usual outputs of a branding agency—design identities, advertising, social media, print literature, websites, email, e-newsletters, photography, etc. But he does so in the context of a bigger picture—a vision for what the brand is, and, more importantly, what it can become. It's a passion that comes from a desire to make things better. Michael's art is an extension of this passion, but it's revealed and expressed in a more visceral way. One example of this can be seen in his "Mechanical Integration" work, where he explores nature and humanity through a series of fine art illustrations that integrate natural life forms with the inner workings of mechanical components. Part of this collection was recently celebrated as a solo exhibition which began in Paris, France, followed by a tour of Europe that concluded in early 2020. Much of that work now remains in galleries and private collections.